KRISTALLNACHT 1938

KRISTALLNACHT
1938

———

Alan E. Steinweis

THE BELKNAP PRESS OF HARVARD UNIVERSITY PRESS
Cambridge, Massachusetts
London, England
2009

Library of Congress Cataloging-in-Publication Data
Steinweis, Alan E.
Kristallnacht 1938 / Alan E. Steinweis.
p. cm.
Includes bibliographical references and index.
ISBN 978-0-674-03623-9 (alk. paper)
1. Kristallnacht 1938. 2. Jews—Persecutions—Germany—History—20th century.
3. Antisemitism—Germany—History—20th century. 4. Germany—Ethnic
relations—History—20th century. I. Title.
DS134.255.S74 2009
940.53′1842—dc22 2009026487

For Fritz Schrafstetter

Contents

Note on Names

Many of the individual stories in this book are based on documents from the post-1945 trials of Kristallnacht perpetrators before German courts. The identities of ordinary persons mentioned in the trial records—that is, persons who are not considered to be historically significant—are protected by German privacy laws and archival policies. Accordingly, I have concealed the identities of individuals described in this book by substituting first names and last initials in place of full names. I have followed this same convention to protect the privacy of ordinary Jewish victims of the Kristallnacht. Readers who wish to conduct further research into the actions and experiences of these persons can refer to the source citations provided in the endnotes.

Introduction: A German Pogrom

Late in the evening of November 9, 1938, Germany erupted into violence. Through the night and well into the next day, marauding Germans destroyed many of the country's synagogues and vandalized thousands of Jewish homes and Jewish-owned businesses. They killed dozens of Jews and physically abused many more. As the riots raged, the police rounded up tens of thousands of Jewish men and shipped them to the concentration camps at Dachau, Buchenwald, and Sachsenhausen, where hundreds of them would perish in the following weeks.

Several names have been used to designate this event. The most common appellation has been Kristallnacht, which translates idiomatically into English as "night of broken glass." It refers to the fragments of shattered window glass that littered the sidewalks in front of Jewish shops that had been vandalized during the night. Nobody has been able to identify the originator of this term. For a long time it was widely held that it had been invented by Joseph Goebbels, the Nazi propaganda minister, as a euphemism intended to divert attention away from the violence committed against people as opposed to property. As a result, many historians, educators, and others who write or speak about the event have avoided the term "Kristallnacht." This has been the case especially in Germany, where there is an understandable sensitivity to the danger of adopting and reproducing Nazi locutions. Many Germans now prefer to use other terms, the most common of which are "November pogrom" and "Reich pogrom night." The aversion to the expression "Kristallnacht" has not been assuaged by the arguments of historians who claim that the term was coined not, after all, by Goebbels, but rather by anonymous citizens of Berlin, who have long been known for their sardonic wit.[1] Outside of Germany, reluctance to employ the term has been much less pronounced, and it has continued to show up in the work of the most highly respected historians. "Kristallnacht" remains the most common appellation for the event by far in the English-speaking world.

But there is also a compelling reason to refer to the Kristallnacht as the "November pogrom." The word "pogrom" originated as a Russian term suggesting acts of breaking, smashing, and plundering. It came into widespread use at the end of the nineteenth century to describe anti-Jewish riots in the Russian Empire. These pogroms were characterized by grassroots antisemitic violence that was condoned, if not organized, by the authorities.[2] Ordinary subjects of the Russian Empire lived in an environment in which antipathy to Jews and Judaism had deep cultural and religious roots. The unusually high representation of Jews in the commercial classes rendered them vulnerable to accusations of greed and exploitation. Russian authorities, for their part, were willing to encourage such hostility against Jews and to tolerate antisemitic riots. Given this background, use of the term "pogrom" is justified in connection with the anti-Jewish violence in Germany in November 1938. For it is essential that we understand the Kristallnacht as the product of interplay between unrest from below and manipulation from above.

In his earliest written statement on the "Jewish question," authored in 1919, Adolf Hitler expressed an aversion to pogroms.[3] As the products of a "purely emotional antisemitism," he argued, pogroms were an insufficient means for bringing about the desired goal of putting an end to Jewish "privilege" and ultimately removing the Jews from Germany altogether. Hitler instead recommended an "antisemitism of reason" by which Jews would be combated by means of a "systematic legal struggle." Hitler did not explain why he thought it was important to emphasize this distinction. He may well have been thinking about the wide-scale pogroms that had been raging in eastern Europe during the chaotic aftermath of the First World War. Hitler knew that pogroms had been a fixture of life in that region since the 1880s, and from his point of view, they had done little to solve the problem posed by the presence and power of Jews. The Russian Empire, where many of the largest pogroms had taken place, had collapsed in 1917, only to be taken over by the Soviet regime, which Hitler, like many antisemites, regarded as an instrument of "Judeo-Bolshevism."

Hitler may well have understood instinctively what Raul Hilberg, one of the great historians of the Holocaust, explained decades later. "A pogrom," Hilberg wrote, "results in some damage to property and injuries to people, and that is all. It does not call for further action." The contrast to a pogrom, Hilberg explained, was "a destruction process" in which "each step [contains] the seed of the next step."[4] This is certainly a valid conceptual distinction. But what endows the Kristallnacht with much of its historical significance is the fact that it was *both* a pogrom *and* a step in a destruction process. Despite Hitler's expressed disinclination toward pogroms, it was he who ultimately signaled the green light for the Kristallnacht. He did so because he believed that, at that moment, a pogrom would help realize his ambition to see Germany rid of Jews.

Only in retrospect can we recognize that the Kristallnacht was an important step in a process that culminated in genocide. At the time of the pogrom, the goal of the Nazi leadership was to compel the Jews to leave Germany, preferably with as little of their wealth as possible. Con-crete plans to commit mass murder of Jews first emerged more than two years after the pogrom, in the middle of World War Two, as Nazi leaders contemplated what they might do with the millions of Jews inhabiting the regions of eastern Europe that Germany had conquered. Only in 1941 when it initiated the "Final Solution"—the mass murder of the Jews—did Nazi antisemitism become *sui generis*.

The Kristallnacht was a monumental development in Nazi anti-Jewish policy for several reasons. It was the single instance of large-scale, public, and organized physical violence against Jews inside Germany before the Second World War. It unfolded in the open, in hundreds of German communities, even those with very few Jewish residents, and took place partly in broad daylight; it inaugurated the definitive phase of so-called Aryanization, that is, the coerced expropriation of German-Jewish property; it led to a dramatic rise in applications for emigration among German Jews, further exacerbating the international Jewish ref-ugee crisis; and it intensified diplomatic tensions between Germany and other countries, which had already suffered considerably as a result of the very recent crisis over the Sudetenland region of Czechoslovakia.

The Kristallnacht has certainly received its fair share of attention in the vast amount of writing on the Nazi persecution of Jews. Quite a few books, both scholarly and popular, have been devoted to the subject in the past several decades.[5] The Kristallnacht has also been examined in some depth in works dealing with Nazi anti-Jewish policy more broadly, and in a much larger number of articles in anthologies and scholarly journals.[6] There are, nevertheless, good reasons to take a new look at this old subject.

This book focuses on the German perpetrators rather than on the German-Jewish victims. It is based on the premise that the manner in which we interpret their actions during the Kristallnacht has impor-tant implications for our broader understanding of German society's involvement in the Nazi persecution of the Jews on the eve of the Sec-ond World War and the "Final Solution." It argues that, with respect to the Kristallnacht, the circle of perpetrators extended well beyond the core group of Nazi thugs. Participation took many different forms and was not limited to physical involvement. Diverse forms of participation amounted to a kind of division of labor among different categories of perpetrators. Although, to be sure, only a minority of Germans participated actively in the pogrom, the size of that minority was significantly larger than is often assumed.

This position is at odds with much of the existing work on the Kristallnacht. Most studies of the subject have conformed, to one degree or another, to a familiar dominant narrative of the event. The key elements of this narrative are as follows: first, the Kristallnacht marked a dramatic departure from what had been a predominantly legal and bureaucratic strategy for persecuting Jews; second, the pogrom is best understood as having been initiated, organized, and coordinated from the top down by the Nazi Party and agencies of the German government; third, the perpetrators of the pogrom consisted almost exclusively of members of the *Sturmabteilung* (Storm Troopers, or SA) and other Nazi Party organizations, with very few "ordinary" Germans spontaneously joining in the riots; and fourth, the majority of the population disapproved of the barbarism and the destruction of property.

The first generally accepted conclusion that requires our attention is that the officially sanctioned violence of the Kristallnacht marked a dramatic departure from what had previously been a legal and bureaucratic strategy for persecuting Jews. The magnitude and intensity of the anti-Jewish rampage of November 1938 were certainly unprecedented in Nazi Germany. But historians of Nazi Jewish policy between 1933 and 1938 have begun to take a critical look at the familiar distinction between legal and bureaucratic antisemitism, on the one hand, and violent antisemitism, on the other. Although a legal-bureaucratic strategy was central to the systematic marginalization of German Jews, instances of violence were much more common than is often assumed. Many historical works have tended to refer to "isolated" incidents, but physical attacks and intimidation were in fact fairly common in Germany after

January 1933. Viewed in light of this continuity, the Kristallnacht can be seen more as a culmination of a brutal trajectory and less as the dramatic rupture it is usually represented as having been.

Also in need of reassessment is the assertion that the pogrom was initiated, organized, and coordinated centrally. Examined in the narrow chronological context of November 9 and 10, 1938, this is indeed how the event can best be understood. But the chronology of Kristallnacht is actually a good deal more complicated. The event that sparked the pogrom occurred on the morning of Monday, November 7. This was the shooting of the Paris-based German diplomat Ernst vom Rath by Herschel Grynszpan, a despondent Jewish teenager. The shooting was reported on German radio later that same day. Before nightfall on November 7, anti-Jewish riots erupted in several locations around Germany, most notably in the region of Kassel and Electoral Hesse. The rioting spread on the following day—November 8—and then again on the day after that—November 9. These localized riots are indeed mentioned in much of the existing scholarship on the Kristallnacht, but they are rarely analyzed in depth. Historians have failed to sufficiently appreciate the causal link between the local anti-Jewish riots of November 7 and 8, on the one hand, and the *national* pogrom that commenced on the evening of November 9, on the other. Important work by the German scholar Wolf-Arno Kropat does emphasize this link and, in so doing, holds out the possibility of a reconceptualization of the Kristallnacht more generally.[7] When looking at the entire period from November 7 to November 10, rather than only at November 9 and 10, as has usually been done, the pogrom appears less like an atrocity that was initiated at, and orchestrated from, the top, and more like the nationalization of a series of localized anti-Jewish actions.

The third element of the standard narrative that requires reconsideration is the notion that the perpetrators of the pogrom consisted almost exclusively of members of the SA and other Nazi Party organizations—in other words, that the circle of Germans who contributed directly to the violence was fairly limited. The core of Kristallnacht perpetrators was indeed formed by members of the brown-shirted SA. But whereas the riots that took place overnight from November 9 to November 10 were dominated by the SA, the circle of perpetrators expanded during the following day. In many localities, entire workforces of business enterprises mobilized to participate in the vandalism of Jewish homes and the desecration of synagogues. Entire troops of the Hitler Youth did the same. Similarly, classes of schoolchildren were marched from their schools and set loose on Jewish targets, egged on by their teachers. Large crowds often assembled to look on as synagogues were destroyed, Jewish shops looted, and Jews roughed up and humiliated. The members of these crowds are usually represented as passive bystanders, but postwar trial testimony as well as accounts from Jewish victims suggests that many of the onlookers were far from passive. Through laughter, applause, heckling, and chanting, they expressed their approval of what they were witnessing, in the process providing psychological support for those who were physically engaged in the attacks. To the extent that the violence can be understood as a ritual performance of antisemitic hatred, many of the onlookers served as the appreciative audience. Moreover, many onlookers ultimately joined the mob and participated directly in the brutality—a point also made abundantly clear in the postwar trials.[8]

The circle of participants becomes even larger when we consider the phenomenon of plundering. When the national leadership gave the green light for the nationwide pogrom the night of November 9, it emphatically prohibited the plundering of Jewish property. This prohibition was violated on a massive scale. Thousands of Germans who had *not* participated in the actual vandalism of Jewish homes and businesses did not hesitate to help themselves to the spoils. Some postwar courts considered such plundering integral to the violence and humiliation perpetrated upon German Jews in November 1938. A large percentage of the looters were women.

Finally, we must look more closely at the contention that the majority of the German population disapproved of the pogrom. The response among the German population as a whole is one of the most important issues surrounding the history of the Kristallnacht. Historians might argue about the extent and nature of popular participation, but there is no question that most Germans were *not* directly involved. A very large number of Germans nevertheless witnessed, or soon became informed about, the pogrom and its immediate consequences. Condemnation of the violence was widespread, but not as universal as the existing scholarship has suggested. The majority of Germans may have disapproved of the pogrom, but the size of the minority who were sympathetic to its aims and methods should not be underestimated. Understanding this complexity of the popular response is important for assessing how the German people felt about the goals and methods of Nazi antisemitism less than one year before the outbreak of World War Two, and less than three years before the Third Reich initiated the mass murder of Europe's Jews.

1

"Our Path Is the Right One"

Scholars of Nazi Germany have long maintained that the Kristallnacht marked a radical break from the Nazi regime's anti-Jewish policy up to that point, which had emphasized legal and bureaucratic measures. This view has been called into question, however, by newer research that has documented widespread physical attacks against German Jews and their property starting with the Nazi seizure of power in 1933 and extending forward into 1938.[1] The magnitude and barbarity of the Kristallnacht were unquestionably without precedent in Nazi Germany. But the outburst of November 1938 was preceded by a clear pattern of grassroots antisemitic violence condoned, and at times encouraged, by Nazi authorities. At the time, both the perpetrators and their critics saw the violence as a challenge to the legal-bureaucratic process for marginalizing Jews. In retrospect, however, we are able to recognize that the grassroots violence actually accelerated that process.

The purpose of Nazi Jewish policy since January 1933 had been the "de-Jewification" of German society. Among the most notable anti-Jewish measures of the 1930s were the Nuremberg Laws of 1935, which defined Jews in racial rather than religious terms; the wide-ranging purges of Jews from German professions and occupations; and the coerced transfer of Jewish property to non-Jewish ownership, a process referred to at the time as "Aryanization." Other measures were designed to isolate the Jews socially and culturally. One of the Nuremberg Laws prohibited marriage between Jews and "Aryans" and criminalized extramarital sex across the racial divide. Other laws promulgated in the 1930s restricted Jewish access to public transportation, parks, and other common spaces.

Governments at all levels took anti-Jewish actions that today might seem trivial, but which at the time possessed a good deal of symbolic value. In Bavaria, for example, Jews were forbidden to wear the traditional lederhosen costumes known as *Trachten*. The spitefulness of such measures, reinforced by a steady stream of antisemitic propaganda targeted at different sectors of German society, helped bring about what some have called the "social death" of German Jews, or the exclusion of Jews from the German "community of responsibility."[2] Jews were not merely deprived of rights, livelihoods, and property but also progressively marginalized as outsiders. The mass explosion of antisemitic violence that erupted on Kristallnacht would not have been possible without this process of systematic social isolation.

The events of November 1938 marked a crescendo in the violence that had accompanied legal and bureaucratic marginalization of Jews from the very beginning. The perpetrators had come mainly from the ranks of the Nazi Party and its brown-shirted auxiliary organization, the SA. The violence tended to occur in waves, the first of which appeared in March 1933, only weeks after Hitler's appointment to the chancellorship of Germany.[3] The emergency powers granted to the Hitler government by the Reichstag Fire Decree of February 28 enabled the Nazis to unleash the SA against their real and perceived enemies. The Storm

Troopers arrested thousands of Communists and others whom they considered threats to the new order, constructing makeshift concentration camps to house their prisoners. The feeling of empowerment that these operations engendered led to other excesses, including attacks on Jews and their businesses.

The attacks began in the Rhine-Ruhr industrial region on March 7, 1933, and spread out from there, reaching Berlin on March 9, Frankfurt and Hamburg on March 11, and southwest Germany on March 13. Typically the attacks began as demonstrations in front of Jewish businesses, where Storm Troopers and other party activists called for boycotts and intimidated customers. Confrontations with customers and shopkeepers then often escalated into beatings and vandalism. This period of unrest saw SA men and others terrorizing Jews on the street and forcibly entering their homes. Fearing disorder, the Nazi leadership quickly took action to put an end to the attacks. While these early actions may have been minor compared with the events of the Kristallnacht, they manifested the potential for brutality and lawlessness that was inherent in the rank-and-file of the Nazi movement and never very far from the surface.

The second wave of antisemitic violence occurred during the first eight months of 1935.[4] It was rooted in the disappointment among Nazi activists that the purge of Jews from German society was not progressing faster and more radically. Jews still owned many businesses, and the exclusion of Jews from occupations and professions remained far from complete. As in 1933, many of the attacks were aimed at Jewish businesses, which saw their windows smashed. Jews were, once again, assaulted on the street. Local government and police officials reacted to the attacks in different ways. Some made a genuine effort to stop them for the sake of ensuring law and order. Often, however, the authorities looked the other way, neglecting to arrest culprits even when they could be identified. The Nazi leadership tolerated these criminal actions as a way to maintain the loyalty of rank-and-file Nazis who had been disappointed by compromises that Hitler and the party had made with established German elites. Violence emanating from the Nazi base also provided a pretext for official antisemitic measures on the part of the state, which could be justified as necessary to appease the antisemitic grassroots.

The Gestapo, or secret state police, was for its part sharply critical of such outbursts, not out of sympathy for Jews, but out of concern that anti-Jewish policy be implemented in an orderly fashion from the top downward. In the summer of 1935, the Nazi leadership finally began to rein in its radical followers. On August 8, Hitler prohibited "wild actions" against Jews. The Nuremberg Laws, which became the legislative foundation for the planned separation of the Jewish and German "races," were issued in September 1935, and were intended, at least in part, to appease restless antisemitic radicals in the Nazi movement.

In 1938 the pattern of antisemitic violence repeated itself once again, but this time on a much larger scale.[5] In March, the German annexation of Austria unleashed a major wave of assaults on Jews, especially in Vienna. Rioters vandalized and plundered Jewish shops, invaded Jewish homes, and assaulted Jews on the street. For the Austrian Nazis who committed these acts, the attacks were a form of celebration as well as an expression of psychological liberation from the restraint that they had previously been forced to exercise.[6]

Incidents of antisemitic brutality and intimidation continued in many locations in Germany into the spring. They were fueled in part by the May Crisis, the first of two periods of anxiety in 1938 stemming from the possibility of a war over the future of Czechoslovakia. The resulting tension generated by *external* enemies inflamed paranoia about the supposed *internal* Jewish enemy. In May and June, antisemitic incidents were especially widespread in Berlin, a city that was still home to tens of thousands of Jews. Columns of Nazi activists roamed the streets, smearing paint on the windows or façades of Jewish shops, marking them for further attack. Although most of the shops were not subjected to further vandalism at that time, the work of the "smear columns" terrified the Jewish population.

These actions in Berlin were endorsed and encouraged by Joseph Goebbels, who, in addition to his position as Reich minister of propaganda, was also the long-serving Nazi gauleiter for the Reich capital. Goebbels detested the continued presence of large numbers of Jews in his city and hoped that the intimidation would help force them out. "We will make Berlin free of Jews," Goebbels wrote in his diary. "I won't relent," he pledged, adding, "our path is the right one."[7] In late June, however, Hitler compelled Goebbels to rein in the radical party activists. The Führer was concerned that the incidents in Berlin—which were impossible for foreign journalists and diplomats to overlook—might worsen Germany's foreign policy situation at a time of rising international tension. On November 9, a similar scenario would play itself out, but with a much different result: this time Hitler would give his blessing to Goebbels's push for anti-Jewish violence.

The terror to which German Jews were subjected in the late spring of 1938 was intensified by the so-called June Action.[8] As political opposition inside Germany had been successfully neutralized, Nazi authorities were now increasingly turning their attention to other groups in German society that were regarded as objectionable. Between June 13 and 18, German police rounded up 10,000 Germans who were classified as "averse to work and asocial" and sent them to concentration camps. The arrests were legally justified as "preventive custody." Among the targets were 1,500 Jews, many of whom fell into the dragnet because they had previously been convicted of a crime. This was the first time that the Nazi regime had rounded up a significant number of Jews and thrown them into camps. Most of the Jewish prisoners were still in the camps in November, when they were joined by a much larger number of Jews arrested during and immediately after the pogrom.

The second major international crisis of 1938 erupted in September, when Germany threatened war against Czechoslovakia.[9] Ostensibly Hitler wanted to protect the rights of the ethnic German minority in the Sudetenland, but in actuality the Führer regarded the annexation of that region as the first step toward his intended goal of dismantling the

Czechoslovak state. The possibility of a European war seemed very real before the crisis was defused by the now notorious Munich Agreement at the end of September. Millions of people around Europe and beyond were relieved that war had been averted, but fanatical Nazis inside Germany were disappointed and frustrated that the day of reckoning with the reviled Czechoslovak state had not come to pass. The outlet for their frustrations took the form of yet another wave of antisemitic violence inside the Reich.

Much of the unrest occurred in southern Germany. It was especially severe in Franconia, the satrapy of the virulently antisemitic gauleiter Julius Streicher. The Security Service (*Sicherheitsdienst,* or SD), which was responsible for assessing public opinion in German society, described some of the violence as having the "character of a pogrom." In the town of Bechhofen, local Nazis demanded that Jews evacuate their homes to make way for "Aryans." When the Jews refused, they were physically hauled out of their homes, beaten, and forced to march through the town barefoot. In a scene that would be common during the Kristallnacht just a few weeks later, many ordinary townspeople, including children, joined the mob as it tormented the Jews.

The unrest in October was especially bad in Vienna. Having joined the Third Reich only the previous March, Austrian Nazis were eager to make up for lost time, and the rapid implementation of antisemitic measures there had been exceptionally cruel. The anti-Jewish riots of October fit into this pattern. In addition to a great number of attempted expulsions of Jews from their homes, there were numerous attacks on synagogues and other Jewish institutions. The attacks occurred daily through the end of October and the first week of November. The regularity of the antisemitic violence in Vienna in the weeks preceding the Kristallnacht may help explain why the pogrom itself took on such barbaric dimensions in that city.[10]

In trying to make sense of the entire wave of antisemitic violence that followed the Sudeten Crisis, the Security Service highlighted one factor in particular. "The actions against the Jewish population," it explained, "are partially the result of the fact that party members believed that the moment of the final resolution of the Jewish question had arrived." This observation about the October violence could just as well apply to the November pogrom. Even most Nazis could hardly imagine the course that the Holocaust would take only a few short years into the future. Many of them imagined the great reckoning with the Jews not as a program of industrial mass murder but rather as a rising up of "the people" in a moment of violent catharsis—in other words, as a pogrom.

2

"This Bloody Jewish Deed"

On October 27, 1938, the Nazi regime initiated the systematic roundup and deportation of Jews possessing Polish nationality. This action was the culmination of a diplomatic tug-of-war between Germany and Poland that had begun several weeks earlier. About fifty thousand such Jews were living in Germany at the time, the vast majority of whom had either arrived before 1933 or been born to parents who had themselves immigrated to Germany. Anticipating that the Nazi regime would attempt to force these Jews to leave for Poland, the Polish government had taken administrative steps to keep them out. The German response was to execute a *fait accompli* in the form of the roundup and deportations. The operation lasted for three days and affected approximately eighteen thousand Jews, who were taken from their homes with virtually no advance notice, crowded into sealed trains, and transported to the German-Polish border. Once shoved across the border by the Germans, the Jews were refused entry into Poland. They were compelled to live in the no-man's-land between the two countries, subject to the elements and with little food.[1]

Among the deported Jews were Sendel and Rifka Grynszpan, along with two of their three children. The Grynszpan family had lived in Hannover since just after the First World War. One of the Grynszpan children, Herschel, had been born in Hannover in 1921. Like his parents, he possessed Polish citizenship. In 1936 he left Hannover for Paris, where he took up residence with an uncle. Having entered France without the requisite visa, he lived under the constant threat of arrest and expulsion. Ordered in early July 1938 to leave the country, Grynszpan went underground in order to avoid capture. At the end of October, in the middle of this predicament, he received terrible news about his family. He read about the anguish of the deported Jews in French newspapers. He also received, on November 3, a postcard from his sister in which she described the cruelty with which the family had been expelled from Hannover.[2]

These were the circumstances that drove Herschel Grynszpan to his act of desperation. At 9:35 in the morning on Monday, November 7, 1938, Grynszpan presented himself to the receptionist at the German Embassy in Paris. A few minutes later, Grynszpan shot Ernst vom Rath, a twenty-nine-year-old junior diplomat. Two days later, on November 9, vom Rath died of his wounds.

Upon his arrest by French police immediately after the shooting, Grynszpan maintained that his action had been motivated by outrage over the German treatment of his family and his people. "I acted," he told interrogators, "because of love for my parents and for my people, who were subjected unjustly to outrageous treatment." He added: "It is not, after all, a crime to be Jewish. I am not a dog. I have a right to live. My people have a right to exist on this earth." Grynszpan stuck to this explanation for his motive for the duration of his time in French custody.

Nazi propagandists lost no time in trying to depict the shooting as the product of a Jewish anti-German conspiracy. A precedent for the case lay close at hand. In February 1936, Wilhelm Gustloff, the leader of the Nazi Party organization in Switzerland, had been shot and killed by David Frankfurter, a Jewish medical student. Although Frankfurter, like Grynszpan, had acted alone, the actual truth about the incident was less important than the need to make it conform to the Nazi master narrative of Jewish malevolence. Pointing his finger at "international Jewry," Hitler denounced the "directing hand that organized this crime, and which desires to organize further ones."[3] A Nazi propaganda campaign styled Gustloff into a martyr for the German cause who had been struck down by diabolical Jewish forces. Both a charitable foundation and a cruise ship were named after him. Ernst vom Rath would undergo a similar elevation to martyr status after his death in November 1938.

There was, however, an important difference between the way the Nazi regime handled the Gustloff and vom Rath killings. Gustloff had been shot on February 4, 1936, only two days before the official opening of the winter Olympic Games in Garmisch-Partenkirchen. The games were supposed to showcase the achievements of National Socialism to thousands of tourists and reporters who would be gathering in Germany for the event. Fearing that violent reprisals against Jews might make a bad impression on these visitors, the regime had secretly ordered the police and local governments to take decisive measures to prevent such assaults.[4] An additional factor in Hitler's thinking at that moment may very well have been the impending unilateral remilitarization of the Rhineland by German troops, a step that he knew was bound to provoke international criticism. These domestic and international constraints on German actions in February 1936 no longer applied in November 1938. To the contrary, from the perspective of Hitler and other leading Nazis, the shooting of Ernst vom Rath offered a welcome pretext for intensifying the persecution of Germany's Jews.

During October and the first week of November 1938, the German press and German radio had carried relatively little in the way of antisemitic content. Much of the reporting had been focused on the aftermath of the Munich Conference and the German acquisition of the Sudetenland.[5] From the diaries of Joseph Goebbels we know that the minister of propaganda had been preoccupied with matters other than Jewish policy during those weeks. In addition to the Sudetenland issue, Goebbels had been stewing in his own marital problems, which had been brought about by his affair with the Czech actress Lida Baarova. The affair had become an open secret, causing embarrassment to the Nazi regime and straining the otherwise very close relationship between Goebbels and Hitler. Despite Goebbels's impatience with the pace of "dejewification," there is no hint in his diary that he had been planning a major anti-Jewish action for November.[6]

Nevertheless, once the shooting in Paris had taken place, the propaganda apparatus under Goebbels acted quickly to distort what had happened and to magnify its significance out of all rational proportion. The attack on Ernst vom Rath in Paris had taken place a little after 9:30 in the morning on Monday, November 7. By the end of the day, official German propaganda had inflated the magnitude of the incident and invested it with global political significance. About four hours after the shooting, the German News Agency (Deutsches Nachrichtenbüro, or DNB) issued its first report about the incident. The DNB was controlled by the Ministry of Propaganda and served as one of the chief sources of news for German newspapers and radio broadcasters. The ministry used the DNB news teletype to inform editors about what stories should be reported and how they should be spun.[7] The headline of the "urgent report" on November 7 suggested that the Nazi propagandists had already decided how they would present the story: "Impudent Jewish Attack in the German Embassy in Paris." The report identified Grynszpan as the assailant, describing him as a Jew of Polish nationality. During an interrogation that took place immediately after the shooting, Grynszpan claimed that he had acted, in the words of the DNB, "to avenge his Jewish racial comrades."

By mid-evening on November 7, barely twelve hours after the shooting, the Propaganda Ministry had begun to promote a thoroughly

worked-out story of the Jewish conspiracy that had supposedly been behind the shooting. The ministry's point person for the press campaign
was Wolfgang Diewerge, a thirty-two-year-old official in the ministry's Foreign Department. Having been trained as a lawyer, and having joined the Nazi Party in 1930, Diewerge had first made his mark
as a Nazi propagandist in 1934 as a correspondent for the *Völkischer
Beobachter*, the Nazi Party newspaper, in Cairo. There he had spear-
headed German news coverage of a defamation lawsuit that had been
filed by Jews against two members of the local German colony; the Nazi
regime referred to this dispute as the "Cairo Jew Trial."[8] Two years later,
in 1936, Diewerge managed the ministry's propaganda campaign relating to the murder of Wilhelm Gustloff, about which he published a
small book presenting Gustloff's killer, David Frankfurter, as an agent
of "World Jewry."[9] He seemed, therefore, to be the perfect man to han-
dle propaganda concerning the vom Rath shooting and Herschel Grynszpan's involvement in it.[10] Diewerge was a true believer in the existence
of Jewish conspiracies. Years after the collapse of Nazism, while active in
the "Naumann Circle" of unreconstructed Nazis in West Germany, he
would continue to insist on the professionalism and objectivity of his
work for Goebbels's Propaganda Ministry.[11]

Diewerge's handiwork was evident in an instruction the DNB issued to the German press at 8:37 PM on November 7. It directed newspapers to give prominent coverage to the shooting in the next day's editions. The story should "fully dominate the front page." Moreover, in
their own commentaries on the incident, the newspapers should point
out that the shooting "must have the most serious consequences for
the Jews." Editors were encouraged to consult Diewerge's book about
the Gustloff affair. They were also directed not to express "anti-French
tendencies" in their reporting, but to keep the spotlight on the "international Jewish criminal riff-raff" that was responsible for the crime.[12]
This instruction was followed up about an hour later with a lengthy
DNB report under the headline "Jewish Murder Bandits." The German people would not have to wait for the conclusion of the French

investigation, the report declared, because "we in Germany know full well" who bears the responsibility for "this bloody Jewish deed." Grynszpan, like Frankfurter before him, was a "tool of international Jewry." German-Jewish émigrés in Paris, supported by international Jewish organizations, had "put the murder weapon" in Grynszpan's hands.

The French investigation had, in fact, barely begun, and the propagandists in Berlin made this claim in the absence of even the most tenuous evidence. The German Embassy in Paris, for its part, had not reported that it had any reason to think that Grynszpan had acted on behalf of anyone other than himself.[13] But evidence might be found later—and, in any event, for ideological antisemites like Goebbels and Diewerge, the truth of the Jewish conspiracy was self-evident to the point of not requiring actual corroborating evidence. Not only was the guilt of "international Jewry" obvious, but so was its motive: "the extermination of National Socialist Germany." The shooting had been designed to promote this aim by poisoning relations between Germany and France in the wake of the Munich Agreement. If it suited its purposes, Jewry would not shirk from fomenting war among the peoples of Europe.

This accusation was as illogical as it was bogus. If Jews had wanted to drive a wedge between Germany and France, sending one of their own to kill a German diplomat in Paris would obviously not have done the trick. The propaganda, however, was designed to operate not rationally but viscerally, and it was itself the process of a mind that was not rational but rather imprisoned inside an antisemitic worldview. Emphasizing that "this crime cannot be left to stand without consequences for the Jews in Germany, regardless of their citizenship," the report concluded that it would be "right and proper" if "Jewry in Germany were to be called to account for the shooting in the Paris embassy."[14]

This language was ominous, but it was also vague. It did not specify precisely how the Jews in Germany would be "called to account" for the alleged transgression of "international Jewry." The ground was obviously being prepared for a wave of new anti-Jewish measures, but the press instructions contained no explicit mention of violence. It was possible to imagine a wide spectrum of actions short of a pogrom: accelerated "Aryanization" of Jewish property, new restrictions on Jewish religious and communal life, the expulsion of Jews from their homes into segregated housing, and even further mass deportations of the sort that had provoked Herschel Grynszpan's outrage.[15]

The first antisemitic riot stemming from the shooting in Paris erupted in the city of Kassel on the evening of November 7.[16] Similar outbreaks occurred the same evening in the surrounding districts of Electoral Hesse (Kurhessen). Kassel was not a major Jewish population center; the city had fewer than 3,000 Jews, who constituted somewhat less than 2 percent of the total population. The rural region around Kassel, however, had an unusually high percentage of Jews. According to the 1925 German census, the so-called Kassel Government District contained 218 communities in which Jews lived. There were quite a few small towns where Jews had made up 9 or 10 percent of the population before the Nazis came to power. Although the Jewish presence in the region had diminished after 1933 as the result of emigration, it remained significant. The occupational distribution of the Jewish segment of the population was skewed overwhelmingly toward trade and commerce. In 1925, whereas 18.4 percent of the population as a whole was engaged in these economic activities, among Jews the percentage was 61.3. The Jewish presence in the commercial economy had been especially conspicuous in many of the smaller towns.[17] The Nazi regime had done its best to fuel the economic resentment against Jews that potentially arose from such circumstances. In August 1937, for example, local authorities sponsored an antisemitic marionette show for workers on the regional Autobahn construction project. The play featured a Jewish cattle-trader as its villain, thus invoking the long-standing antisemitic stereotype of the exploitative *Viehjude*.[18]

The Kassel region had been the scene of more than its share of violent antisemitic incidents since 1933, and the region's reputation as a bastion of antisemitism was a local point of pride.[19] By itself, however, this does not explain why the violent response to the Paris shooting began specifically in Kassel. Equally important, a local Nazi Party official in Kassel took it upon himself to organize the riots.[20] The official in question was probably the propaganda leader for the Nazi Party Gau, or administrative region, of Electoral Hesse, Heinrich Gernand. Acting without the authorization of his superior, Gauleiter Karl Weinrich (who, in fact, would oppose the nationwide pogrom that would begin forty-eight hours later), Gernand telephoned local and regional functionaries with instructions to initiate attacks on the Jewish community. Although Gernand might have acted on the basis of a direct order from the Propaganda Ministry in Berlin, there is no concrete evidence to substantiate this possibility.[21] The most likely scenario is that Gernand, accurately or otherwise, interpreted the propaganda emanating from Berlin as a signal to unleash the local party faithful against the local Jewish population.

An alternative interpretation has held that the outbursts in Kassel on November 7 and 8 were a kind of "pilot pogrom" orchestrated by Joseph Goebbels.[22] But the evidence does not seem to bear this out. Goebbels had started his workday on November 7 in his ministry office in Berlin, dealing with music-related matters. He had then traveled to Munich to attend several days of Nazi Party festivities associated with the annual commemoration of the Beer Hall Putsch. Once in Munich, he had kept busy meeting with old party comrades and other high-ranking Nazi officials who were also in Munich for the commemoration. Over the course of the day, Goebbels may have discussed the shooting at the Paris embassy with any number of interlocutors, but, if he did, he made no mention of it at all in his diary. Moreover, Kassel and Electoral Hesse were not the only places in Germany where a substantial number of local Nazis could be easily mobilized for an anti-Jewish action, as subsequent events would dramatically demonstrate. Goebbels exercised tremendous personal authority in Berlin, where he was the gauleiter, so it

is unlikely that he would have chosen Kassel as the site for a "pilot" pogrom when he could have easily used his own territory for such a purpose. Therefore, while there is no question that Goebbels was the chief
instigator of the nationwide pogrom of November 9 and 10, it is doubtful that he was primarily responsible for the November 7 riot in Kassel.

The violence that took place in Kassel and in the surrounding communities on the evening and night of November 7 was summarized in
reports filed by the Security Police a couple of days later.[23] The riot began at the Jewish-owned Café Heinemann, which was broken into by a
mob and "totally destroyed." From the café the mob, growing in size,
according to the police, to about one thousand people, moved to the
local synagogue. The nucleus of the mob was drawn from the SA, reinforced by an SS unit from the nearby town of Arolsen. A significant
percentage of the rioters consisted of ordinary townspeople who were
not directly connected to the Nazi Party structure. While most of them
were onlookers, some joined in the violence. Part of the mob forced its
way into the synagogue and "completely devastated the interior." They
then threw some of the furniture onto the street and set it ablaze. The
police intervened, according to the report from the Security Police, but
were hampered by a lack of personnel, as many local policemen had
been temporarily reassigned to Munich to help maintain order at the
upcoming Nazi Party commemoration. The police stood by, looked on,
and did nothing.[24] An eyewitness remembered seeing the police commissioner of Kassel observing the violence passively.[25] Once finished at
the synagogue, the mob broke up into small groups, which radiated out
into the adjacent streets and smashed the windows of Jewish-owned
businesses. The vandalism was accompanied by looting. In an attempt
to put a halt to the riot, the regional governor called in the motorized
police. By the time the violence had died down, about twenty Jewish
shops had been destroyed and looted.

As the pogrom wound down in Kassel, it spread to other localities
in the region. According to the police, almost all the windows of Jewish
homes were smashed overnight in the towns of Rotenburg, Fulda, Be-

bra, Sontra, and Baumbach. In Rotenburg, the synagogue was vandalized, its furnishings tossed out onto the street and destroyed. In Bebra, mobs invaded Jewish homes, destroying property and terrorizing the Jewish inhabitants.

A detailed account of that night's events in Bebra emerged in December 1946, when eight residents of the city were tried for their participation in the pogrom.[26] On the evening of November 7, local Nazi officials held a meeting in the sports hall of the nearby town of Hof. The local leader of the party, Erich Braun, announced that an "action" was to be organized in retaliation for the vom Rath shooting. Braun was following the instruction he had received from the Nazi Regional Office in Kassel (probably from Heinrich Gernand). Groups of party activists were to be sent into Bebra and other towns to "whip up" the local population and make certain that the riot developed "in the desired direction" and to "the aspired-to dimensions." The requisite provocations were delegated to members of the SA and the SS. By all accounts, they performed effectively. The court established in 1946 that, on that night in November 1938, "uncontrollable mobs" roamed the streets of Bebra, shouting, chanting, and breaking into Jewish homes, where they destroyed property and molested inhabitants.

One member of the mob in Bebra was Otto R., a thirty-six-year-old railroad employee. Otto R. was a member of the SA; in 1946 the court characterized him as having been a "typical" member of this organization, a person who "lacked intellectual independence," who was "easily controlled," and who was unwilling to buck his superiors lest he jeopardize his secure job with the railroad. Otto R. had attended the Nazi Party meeting in Hof earlier on the evening of November 7. When local party leader Erich Braun announced that an anti-Jewish action would be organized, Otto R. joined the group that would operate in Bebra, where he lived. Together with others, he invaded and vandalized several Jewish homes. In one of these homes, Otto R. and his comrades roughed up and humiliated Siegfried A. They mocked the elderly Jewish man by forcing him to read and translate a Hebrew text that was

held up in front of him upside down, all the while denying him access
to his reading glasses.

If Otto R. was a representative member of the core group of Nazi
rioters on the first night of the pogrom in Bebra, then Johannes L. was a
representative member of an equally important group of perpetrators,
the spontaneous joiners-in. Johannes L. was a fifty-three-year-old railroad conductor. He was not a member of the SA or any other Nazi
Party organization. He and his wife and daughter were already in bed
on the night of November 7 when they were awakened by the noise of
the rioters. They dressed, went outside, and joined the mob. Johannes
L. became part of a group that invaded several Jewish homes. He was
present in the home of the Jewish couple Herr and Frau K. when one
of the rioters poured the contents of a night pot over Herr K.'s head.
During the night, Johannes L. returned to his home several times, repeatedly trying to persuade his neighbors, Herr and Frau B., to come
outside and participate in the action. Aside from Johannes L., three additional defendants at the 1946 trial were accused of having joined in
the violence spontaneously.

On November 8, one of the local newspapers attributed the previous night's pogrom in and around Kassel simply to "the population,"
attempting to create the impression that the people of Electoral Hesse
had risen up spontaneously against the local agents of "World Jewry."[27]
The pogrom of November 7 in and around Kassel was, however, at its
core, an undertaking of the Nazi Party. While neither the police nor the
press was willing to acknowledge this fact at the time, it emerges clearly
from postwar judicial proceedings, such as the one in Bebra. Nazi rioters committed the lion's share of the vandalism and led and egged on
the other members of the mob. But an important point deserves emphasis here because it is central to understanding the way the Kristallnacht would eventually play itself out throughout Germany in the coming days: the Nazi rioters in Kassel received significant support from
members of "the population," such as Johannes L.

Indeed, the pogrom in Electoral Hesse on the evening and night of
November 7 possessed a number of features that would be common in

the nationwide pogrom of November 9 and 10. Although, to be sure, the attack was organized, it was done so on the spur of the moment. While instigated by the Nazi Party, it attracted a significant number of non–party members. And although the SA accounted for most of the core members of the mob, units of the SS were present as well. The violence spread from one town to the next, often beginning in a regional capital or county seat, and then spreading out into the hinterland. Within each community, the mob was mobile, roaming through towns and neighborhoods, targeting synagogues, Jewish homes, and Jewish businesses. The vandalism of property was accompanied by physical abuse of Jews, which often came in the form of personal humiliation. The police, for the most part, intervened half-heartedly, too late, or not at all.

The newspapers that appeared across Germany on the morning of November 8 devoted extensive coverage to the vom Rath shooting but not a word to the anti-Jewish riot in Kassel. The tone of the reporting was set by the Nazi Party newspaper the *Völkischer Beobachter*. The paper devoted no fewer than eight stories to the shooting. A large banner headline declared the shooting a "heinous Jewish attempted murder." Another front-page headline described it as a "crime against the peace of Europe." A second leading Nazi newspaper, *Der Angriff*, demanded that the Jews be made to suffer "the sharpest consequences." In the Berlin *Lokalanzeiger* the headline cried out, "we demand clear justice." Germans, the newspaper commented, should expect a "full and genuinely just punishment" of the Jews for the attempted murder. In an effort to establish a connection between the threat posed by Jews and that presented by Communism, the *Deutsche Allgemeine Zeitung* pointed out that vom Rath had been shot on the anniversary of the Bolshevik revolution. The message was unambiguous: international Jewry had conspired to have Ernst vom Rath killed to intimidate Germany and to sabotage any chance for a French-German rapprochement.

These reports echoed the instructions the German News Agency sent to newspaper editors on the evening of November 7. It is doubtful that most of the editors possessed knowledge of the first violent outbreaks as they prepared their editions for November 8.[28] The newspaper articles of November 8, therefore, cannot be interpreted as an explicit endorsement of the pogrom in Kassel. Nonetheless, the overall effect of the press coverage was to manufacture antisemitic outrage. The stories that appeared on November 8 not only contributed to the violent incidents that occurred during the subsequent night but also helped to produce the frenzied psychological atmosphere in which the officially approved and centrally orchestrated violence of November 9 and 10 would play itself out on a nationwide scale.

During the course of the day on November 8, the Nazi propaganda narrative of the Paris shooting took on an additional gloss. Even though Ernst vom Rath had been a fairly low-ranking member of the German diplomatic corps, an effort was now made to shape him into a figure of considerable significance. The propagandists in Berlin intended to magnify the victim so that his importance corresponded to the heinousness of the crime. During the night, Hitler had ordered his personal physician, Dr. Karl Brandt, and another doctor, Professor Dr. Georg Magnus, to travel to Paris to check on vom Rath's condition. Brandt and Magnus reported back to Berlin frequently, and German newspapers and radio broadcasters were kept informed of the medical situation through a steady stream of wire reports from the German News Bureau.[29] Each of vom Rath's blood transfusions was reported to the public along with the message that his injuries were very serious.[30] Although vom Rath was still alive, he was presented to the German public as a martyr-in-waiting. The presence of the Führer's personal physician at his side was supposed to assure the German people that vom Rath's fate was important to Hitler personally. To further drive home this point, Hitler promoted vom Rath from his relatively low rank of Legationssekretär to the more senior position of Gesandtschaftsrat First Class on November 9. The German press was duly instructed to refer to vom Rath using only the new, higher rank, and to avoid mentioning the promotion.[31]

Although the supreme leadership of the Third Reich had not yet decided to embrace a nationwide pogrom, on November 8 the Nazi Party organization in Electoral Hesse conspired to incite a second night of antisemitic violence. At dusk, the streetlights mysteriously failed to come on in several towns. The ensuing vandalism was then provoked and encouraged by well-coordinated and, in some cases, uniformed units of the SA and the SS. Testimony given in postwar trials confirmed that regional and local officials of the Nazi Party had planned the second night of violence.[32] The geographic scale of the terror and destruction on November 8 was larger than that of the previous night. The violence extended to more than two dozen towns in eleven counties. Most of the towns were small, obscure places such as Spangenberg, Beiseförth, Melsungen, Abterode, and Guxhagen, where the Jewish communities consisted of only a few families. As on the first night, the targets were synagogues, Jewish-owned businesses, Jewish homes, and Jews themselves. These attacks took place despite the fact that, earlier in the day, the regional governor had ordered the police to intervene.[33] How seriously the police actually attempted to do so is an open question; in any event, they made little difference.

Abterode was a predominantly agricultural town of about eight hundred residents in 1938.[34] The local SA troop consisted of about thirty members. Reflecting a pattern that was typical for many rural regions of Germany, the Jews of Abterode made their living from cattle trading and other small-time commercial activities. Even as late as November 1938, many of the townspeople carried on business relationships with Jews. On the evening of November 8, the Nazi town leader of Abterode gathered about forty people for a meeting in a local restaurant. The group included his subordinate party functionaries and some members of the SA. Even as the Nazi town leader was in the process of informing his audience that "something was planned for this evening," the violence in Abterode had already begun. Nazi units from neighboring towns had arrived and initiated the pogrom by attacking the synagogue and a small Jewish-owned department store. At the synagogue, they vandalized the interior and threw sacred objects onto the street, subsequently setting them ablaze. At the store, members of the SA caused extensive damage and confiscated business records to identify who among the local townspeople had been patronizing the Jewish business. The dimensions of the violence swelled as many of the residents of Abterode joined in. Mobs seized Jews from their homes and marched them forcibly through the streets, subjecting them to ridicule, taunting, and physical abuse. In 1949, a court in Kassel concluded that a large portion of the population of Abterode had participated in the pogrom, even if only as onlookers who encouraged the mob verbally, or even if only by virtue of their obsequious acquiescence in the cruelty.

As in other towns, the antisemitic violence in Abterode was aimed at "the Jews" in the aggregate, at a people who had been demonized by Nazi propaganda as an alien and threatening race. The desecration of the synagogue—an almost universal occurrence on the Kristallnacht— served as the most conspicuous expression of this assault on "Jewry" as a collectivity. But in Abterode, as in other small towns, many of the perpetrators of the pogrom knew their victims personally and, at least in part, were motivated by self-interest. The pogroms of November 1938 offered Germans an opportunity to settle scores with Jewish neighbors or business competitors. In many such instances, the existence of a personal motive to join in the pogrom did not necessarily substitute for an ideological motive. Instead, personal and ideological motives functioned as mutually reinforcing factors. In the antisemitic public sphere fostered by the Nazi regime, ordinary Germans were encouraged to interpret personal disagreements with individual Jews as manifestations of a larger German problem with the Jewish people as a whole.

Among the Jewish victims in Abterode singled out because of long-standing grudges was Max R., a local cattle-trader. Over the years, Max R. had had his share of disagreements with clients and customers. On the night of November 8, he was dragged out of the home of his in-laws and marched along the street, where he was mocked, cursed, and battered. A group took him upstairs into the gallery of the synagogue and prepared to throw him over, into the nave. In the end he was saved by some of the more cool-headed members of the mob.

Max R.'s tormentors in the synagogue included forty-one-year-old Heinrich P., who worked as a representative for an agricultural machine factory. He was not a member of either the Nazi Party or the SA. Earlier in the evening, Heinrich P. had heard a rumor that the Jews would be forced to settle debts that they owed to the local townspeople. Believing that Max R. owed him thirty Reichsmarks, Heinrich P. went out to find him. He tracked Max R. down at the home of his in-laws. As the two men argued, a gang broke into the house and dragged Max R. away to the synagogue. Heinrich P. joined the gang and helped shove Max R. upstairs into the synagogue gallery. As the gang threatened to toss Max R. from the gallery, Heinrich P. demanded his thirty Marks. The terrified Max R. handed over whatever cash he happened to have on him.

Once released by the gang in the synagogue, Max R. sat down on the ground in front of an adjoining building, exhausted. There he was approached by Martha S. Like Heinrich P., Martha S. did not belong to the Nazi Party and had not been involved with the secret preparations for the attack on the Jews of Abterode. Also like Heinrich P., she believed that she had a score to settle with the Jew Max R. The family of Martha S. had been involved in a lengthy lawsuit against Max R., which had ultimately been settled in favor of the Jew. Afterward, Max R. had occasionally teased Martha S. and other members of her family about the case. On November 8, Martha S. sensed her chance to deliver to Max R. his comeuppance. When she saw him on the street, she approached him, announced, "This is for then," and struck him hard on the side of his head.

Similar scenes of personal retribution played themselves out in numerous small towns across Electoral Hesse. Felsberg was the home of Christoph S., a forty-six-year-old worker on the Reich Autobahn Construction project.[35] He was not a member of the Nazi Party or the SA. Over the years he had had many interactions with members of Felsberg's small Jewish community. His apartment was located directly adjacent to the building housing the town's synagogue and Jewish school. Christoph S. shared the Jewish school's underground cellar, in which he stored his potatoes.

When the pogrom hit Felsberg at around 8:30 PM on November 8, Christoph S. was drinking in a pub. The main provocateurs of the brutality that ensued were members of an SA troop from the nearby town of Melsungen. When he heard that a mob had attacked the synagogue, Christoph S. went to investigate. Inside the synagogue he looked on as the interior was demolished and as furniture and other items were hauled away as plunder. It was then that Christoph S. decided to avenge a personal humiliation at the hands of a Jew. He ran the short distance to the house where he knew that Resi D. had her apartment. When he found Resi D., he assaulted her, striking her multiple times on the head, neck, and back. What had Resi D. done to bring this retribution upon herself? In 1936, Resi D.'s husband, a shoemaker, had repaired a pair of shoes for Christoph S. The price for the work had been eighty pfennig. Christoph S. had paid the money to Resi D., unaware that she had separated and become estranged from her husband. When Resi D. decided to keep the money for herself, Christoph S. had to pay the eighty pfennig a second time, directly to the shoemaker. Christoph S.'s anger was fueled not so much by the eighty pfennig as by the teasing to which Resi D. had subjected him after she had refused to turn the money over to her husband. His rage on November 8 stemmed from his embarrassment over having been duped and humiliated by a Jewish woman in front of his Felsberg neighbors.

Christoph S. was just one of a large number of ordinary Felsberg residents who participated in the pogrom. Although the violence in the town had been initiated by an SA unit that had come from the outside, local members of the SA and the party dropped what they were otherwise doing and joined in. Max W. was a thirty-eight-year-old farmer who was chief of the town's Hitler Youth troop. At his trial in 1948 he confessed to having been "a convinced enemy of the Jews." Max W. was at a family function when he heard about the pogrom. He stayed in the restaurant a while longer before injecting himself into the action. Despite having arrived late, Max W. was responsible for several brutal beatings that were inflicted upon the Jews of Felsberg on November 8. His victims included Isaak K., a fragile seventy-five-year-old Jewish man, whom Max W. roughed up during a chance encounter on the street. Max W. also mobilized the members of the Hitler Youth who were under his command. In Felsberg gangs of teenage boys participated directly in the violence against Jews and their property. This would be a common phenomenon throughout Germany on November 9 and 10.

Similarly, the open plundering of Jewish property characteristic of the pogrom in Hesse would reproduce itself on a massive national scale the following night. This occurred both during the pogrom, as looters helped themselves to valuable items in synagogues, homes, and shops, and afterward as well, when neighbors emerged from their homes in the wee hours of the morning to scavenge through the debris that littered the streets. One especially aggressive looter was Johannes S., a thirty-one-year-old laborer who lived in the Hessian town of Hoof.[36] He had previously belonged to the Nazi Party and the SA but was no longer a member of either by November 1938. Johannes S. was at home on the evening of November 8, drinking schnapps with a few relatives, when he heard the commotion in town. He went outside to investigate, and then eagerly joined the mob. He entered the synagogue and tried to steal the light bulbs from the chandelier. Soon he moved with the mob to the home of the Jewish family G., where he stole some expensive fabrics. His next stop was the home of the family K., where he took a small pouch of money away from Herr K. and tried, unsuccessfully, to rip the electrical meter off the wall so that he could take that with him as well. Only at 3:00 AM did Johannes S. conclude his tour of looting and return to his home.

When the national leadership signaled the green light for a pogrom throughout the Reich late in the evening of November 9, it issued an explicit directive prohibiting looting. It did so precisely to preempt the kind of mass plundering that had occurred in Hesse on November 8.

For the antisemitic violence to be perceived as an expression of outrage by honorable Germans, it was important to avoid the appearance that the rioters were motivated by petty greed. But petty greed did indeed serve as a motive for many Germans on both nights. Greed, however, operated in a mutually reinforcing relationship with antisemitic ideology, much as did the impulse to use the pogrom to pursue personal grudges. Since 1933, a basic tenet of Nazi anti-Jewish propaganda had been that the Jews had acquired their wealth not legitimately but rather through the exploitation of honest, hard-working Germans. In an atmosphere in which ordinary Germans were encouraged by their government to perceive Jewish wealth as stolen property, it should not have been surprising that many jumped at the opportunity to steal it back.

In small towns like Felsberg, Abterode, and Hoof, Jews could do little to protect themselves against the attacks. Their identities, homes, and businesses were known to the local Nazi activists, there were few places to hide, and they were vastly outnumbered. The perpetrators of the pogrom operated as a mob or in groups, and their victims were usually either individuals or families. Striking back at one's assailants tended not to ward them off but rather to provoke an escalation of the violence. This is what happened in Felsberg to Resi D., whose beating at the hands of Christoph S. only intensified after she bit his finger. Some Jews depended on refuge granted to them by decent friends and neighbors. A number of the Jews in Felsberg gathered in the apartment of Frau F., who protected them against the mob until she herself was physically threatened. Also in Felsberg, Herr S. stood in front of the house where the Jew Isadore W. lived, preventing the mob from entering. Herr S. had just bought the house from Isadore W., and he wanted to protect his newly acquired property. The town of Felsberg also had at least one policeman who took his job seriously. As the Jew Sigmund W. and his wife were being forced down a street by the mob, Officer T. took them under his protection. The policeman was cursed by one of the rioters, who shouted, "Get with the times! Are you also a friend or a slave to the Jews?"

Felsberg was the town that saw the single recorded death arising from the pogroms in Hesse before November 9. The Jew Robert W. had been suffering for some time from kidney and liver ailments, and his body was already very weak. He suffered a heart attack and died while being forcibly marched through the town. The absence of fatalities otherwise arising from the violence in Hesse on November 7 and 8 is notable. There were, to be sure, a few close calls, such as Max R.'s narrow escape in the gallery of the synagogue in Abterode. A factor more important than luck, however, may have been the self-restraint exercised by the perpetrators, who certainly had been, in a physical sense, in a position to kill on a wide scale. They continued, however, to recognize the line separating murder from lesser forms of physical violence. The Nazi leadership had not yet determined for itself, nor had it signaled to its followers, that this line could or should be crossed. Nevertheless, what happened to the Jews of Kassel and Electoral Hesse on November 7 and 8 demonstrated just how easy it would be to mobilize popular antisemitism on short notice, and how vulnerable Germany's Jews would be in the face of a pogrom.

3

"Now the People Shall Act"

November 9 was a big news day in Germany, but not because of what had transpired in Hesse. In fact, the morning newspapers contained very little about the pogroms of the previous two nights. The Munich edition of the *Völkischer Beobachter* carried a one-sentence item on the bottom of page three, while the north German edition of the same newspaper carried no word on the subject at all. Nor were the events mentioned in the November 9 edition of *Der Angriff;* indeed, as the day progressed, the DNB teletype remained silent on the violence, reflecting the intention of the Propaganda Ministry not to play it up. The attention of the German press was focused instead on other issues. By far the most significant of these was the annual commemoration of the Beer Hall Putsch of November 9, 1923. This was the most important ritual on the Nazi calendar, one for which the entire leadership of the Nazi Party had gathered in Munich. Newspapers also devoted considerable coverage to the previous day's midterm congressional elections in the United States. The Democrats had suffered severe losses, which the German press depicted as a humiliation for Franklin Roosevelt, a figure despised in Nazi circles for his close relationship with Jewish advisors.

While ignoring the pogroms, the press did report on other aspects of the vom Rath shooting. It covered in some detail the debate that the shooting had provoked in France concerning restrictions on immigrants. Herschel Grynszpan, it turned out, had not had a valid visa for France, which raised the question of whether more should be done to control the flow of German-Jewish refugees into the country. It was bad enough that these refugees engaged in anti-German propaganda, but now one of them had resorted to violence. The point emphasized by the German press was that the French might have finally woken up to the danger that the presence of perfidious Jews posed to their peace and security.[1]

The German reporting on the French response to the shooting was intended to dovetail with another foreign policy story. Every year on November 8, the eve of the annual Nazi commemoration, Adolf Hitler delivered a major speech in the Bürgerbräukeller in Munich, the site of the 1923 putsch attempt. In 1938, Hitler used the speech as an opportunity to attack British politicians, who, he claimed, were attempting to torpedo the Anglo-German rapprochement that had been in place since the Munich Agreement. Privately, Hitler had already decided that a German war against Britain and France was probably inevitable. The goal of his foreign policy was not to prevent such a war but rather to throw anti-German hardliners in both countries off balance, and to make sure that the German people understood that the war had been forced upon them by international Jewry and its lackeys. Hitler conceded in his speech that both Britain and France were, for the moment, under the control of leaders who wanted peace with Germany. But, as he pointed out, power could shift at any moment to those who made no bones of their desire for a conflict. His main targets were Winston Churchill, Anthony Eden, and Duff Cooper. Hitler did not mention the vom Rath shooting, but he drew an implicit linkage between Germany's enemies in Britain and the influence of "international Jewry."[2]

Although the pogroms of November 7 and 8 were not given prominent coverage in the German press, news about them traveled fast, via telephone and word-of-mouth. Word spread especially quickly in Jewish circles, deepening the general sense of foreboding that had overcome German Jewry since the first reports of the incident in Paris.[3] On November 8, an envoy from the German-Jewish community, Wilfried Israel, met with the British chargé d'affaires in Berlin, Sir George Ogilvie-Forbes. Israel described the widespread "apprehension that reprisals will be taken on Jews in Germany."[4] Similarly, on November 9, Chaim Weizmann, the president of the World Zionist Organization, telephoned Lord Halifax, the British foreign minister, expressing his fear, based on reports from contacts in Germany, that "pogroms were about to start."[5] The certainty among Jews that something very bad was in the offing was mixed with anxiety about precisely what form it would take. "No Jew in Germany could doubt," a Jew from Berlin later recalled, "that the most negative developments were to be expected." But, he added, "no Jew could yet comprehend that the consequences would be so horrifyingly destructive." Word-of-mouth reports about the violence in Hesse reinforced the worst of the fears, but at the same time, some Jews were relieved to see that Hitler had not referred to the Paris shooting in his Bürgerbräukeller speech on November 8, the text of which was printed in the next day's newspapers.[6]

Despite all the provocative rhetoric in the German press since November 7 about "consequences," there had been only one concrete governmental action. On November 8, the police commissioner of Berlin, Count Helldorf, had issued an order requiring the Jews of the city to surrender their firearms to the police. Helldorf had cooperated closely with Goebbels in harassing the Jews of Berlin, most notably during the antisemitic campaign of June 1938. In the autumn, the police in Berlin (and elsewhere) had exploited gun-licensing procedures to seize weapons from Jews. On November 8, Helldorf announced that all Jewish-owned weapons would be confiscated, citing the "Jewish murder attack" in Paris as well as the need to guarantee "public security and order in the Reich capital."[7] A considerable number of Jewish homes in Germany did indeed contain weapons, but these were overwhelmingly daggers, sabers, and pistols that Jewish men had kept as mementos from their military service in World War One.[8] The notion that Jews needed to be disarmed because they constituted some sort of physical threat was preposterous. It fit well, however, with the antisemitic narrative that German propaganda had constructed to explain the vom Rath shooting. It would also serve a practical purpose during the pogrom on November 9 and 10, when Jewish homes were not infrequently broken into and ransacked on the pretext of a search for illegal weapons.[9]

By November 9 the Nazi regime had also decided to exploit the vom Rath shooting as an excuse for imposing new restrictions on the Jewish press. Many Jewish newspapers in Germany had already been shut down since 1933, but several remained, the most notable being the *Jüdische Rundschau,* the *Israelitisches Familienblatt,* and the *C. V. Zeitung.* On November 9, the editors of the major Jewish newspapers in Berlin received a summons to appear at an office of the Gestapo the following morning.[10] They did not know what to expect, but the news would probably not be good. When the editors arrived at the Gestapo office on the morning of November 10, they were held for a while and then told to return again the next day; the Gestapo in Berlin was too busy with the mass arrest of Jews that was taking place throughout the country. Only on November 11 were editors finally informed that their newspapers were to be shut down completely.[11] Whether this radical measure is what the Gestapo had had in mind already on November 9 is not known, but it is clear that some kind of crackdown on the Jewish press was already in the works before the outbreak of the nationwide pogrom.

On November 9, the entire Nazi leadership congregated in Munich to observe the anniversary of the Beer Hall Putsch of November 9, 1923. This annual commemoration consisted of a series of highly ritualized and minutely choreographed marches and ceremonies, some of which possessed the pseudo-religious quality of a Nazi Passion Play.[12] They were designed to retrace the route of Hitler's movements fifteen years earlier, to honor the Nazi martyrs who fell during the putsch, and to celebrate the victory of the Nazi movement over its adversaries. The symbolic core of the commemoration unfolded between noon and 2:00 PM. Hundreds of Nazi "Old Fighters" gathered at the Bürgerbräukeller, the beer hall in which the 1923 putsch attempt had begun, where they were met by Hitler. Forming a column, they marched through the swastika-draped streets of Munich. The procession made its way to the Feldherrnhalle at Odeonsplatz, following, as though it were a Nazi version of the Via Dolorosa, the same route that the martyred Nazi putschists had taken in 1923. At the Feldherrnhalle the faithful were presented with the "blood flag," which had been carried in 1923, and which now possessed the status of a sacred relic. Serving as a kind of high priest, Hitler presided over a ceremony honoring the sixteen Nazis who had been killed during the putsch. The scene then moved not far away to Königsplatz for its climax. After 1933, the Nazi Party had converted this gigantic square into the site of its national headquarters, adjacent to which it had erected two temples, in Nazi neoclassical style, containing the sarcophagi of martyrs of the movement. In a solemn ceremony before thousands of uniformed Nazis standing silently in formation, these fallen Nazis were now granted a final muster. The ceremony then concluded on a triumphal note, as giant Nazi flags were hoisted from half to full mast, accompanied by a rousing rendition of the "Horst Wessel Song." The entire two-hour event was broadcast live on German radio.

In 1938 this ritualized commemoration of Nazi martyrdom converged with the propaganda campaign targeting "World Jewry's" alleged responsibility for the shooting of Ernst vom Rath. By coincidence, vom Rath died from his injuries late in the afternoon on November 9.[13] He now became the newest martyr for the Nazi cause—the latest German victim of Jewish terror. In Nazi historical memory, the Jews had been among those chiefly responsible for Germany's defeat in World War One, for the Treaty of Versailles, and for the despised Weimar Republic—the very offenses that Nazis believed provoked the putsch in 1923. For many of its Nazi perpetrators, then, the antisemitic violence that was about to erupt would serve as a ritualized act of collective vengeance on a day specifically devoted to the memory of Nazi suffering at Jewish hands.[14]

The early afternoon ceremony was the first of three major events slated for the November 9 commemoration in Munich. The next event on the schedule would be a dinner and "comradely evening" for high-ranking Nazi officials in the Old Town Hall, beginning at 7:00 PM. Then, at midnight, Hitler would preside over a torch-lit swearing-in ceremony for new SS recruits. For the Nazi leadership, much of the afternoon could be devoted to other tasks. Joseph Goebbels returned to his hotel and worked on a book he was writing.[15] Hitler spent the afternoon engaging in military-related discussions at the comfortable private apartment he maintained in Munich at Prinzregentenplatz.[16]

Fateful decisions that would be made later in the day in Munich were affected by two developments that unfolded elsewhere on the afternoon of November 9. The first of these occurred in the city of Dessau, where a local antisemitic pogrom broke out in mid-afternoon. The violence may have been provoked by the local Nazi Party newspaper, which on the previous day had published a list of the 204 Jewish families that remained in the city. At about 3:00 PM on November 9, mobs attacked and set fire to the synagogue and the headquarters of the Jewish community. In the synagogue, one member of the mob played music on the organ to accompany the vandalism. The rioters ransacked and looted Jewish shops, roughing up the Jewish shopkeepers in the process. They also destroyed the chapel at the Jewish cemetery. Plundering of Jewish property was widespread, especially by women. These attacks began about an hour after the conclusion of the nationally broadcast commemoration ceremony in Munich and took place in broad daylight.[17] Several hours later, a press report issued by the German News Agency mentioned the "spontaneous demonstrations," noting that police had been called in to protect the Jews.[18]

The second development was the death of Ernst vom Rath, who

passed away in his hospital bed at 5:30 PM, Berlin time (4:30 PM Paris time).[19] Karl Brandt telegraphed the Reich Chancellery about the death fifteen minutes later.[20] He may also have telephoned Hitler directly; in any event, Hitler received the news in his Munich apartment fairly quickly. The DNB transmitted the news over its press wire at 6:15 PM, forty-five minutes after vom Rath's passing.[21] By the time Hitler left his apartment to attend the "comradely evening" in the Old Town Hall around 7:00 PM, vom Rath's death was widely known in Germany.

At some point during the evening of November 9, Adolf Hitler signaled his assent to a nationwide antisemitic pogrom. Exactly when he did so, and under what circumstances, has been the subject of a great deal of conjecture by contemporaries and historians alike. One possibility is that Hitler made his decision before leaving his private apartment to attend the "comradely evening." According to one witness, a high-ranking officer in the SA, when Hitler left his apartment on his way to the Nazi festivity, he was asked about police intervention against anti-Jewish rioters. Hitler was said to have responded that the authorities should avoid being too firm with the "outraged people," thus giving his assent to the violence. Moreover, according to the same witness, Hitler was at that very moment accompanied by Joseph Goebbels, who a little while later would announce the Führer's decision to the elite of the party in the Old Town Hall.[22] Although this scenario is plausible, Goebbels did not mention it in his diary; nor did he refer to a visit to Hitler's apartment.

Joseph Goebbels, for his part, had decided that the time had come to unleash the antisemitic passions of the German people. This is abundantly clear from his diary. By November 9, after two nights of violence in and around Kassel, Goebbels had embraced the possibility of a nationwide pogrom. A diary entry for that day suggests that he recognized a cause-and-effect relationship between his ministry's propaganda campaign and the pogroms of November 7 and 8. He clearly approved of the violence: "In Paris, a Polish Jew Grynspan [sic] shot the German diplomat vom Rath in the embassy and wounded him seriously. As revenge for the Jews. The German press is now screaming out. Now we intend to talk straight. Large antisemitic rallies in Hesse. The synagogues are being burnt down. If we could now just once unleash the wrath of the people!"[23] Goebbels noted the afternoon pogrom in Dessau and the death of vom Rath. Responding to the latter, he wrote, "Now it's cooked." He then described the scene that played itself out in the Old Town Hall during the festivities: "I go to the party reception in the Old Town Hall. A gigantic event. I describe the situation to the Führer. He decides: let the demonstrations continue. Withdraw the police. For once the Jews should feel the rage of the people. This is correct. I issue corresponding instructions to the police and the party. Then I speak briefly to the officials of the party. A storm of applause. They all rush to the telephones. Now the people shall act!"[24]

This account suggests that Hitler made his decision only during the course of his conversation with Goebbels at the "comradely evening" in the Old Town Hall, rather than beforehand. Such an interpretation is supported by the postwar statements of several Nazis who were present at the event. Although none of them could actually hear what Hitler and Goebbels were saying to each other, they witnessed the two men engaged in a vigorous conversation immediately before Hitler abruptly rose and left the hall. Goebbels then stood up to announce that the Führer had authorized a pogrom.[25]

A triangulation of all the available evidence, therefore, leads to the conclusion that Hitler did indeed know about vom Rath's death before he arrived at the "comradely evening," but only decided there and then, at least in part in response to Goebbels's urgings, to authorize the pogrom. Here it would be useful to step back from the detailed reconstruction of events to try to understand why a national anti-Jewish pogrom made sense to Hitler at this particular moment. Hitler's views on the need to rid Germany of its Jews converged with his planning for the coming war, which he understood, given his own ambitions for German expan-

sion, was probably inevitable, and for which Germany had to be prepared. Having long been convinced that Germany's defeat in World
War One had been the result of a stab-in-the-back by, among others,
Jewish traitors, Hitler was now determined to complete the "dejewification" of German society before the outbreak of the next war. He was no
less frustrated than Goebbels and other members of the Nazi movement
that by late 1938, after almost six full years of Nazi rule, less than one
half of German Jews had emigrated from the German Reich. He was
also keenly aware of the many thousands of additional Jews Germany
had acquired through the annexation of Austria in March 1938. In earlier years, Hitler had proceeded on Jewish policy deliberately and strate-
gically. Germany had been in the process of re-arming and of dismantling the constraints of the Treaty of Versailles. The country remained
vulnerable, and international criticism of the Nazi regime's anti-Jewish
policy had to be held in check. Under these circumstances Hitler had
tolerated antisemitic violence inside Germany as long as it remained
relatively sporadic and did not seem to be officially sanctioned or encouraged. For similarly pragmatic reasons, he had also allowed the continued Jewish ownership of businesses, despite continual whining from
within his own Nazi movement. The process of "Aryanization" had, to
be sure, reached an advanced stage by late 1938, but Jewish shops continued to be annoying eyesores to German antisemites.

By November 1938, Hitler no longer felt that such caution was necessary. In the Sudeten crisis, Germany had had a close brush with war,
and the Munich Agreement, in Hitler's mind, had only delayed the
armed conflict, not reduced the probability that it would indeed occur,
and soon. He instructed his military advisors to prepare for the destruction of Czechoslovakia.[26] The German economy would also have to be
prepared for an extended period of armed conflict. These preparations
were explicitly linked to an acceleration of the "Aryanization" of Jewish
wealth and intensified measures to compel the Jews to leave Germany.[27]

The deportation of Polish Jews from Germany in late October was
a further indication of a hardening of Hitler's resolve. The Führer certainly had the opportunity to intervene against the action had he feared

negative consequences for Germany's image. But Hitler no longer recognized a need for discretion in matters of Jewish policy. There is further evidence of Hitler's hardening in the autumn of 1938. On November 4 Hans Heinrich Lammers, the head of the Reich Chancellery, informed Minister of the Interior Wilhelm Frick that Hitler had decided to put an end to individual exceptions from anti-Jewish measures.[28]

Hitler had remained publicly silent on the "Jewish question" in the immediate aftermath of the vom Rath shooting. He had not referred to the subject either in his remarks in the Bürgerbräukeller on the evening of November 8 or in the ceremonies at the Feldherrnhalle and Königsplatz on the afternoon of November 9. On the night of November 8, after the Bürgerbräukeller speech, Hitler had withdrawn to the Führerbau, his official Nazi Party headquarters, with Joseph Goebbels, Rudolf Hess, and several other prominent Nazis. From there, he moved with some of his comrades to Café Heck, where he remained until 3:00 AM. According to an entry in the Goebbels diary, the Nazi leaders discussed a wide variety of issues into the early morning hours. Although it is likely that the "Jewish question" came up for discussion, we have no way of knowing for certain.[29]

During the day on November 9—probably in the afternoon, after the big ceremony at the Königsplatz—Hitler had at least one very substantive conversation on Jewish policy with Hermann Goering. Hitler expressed his frustration over the inaction of foreign governments that criticized Germany's approach to its Jews. Hitler told Goering that he intended to put those governments on the spot: they should stop complaining about Germany's treatment of its Jews and actually take them as refugees. Hitler also mentioned Madagascar as a possible refuge for the Jews. Alternatively, he suggested that wealthy Jews could buy land for Jewish resettlement in the United States or Canada. To Goering it was clear that the Führer had decided to approach Jewish policy with a heightened tenacity.[30] By the time Goebbels lobbied for a pogrom on the evening of November 9, Hitler was already receptive to a crackdown on Germany's Jews.

At the "comradely evening" in the Old Town Hall, Hitler would normally have remained with his Nazi comrades late into the evening and made some remarks. His abrupt and premature departure this time around reflected a desire to distance himself from the violence that he had just authorized in his conversation with Goebbels. As the head of state and supreme leader of the German people, Hitler required what today would be called "plausible deniability." It was important for him to be shielded from a direct connection with actions that were clearly considered criminal under German law. The German public and the world would be told that the pogrom had been a spontaneous uprising of the German people, and not an act in which the German government had played a role.

The Führer may well have succeeded in obscuring his role in approving the pogrom. We see evidence for this in the diary of Hertha Nathorff, an insightful Jewish physician in Berlin who kept a detailed chronicle of the events of that time. As late as November 17, Nathorff was attributing responsibility for the pogrom to Goebbels rather than to Hitler, a perception that other German Jews undoubtedly shared.[31] Foreign journalists reporting on the pogrom also seemed to be unaware of Hitler's central role in the decision to unleash the violence.[32]

Once Hitler had left the Old Town Hall, Goebbels stood up to address the assembled officials of the Nazi Party. His listeners included most of the gauleiter as well as high-ranking officials from Nazi Party organizations such as the SA, the SS, and the Hitler Youth.[33] It was about 9:30 or 10:00 PM.[34] No verbatim transcript of Goebbels's remarks exists, so they must be reconstructed as best as possible from a number of post facto accounts. Goebbels directed that Jewish businesses be destroyed and synagogues set ablaze. The police were not to interfere, and fire departments were to intervene only to protect "Aryan" property. Looting was to be prevented. Weapons were to be confiscated from Jews.

One especially detailed account of Goebbels's instructions is contained in a report produced in February 1939 by the High Court of the

Nazi Party, which had carried out an investigation of some aspects of the Kristallnacht.[35] The version of events presented in the report is consistent with the above-quoted entry in Goebbels's diary on one key point: Goebbels told the assembled party leaders that, even though Hitler had made his decision in response to Goebbels's suggestion, the authorization to unleash a pogrom had come from the Führer himself. The report of the High Court provides additional important details about the instructions Goebbels issued to the Nazi leaders. Goebbels stated that Hitler had decided that the anti-Jewish riots "were not to be prepared or organized by the party," and "insofar as they originated spontaneously, were not to be interfered with." The High Court unambiguously concluded that Goebbels's formulation had been a transparent attempt at establishing plausible deniability for himself, Hitler, and the party. "The verbally communicated instructions of the Reich propaganda leader," the report stated, "were interpreted by all of the party leaders who were present to mean that the party not appear to be the originator of the demonstrations but should, in fact, organize and implement them."

The Nazi gathering in the Old Town Hall broke up after Goebbels had finished speaking. The gauleiter and other party officials had to pass the instructions on to their home districts. They had to do this verbally, over telephone lines. Roughly three dozen gauleiter, plus regional leaders of the SA, had to find phones and place calls to their home offices late in the evening on the day of a national Nazi Party celebration. The phone lines available in the Old Town Hall were limited, so many of the officials had to rush back to their hotels to call from there. Long queues formed in front of telephone booths, and the phone calls from Munich to all regions of the Reich remained continuous throughout the night.[36] The scene was hectic and more than a little chaotic. Moreover, the party officials had no printed instructions to recite over the phone. They had to reconstruct what they had heard from Goebbels from memory, or perhaps from hastily scribbled notes. In many districts, subordinates had to be tracked down in a pub or hauled out of bed to take the call. They then had to convey the verbally received instructions to party officials at the next level down. This process was repeated throughout the night within the regional and local Nazi Party structure. While the word could be spread fairly quickly in the cities, in rural regions the process took longer and was more cumbersome.

The improvised and messy process for disseminating the pogrom authorization inside the Nazi Party is significant. It helps to underscore the fact that Hitler and Goebbels had not decided upon the nationwide pogrom earlier than the night of November 9. Had they made the decision earlier in the day, or even before November 9, some kind of written instruction would probably have been prepared in advance for distribution via telex at the right moment. Indeed, in his speech in the Old Town Hall, Goebbels had said that he would order written instructions later on, and he did in fact do so. But these instructions (a copy of which has not survived) were not telexed to the regional party offices until 1:40 AM. By this time, the verbal instructions had been transmitted over the phone throughout much of the country, and the pogrom was already well under way.[37]

The improvised dissemination via telephone of a verbal order, in the middle of the night, and within the geographically far-flung and organizationally complex Nazi Party, was a recipe for confusion. Several degrees of separation stood between Joseph Goebbels and the low-level SA men and other Nazis who were expected to carry out the instructions. Each link in the chain of command was a potential point of miscommunication.[38] Some of the more heinous crimes committed against the Jews of Germany on November 9 and 10—specifically many of the murders—resulted, at least in part, from orders that had been garbled or misunderstood as they were passed downward.

For the pogrom to succeed, Germany's police would have to be neutralized. By November 1938, command over all categories of police had been centralized under the SS, and in particular in the person of Heinrich Himmler, who carried the title "Reich leader of the SS and chief of the German police." Like the other top Nazi leaders, Himmler had been present in Munich for the November 9 commemorations. On November 8 he had presided over a meeting of SS generals, which took place every year in conjunction with the festivities in Munich. Himmler's speech to his generals ranged widely, touching on questions of foreign policy, military issues, and the role of sports within the SS. His remarks were very much colored by the recent Sudeten crisis. Although a war had been avoided this time around, Himmler was certain that one would come. "We must be clear about one thing," he told his generals, "that in the next ten years we will certainly face extraordinary challenges of a critical nature." Germany would be confronted not only with a "struggle of nations" but also with the "ideological struggle against Jewry, Freemasonry, Marxism, and the churches." Himmler left no doubt that, among these enemies, the Jews were the most dangerous; they were, in his words, the "source of everything negative" in the world. Speaking in the immediate aftermath of the shooting of Ernst vom Rath, on a day when the front pages of German newspapers were dominated by vitriol about the world Jewish conspiracy, Himmler commented to his SS generals that "the Jew will not be able to survive in Germany. This is a question of years." "We will chase them out," he told them, "with unprecedented ruthlessness."[39]

If Himmler was in no mood to soft-pedal when it came to Jewish policy, neither was the SS more generally. Just a few days earlier, on November 3, the official newspaper of the SS, *Das Schwarze Korps,* had published an exceptionally militant antisemitic article.[40] Written as a follow-up to the previous month's expulsion of Polish Jews, the article contended that "World Jewry" had declared war against the Third Reich. Accordingly, German Jews would have to be held accountable for "the damages that World Jewry has inflicted, and still desires to inflict, on us." The article went on to advocate the internment of unemployed Jews and the concentration of Jews into segregated housing facilities.

Notably, the article in *Das Schwarze Korps* did not mention, or even hint, that a pogrom would be an appropriate measure. It has become somewhat axiomatic in the scholarship about Nazi Jewish policy that the SS tended to disapprove of uncontrolled antisemitic violence from below, preferring instead to advocate systematic measures carried out in an orderly, efficient manner by experts with the proper knowledge and training.[41] There is a good deal of truth to this generalization, and probably neither Himmler nor the author of the *Das Schwarze Korps* article was thinking in terms of a pogrom in early November 1938. But there were "Jew" experts in the SS who had recognized the potential utility of mass anti-Jewish violence. One of these was Adolf Eichmann, who had set down his ideas on the subject in a memorandum in January 1937.[42] At the time, Eichmann was the specialist for "Zionists" in the "Jewry" department of the SD, which was part of Himmler's police empire. In a survey of the various methods available to the Nazi regime for its campaign against the Jews, Eichmann devoted a small section to "Intimidation." "Popular rage," Eichmann noted, "is the most effective means to undermine the Jews' sense of security." This had been proven through experience, he claimed, noting that even Jews in Palestine had come to consider Germany too dangerous to visit. Moreover, Eichmann contended, the collective psychology of the Jews had been shaped by centuries of experience with pogroms. A Jew fears nothing so much as a "hostile mood that can turn against him spontaneously at any moment."

The idea of a pogrom had not, therefore, been foreign to the thinking of the SS. This having been said, it remains unlikely that either Himmler or his close subordinate Reinhard Heydrich, the head of the Reich Security Main Office, was brought into the planning of the Kristallnacht until *after* Goebbels and Hitler had made the fundamental decision to proceed with the violence. The evidence that speaks most directly to this question consists of the orders transmitted to police offices around Germany through the night of November 9–10. The first such order was issued to Gestapo offices by Heinrich Müller, the head of the Gestapo, at 11:55 PM on November 9, roughly two to two and a half hours after Goebbels had given his speech in the Old Town Hall.[43] The content of this order will be examined below, but here it is important to emphasize that a second order, essentially similar, but much more detailed, was sent out to the same recipients (plus offices of the

SD) almost one and a half hours later, at 1:20 AM, by Müller's superior, Reinhard Heydrich.[44] The existence of the second, more thorough, order suggests that its predecessor had been formulated in haste, and that Heydrich had found it necessary to draft an improved version between midnight and 1:20 AM. Had Himmler and Heydrich been involved with the planning of the pogrom with Goebbels earlier in the day, as one historian has argued, then it is unlikely that Heydrich would have had to improvise in this fashion in the middle of the night.[45] It is also worth noting that these orders were issued to the Gestapo and the SD, which represented only two of Germany's many police organizations. The corresponding directive to the Order Police, who were responsible for normal policing duties, by their chief, Kurt Daluege, was not issued until 6:30 in the morning on November 10.[46] There is, in short, no evidence of advanced knowledge of the nationwide pogrom within the German police apparatus at any level.

Both Himmler and Heydrich had been in attendance at the "comradely evening" in the Old Town Hall, but there is no way to know for sure whether they were still present when Goebbels rose to give his instructions for the pogrom. We know that when Hitler left the hall, many who were present interpreted the Führer's departure as an opportunity to take their leave as well. Himmler and Heydrich may have been among them.[47] Their absence from the hall at the time of Goebbels's speech is supported by another important piece of evidence. In 1946 Luitpold Schallermeier, who in 1938 had been an SS officer on Himmler's personal staff, submitted a statement to the International Military Tribunal.[48] Although Schallermeier's statement was clearly intended to exculpate the SS from responsibility for the Kristallnacht, and much of it can easily be proved false, it remains an important document because it is among the very few items of evidence that we have regarding the movements of Himmler and Heydrich on the evening of November 9.[49]

Schallermeier asserted that the two men learned of the pogrom authorization only after the fact. This claim is consistent with the improvised and relatively late manner in which the SS issued its orders to the police. It is also important to note that, according to Schallermeier, Himmler was present with Hitler in the Führer's Munich apartment between 11:00 PM and midnight on November 9, shortly before Heinrich Müller issued the first set of instructions to the German police.[50] We also know that Hitler and Himmler appeared together at midnight at a swearing-in ceremony for new SS recruits at the Feldherrnhalle.[51] All of this suggests that Himmler was engaged in direct conversations with Hitler about the content of the instructions that would be transmitted to the police. It was under Himmler's command that the German police would soon be ordered to stand aside during a systematic, nationwide act of lawbreaking, and to carry out the mass arrest of tens of thousands of Jews. An action of that magnitude required the permission of the Führer.

The telex that Heinrich Müller sent to Gestapo offices at 11:55 PM, therefore, reflected a decision made at the very top. The telex was quite brief and emphasized four points. First, it gave notice that "actions" against Jews would take place shortly, and that they would be targeted especially against synagogues. Second, it directed the Gestapo to seize "important archival materials" from synagogues. Third, it instructed the Gestapo to prepare for "the arrest of about 20,000 to 30,000 Jews throughout the Reich. Priority should be given to arresting affluent Jews." Fourth, the Gestapo should take "severe measures" against Jews found with weapons. The instructions also allowed units of the SS to be mobilized to take part in the action.

By far the most notable of these provisions was the third one, which stipulated the mass arrest of Jews. We have clear confirmation from Joseph Goebbels's diary that this measure in particular was authorized personally by Hitler: "The Führer has ordered that 25–30,000 Jews be arrested immediately," he wrote in his diary.[52] Reinhard Heydrich's follow-up order, issued at 1:20 AM, fleshed out Müller's rather vague directive regarding the arrests. Heydrich's order was a good deal more precise and was based on a more careful consideration of the problems inherent to such a massive operation. It specified that police should carry out the arrests only after they were no longer needed to prevent looting and to protect "Aryan" property. Rather than citing a specific figure of Jews to be arrested, as Müller had done, Heydrich directed that only so many Jews should be taken into custody as could be accommodated by the available "detention space." Heydrich evidently feared that the arrest of 30,000 Jews would overburden the prison and concentration camps system. Like Müller, Heydrich specified that the arrested Jews should be propertied or affluent. Heydrich added two further provisos to the arrests. His order identified those to be arrested as "healthy male Jews of not too advanced age." Moreover, the arrested Jews were "not to be maltreated."

These instructions reflected the intention of taking a large number of affluent Jews hostage as a means of pressuring them to agree to an expeditious "Aryanization" of their property and departure from the country. They also reflected a desire to make certain that the arrest and imprisonment of the Jews played itself out in a more orderly fashion than the torching of synagogues and the demolition of Jewish businesses. In Heydrich's mind (and probably also in Himmler's) there would be a tidy division of labor between the German police, who would carry out their responsibilities in an efficient and professional manner, and the SA, which would be entrusted with the more primitive tasks of vandalism. As things would turn out, however, Heydrich seriously overestimated the efficiency and order with which his own people would proceed. As the pogrom played itself out, many of the Jews who were arrested and sent to the concentration camps were *not* affluent. The jails and concentration camps *did* become seriously overcrowded with Jews. And many of these Jews were *not* relatively young and healthy, but rather too old and frail to survive the ordeal.

At exactly midnight, five minutes after Heinrich Müller transmitted the first of the orders to the police, Hitler and Himmler appeared at the Feldherrnhalle, where 10,600 recruits were to take their oaths as new members of the SS. The swearing-in of the SS at the Feldherrnhalle was the capstone of the November 9 commemoration and was attended by other Nazi leaders who were present in Munich, including Goebbels.[53] After the brief ceremony, Hitler returned to his private apartment. He received a visit from Karl Freiherr von Eberstein, the police commissioner of Munich, and had at least one long telephone conversation with Goebbels.[54] While we do not know what was said, it is clear that Hitler was being kept informed about the pogrom that was beginning to unfold in the streets of Munich. Attacks on Jewish targets had already begun before the midnight SS ceremony. At 11:59 the fire department recorded the first of many alarms caused by arson against Jewish sites in the city, in this case a clothing store owned by Hans Weber.[55]

For his part, Joseph Goebbels was out and about in Munich, doing his best to foment trouble. He recorded his actions and movements in his diary in some detail.[56] He spent most of the night receiving reports, first at the headquarters of the Nazi Gau of Munich and Upper Bavaria, and then at the Künstlerklub. Irked by the hesitation of "luke-warm slackers," as he described them in his diary, Goebbels worked to "stir things up." One of the slackers, in Goebbels's view, was Adolf Wagner, the local Nazi gauleiter. "Wagner," Goebbels wrote, "has cold feet and trembles for his Jewish shops."[57] But Goebbels was determined: "I won't let myself be dissuaded." Goebbels was also in touch with his home Gau of Berlin, where he ordered the destruction of the large synagogue in Fasanenstrasse. This order was carried out, and through the night Goebbels received word that the violence in Berlin and elsewhere was spreading: "Reports are arriving from the entire Reich: 50, then 75, synagogues are burning." Returning to his Munich hotel, Goebbels could hear the smashing of shop windows. "Bravo, bravo," was his response.

For at least part of the night, Goebbels was accompanied by Julius Schaub, Hitler's personal adjutant and trusted confidante.[58] Schaub was a true Nazi "Old Fighter" who had participated in the 1923 putsch. He had done so as a member of the Stosstrupp Hitler, which had been founded in the spring of 1923 as a kind of personal bodyguard for the Nazi leader. When the SS was created in 1925, it drew its original members from the disbanded Stosstrupp. The Stosstrupp had long ceased to exist by November 1938, but veterans of the unit gathered each year in

Munich on November 9 to commemorate their role in the putsch. In its heyday, the unit had been known both for its toughness and for its loyalty to the Nazi cause.[59] The 1938 commemoration offered the Stosstrupp veterans a special opportunity to celebrate their tradition. They were the vanguard of the pogrom in Munich. Goebbels described their exploits in his diary: "The Stosstrupp Hitler goes right to it, in order to clean up in Munich," he noted, adding later that it had "accomplished terrifying work." The destructive enthusiasm of the Stosstrupp veterans extended to Julius Schaub. Goebbels described Hitler's adjutant as "in full swing" that night, with his "old Stosstrupp past awoken."

Even in his private diary, the propaganda minister became carried away by his own rhetoric. His claim that "the entire German people is in rebellion" against the Jews reflected less the complicated reality of what was happening around Germany than the narrative that Goebbels desired to superimpose onto it. "The popular anger is now raging," Goebbels wrote, convinced that he had simply given the German people an opportunity for which they had been yearning. By the morning of November 10, when Goebbels had learned that the "terrifying rage" had swept through the entire country, he had a sense of vindication. "This was only to be expected," he observed. "The dear Jews," he added, "will think carefully before they bump off German diplomats." Such, he concluded, was the "point of the exercise."

The national pogrom that had just been unleashed was not, contrary to Goebbels's self-delusion, a spontaneous mass uprising of the German people. But neither was it a carefully executed operation that had been planned in advance, as some continue to believe.[60] Although the scale and intensity of the violence might seem difficult to explain in the absence of long premeditation and careful organization, the evidence speaks overwhelmingly against such an interpretation. The decision to initiate the pogrom was made only on the evening of November 9, and the ensuing action was a massive improvisation. The explanation for its destructiveness lies not in advance preparation but in the readiness of tens of thousands of Germans to commit violence against their Jewish neighbors.

4

"The Time for Revenge Has Now Arrived"

On Wednesday, November 9, the sun set over Germany at 4:44 PM. The weather in most of the country was unusually mild for late autumn. A system of high pressure originating in southern Europe resisted the influx of colder air from Scandinavia. In most parts of the country, overnight temperatures fell only as low as the high single digits on the Centigrade scale. The skies were mainly overcast, though it was dry in most places, the few exceptions experiencing only light drizzle. It was a night during which it would not have been uncomfortable to be outdoors.[1]

The pogrom that swept across Germany starting late that evening was instigated, sanctioned, and organized by the country's leadership; carried out mainly by members of the Nazi Party and its auxiliary groups; and enabled, and at times facilitated, by the police. The riots were by no means simultaneous across the land, but began, peaked, and ended at different times in different locations over a period of roughly twenty-four hours. They extended beyond that period in a few exceptional cases, most notably in the "Free City" of Danzig, where Nazis launched their assault against local Jewish targets only on November 12.[2]

Viewed in its entirety, the pogrom seemed frenzied and chaotic, yet it did possess a certain unifying structure and rhythm. As the violence cascaded across the Reich, it generally followed the lines of the organizational chart of the Nazi Party and the SA. The first to receive the instructions from Munich were the main regional offices of the party, located in large towns and cities. While the local Storm Troopers mobilized for their destructive tasks, the instructions worked their way downward through the party and SA hierarchies in a process that often took a long time and, in quite a few cases, was not complete until late in the day on November 10. During the hours of darkness the main core of culprits consisted of the Storm Troopers, but as night turned to day, a considerably wider circle of perpetrators was drawn into the action. It was also during the day on November 10 that the majority of mass arrests took place. Ultimately about 30,000 Jewish men were sent to the concentration camps at Buchenwald, Dachau, and Sachsenhausen.

Even as it was a nationwide event possessing certain unifying characteristics, the Kristallnacht was an aggregation of hundreds of individual, local pogroms, each of which unfolded according to a unique convergence of factors. Among the most important of these were the size, economic profile, and visibility of the local Jewish community. Notwithstanding the symbolic significance of Jews and Jewish-owned property as targets of Nazi aggression, the local pogroms were also shaped in part by the personal and economic relationships between Jews and their non-Jewish neighbors. Much also depended on the temperament, tactical judgment, and ideological zeal of the local Nazi leadership, which possessed a good deal of latitude when it came to interpreting and implementing the instructions received from above. On the other side of the equation was the presence—or absence—of local non-Jews who, for whatever reason, objected to the violence and had the courage to intervene against it. Similarly, we must consider the role played by local government officials—be they police, firefighters, or other civil servants—who often struggled to balance professional integrity against the pressure to carry out orders that they recognized to be immoral and illegal. Finally, the contours of the violence at the local level were shaped to a considerable degree by the ways in which the Jews themselves reacted to the assault. Organized resistance was out of the question, given their precarious situation in Germany after almost six years of Nazi rule. But many Jews remained anything but passive, taking some form of action to protect themselves and their families.

One of the most remarkable features of the Kristallnacht was its geographic comprehensiveness. The violence erupted not in dozens but in *hundreds* of communities, the vast majority of them small cities and towns where only a handful of Jews were present. Jewish population centers such as Berlin and Frankfurt were major sites of terror and destruction, to be sure, but a significant percentage of German Jews had lived for a long time not in these large cities but rather in more provincial places. The list of places in which pogroms occurred on November 9 and 10 includes many towns unknown even to experienced scholars of German history, towns such as Allendorf, Bad Vilbel, Echzell, Falkenstein, Goddelau, Hungen, Illvesheim, Kirch-Beerfurth, Küstrin, Laubach, Messel, Nieder-Mockstadt, Obbornhofen, Platjenwerbe, Ritterhude, Strümpfelbrünn, Treysa, Weisweiler, and Zwingenberg. In all these places Germans were prepared to inflict violence upon their Jewish neighbors. The number of Jews in these, and many other, obscure towns had dwindled since the Nazis had come to power. Many had relocated to cities, seeking the protection and comfort of the larger Jewish communities there. But a few Jewish families remained in November 1938, and they were easy targets during the pogrom, as were their small synagogues.

The acts of violence on November 9 and 10 were committed primarily by members of the SA. This had also been the case in Hesse on

November 7 and 8. The SA had not played so decisive a role in Germany since the "Night of the Long Knives" in June 1934. Hitler's decision at that time to decapitate the Storm Troopers by ordering the arrest and murder of Ernst Röhm and other leading figures had been intended to neutralize the SA's potential for revolutionary violence. Hitler had deemed this a necessary step for ensuring the collaboration of the German economic and military elite with his regime. Although the organizational influence of the SA had diminished, its continued existence as a mass organization remained vital to the Nazi regime. For many rank-and-file Nazis, participation in the marches, rallies, charity drives, and other activities sponsored by the SA continued to be an important form of political involvement. The commemoration of the Beer Hall Putsch every year on November 9 was a highlight for many members of the SA. Not only were the attendant ceremonies elaborate, but the event being celebrated recalled the bygone days when the SA was at the very center of the Nazi movement. On November 9, 1938, not a few Storm Troopers recognized a moment when they could, once again, play a decisive role in the affairs of the German nation.

On the evening of November 9, Storm Troopers throughout Germany engaged in rowdy drinking as part of the annual observance of the Beer Hall Putsch. Directives to mobilize for the anti-Jewish action often arrived in the middle of these celebrations. Thus it was not merely the institutionalized antisemitism of the SA that explains the readiness of the Storm Troopers to behave barbarically on the night of November 9, but also its deeply rooted masculine culture of beer-hall hooliganism. The keyed-up and drunken state of some Storm Troopers helps explain why in certain instances the violence intensified beyond the bounds stipulated by the Nazi leadership on the evening of November 9, reaching the level of murder, rape, and widespread theft of Jewish property.[3] It should be emphasized, however, that most of the crimes perpetrated during the pogrom were committed by men who were not acting under the influence of alcohol.

The rioting Storm Troopers were, in most cases, men ranging in age from their mid-twenties to their mid-forties. Most had joined the Nazi Party after January 1933, though a significant minority consisted of "Old Fighters," whose affiliation with the SA or the Nazi movement stretched further back. Although all segments of the German socioeconomic hierarchy were represented among the rioting Storm Troopers, the vast majority could be categorized as members of the lower middle and working classes. A great many were shopkeepers and skilled workers. All told, the Storm Troopers who committed acts of violence during Kristallnacht constituted a representative sample of the SA membership at the time.[4]

Although the Storm Troopers constituted the core of the rioters, the circle of perpetrators widened considerably as the pogrom unfolded, coming to include many other categories of people. November 10 was originally supposed to be a normal school and work day in Germany. As the day progressed, however, significant numbers of German youths engaged in physical attacks on Jews and their property. In most cases they had been mobilized by local officials of the Hitler Youth or by their schools. Classes of schoolchildren were marched from their schools and set loose on Jewish targets, encouraged by their teachers. In several postwar trials, and in the testimony of many Jews, victims and witnesses noted that the children made a party out of the vandalism and were difficult to bring under control once local authorities intervened to put a halt to the destruction. The exploitation of children as agents of group violence was especially shameful, which explains not only why it was emphasized in many of the postwar Kristallnacht trials but perhaps also why it has gone virtually unmentioned in the memoirs of Germans who grew up in the Third Reich. There were many similar instances in factories and other places of work, where mobs of employees were organized on short notice to participate in the riots. More often than not, the employer was himself one of the lead instigators of the action.

Exactly as had been the case in Hesse on November 7 and 8, widespread looting followed vandalism against Jewish-owned property. Most of it was spontaneous, and all of it occurred in direct contravention of explicit prohibitions issued by the party and the police. Large numbers of Germans who had had no direct involvement in the actual violence showed little reluctance to help themselves to its material spoils. Some postwar prosecutors regarded such looting as an integral component of the violence and humiliation perpetrated upon German Jews in November 1938, and they pressed charges in quite a few cases, as we will see. Notably, many of those who had engaged in the looting were women, providing a compelling illustration of how the gendered division of labor that characterized German society more generally could also extend into the sphere of persecution.

The images that have come to dominate memory of the Kristallnacht are those of damaged and destroyed buildings, mainly synagogues but also Jewish-owned shops. This focus on property has at times obscured the massive terror against *people* that was unleashed during the pogrom. Nazi officials later determined that ninety-one Jews had been killed during the violence.[5] This figure was based on police reports and included neither Jewish suicides nor the significantly larger number of Jews who were arrested in connection with the pogrom and would die in concentration camps in the following weeks and months.[6] When it initiated the pogrom, the Nazi leadership did not specifically call for Jews to be killed. The instructions the national police leadership disseminated stipulated systematic vandalism of Jewish property and mass arrests of Jews, but not killing. Murder was not the official intention. But even after the first reports of killings reached the national leadership in the early hours of November 10, nobody saw fit to issue an order specifically prohibiting such acts. When a Nazi official in Munich suggested to Goebbels that the killing of Jews might cause the pogrom to spiral out of control, the propaganda minister answered that one should "not get excited about a dead Jew."[7] In the end, nobody at the pinnacle of the Nazi regime was, or should have been, surprised that the orgy of violence claimed Jewish lives.

This was indeed the barely disguised conclusion of the High Court of the Nazi Party, which subsequently investigated a number of cases of murder, rape, and looting arising from the pogrom.[8] Its judgment, issued in February 1939, remained secret until it was discovered in Nazi archives after the war. The court found that the potential for murder was inherent in the instructions Goebbels issued on the evening of November 9. As the court explained, during the "time of struggle" before 1933, Nazi leaders had learned how to protect the party from the legal repercussions of illegal demonstrations and other actions. They did so by formulating orders in a vague and imprecise manner so as to preserve plausible deniability for the party when its members were instructed to do something illegal. For their part, the lower-level members of the movement had learned how to read between the lines of such orders, understanding that the wishes of the party leadership did not necessarily correspond to the text of their instructions. This method of communication had become institutionalized inside the party, and it continued to operate into the period of Nazi rule. It should not have been a shock to anyone, the Nazi High Court maintained, that on November 9 and 10, 1938, a number of rank-and-file party members, and especially Storm Troopers, interpreted their instructions as a green light for murder. The court pointed out some of the vague and, in its opinion, "unfortunate" formulations that had impressed themselves on low-level Nazis in the days and hours leading up to the pogrom: "Not the Jew Grünspan [*sic*] but all of Jewry bears the guilt for the death of party comrade vom Rath"; the German people will "take revenge against all of Jewry"; and all SA men "know what they have to do." Some Storm Troopers logically and understandably concluded, argued the court, that "Jewish blood had to flow" and that "according to the will of the leadership, the life of a Jew does not matter."

One might be tempted to dismiss this ruling as an attempt by the High Court to whitewash the Nazi leadership's responsibility for ordering murder, but this was clearly not the case. The ruling was crafted first and foremost to justify leniency toward a number of ordinary Nazi perpetrators, and it was critical (even if only implicitly) of the recklessness Goebbels displayed on the evening of November 9. The substance of the court's opinion corresponds to a great deal of the evidence we have for how some Germans came to murder Jews during the Kristallnacht.

The inevitability that the violence unleashed by the Nazi leadership would result in murder can be illustrated by a case drawn from northern Germany.[9] Among the Nazi dignitaries Goebbels addressed in the Old Town Hall in Munich on the evening of November 9 was Johann Heinrich Böhmcker. A party "Old Fighter" since the mid-1920s, Böhmcker had risen to become the Nazi boss of Bremen, where he was both mayor and head of the SA. When Goebbels finished speaking, Böhmcker rushed to a telephone to convey Goebbels's instructions to his subordinates in Bremen. Böhmcker's call was taken by his chief of staff, a man named Römpagel. Böhmcker told Römpagel that the Bremen SA was to "destroy all Jewish businesses immediately." SA men were then to ensure that no plundering occurred. The instructions from Böhmcker, which Römpagel took down in writing, continued: "Jewish synagogues are to be set ablaze immediately." The fire department should be allowed to intervene only when fires threatened "Aryan" property. The police were not to interfere at all. Böhmcker was emphatic on this point: "The Führer desires that the police not interfere." Finally, Böhmcker ordered the SA in Bremen to confiscate all weapons from Jews. Should Jews mount resistance, they should be "gunned down."

It was now Römpagel's responsibility to disseminate the instructions through the SA organization in Bremen. Before reaching the rank-and-file SA man on the ground, the order had to be relayed downward through an elaborate chain-of-command. Chief of Staff Römpagel would first have to notify the commanders of each SA brigade in Bremen. The brigade commanders would then, in turn, have to transmit the order to the head of each *Standarte*. The order would continue to work its way downward through the *Sturmbann* level and finally to the most local unit of the SA, the *Sturm*. Late in the night of November 9, this procedure was carried out for the most part verbally, usually via telephone.

In the small town of Lessum, just outside of Bremen, the telephone chain that began with Johann Heinrich Böhmcker in Munich ended with Fritz K. A textile salesman by training, and a Nazi since 1932, thirty-two-year-old Fritz K. served both as the mayor of Lessum and as the head of the local SA-*Sturm*. At around 3:00 AM, Fritz K. was fast asleep in his home. He was awakened by a banging on the front door. The culprit was the superintendent of the Lessum Town Hall, where Fritz K. was needed to take an urgent phone call. Fritz K. dressed quickly, rushed to the town hall, and took the receiver. The person on the other end of the line was Walter S., an officer in SA-*Standarte* 411 in Bremen. Walter S. asked Fritz K. whether he had received the order for the anti-Jewish action. Fritz K. had no idea what Walter S. meant. Walter S. angrily described what had been taking place all over Germany while Fritz K. and the SA men under his command in Lessum had been asleep.

There had been a break in the chain of communication. Fritz K. had not received the order from his immediate superior, Ernst R., the commander of *Sturmbann* 3 of *Standarte* 411. Figuring out why this had happened was now less important than fixing the problem, which meant immediately activating the SA in Lessum against the local Jewish community. Walter S. described the order that had been transmitted from Munich by Johann Heinrich Böhmcker. He told Fritz K. that, as an act of revenge for the murder of Ernst vom Rath, all Jewish shops were to be destroyed and that synagogues were to be set ablaze. Fritz K., who had been caught off guard by Walter S.'s instructions, responded with questions. He asked Walter S., "What do we do with the Jews?" Walter S. responded curtly before hanging up in frustration: "Get rid of the Jews . . . now act!"

The anger of Walter S. combined with the confusion of Fritz K. to produce a fateful miscommunication. Immediately after the phone call had ended, Fritz K. returned home and told his wife that he had received an order to kill the Jews of Lessum. Fritz K. had trouble believing the order, and his doubts were reinforced by those of his wife. But believing that he had to act, Fritz K. began to gather the men of his SA-*Sturm*. He informed them that a massive operation was under way all over Germany, and that "all of the Jews must go." He told them to be ready for action but ordered them to wait until he could confirm the substance of the order.

While his men waited, Fritz K. drove to the home of his immediate superior, Ernst R., in the neighboring town of Vegesack. Ernst R. was also in a state of confusion about the night's events. Together he and Fritz K. telephoned the SA head office in Bremen. They were connected not with Römpagel, who had originally disseminated Böhmcker's order from Munich, but rather with the officer who happened to be on duty at the moment. The officer did not seem to know very much about the details of the order, but he did assure Ernst R. and Fritz K. that "the night of the long knives has arrived."

Fritz K. returned to Lessum, where his SA men were waiting. He gave them the news: the local Jews were to be killed.[10] Several members of the *Sturm* objected to the order. One of these was August F. Born in 1885, August F. had trained as an engineer and had served on German U-boats during the First World War, for which he had received an Iron Cross First Class. After the war, while working as a machinist in and around Bremen, August F. had gravitated into the right-wing orbit. He joined the paramilitary Stahlhelm in 1928, later to become a Nazi Storm Trooper by default when the Stahlhelm was absorbed into the SA. When August F., along with other members of his SA unit, objected to the order to kill Jews, Fritz K. reminded them of their oath of loyalty to Hitler.

One of Fritz K.'s men then asked how the Jews should be killed. Should they perhaps be clubbed to death? Ultimately they decided on firearms, and several of the men were dispatched to fetch their pistols. One of these was Storm Trooper J., who, after returning to the group with his pistol, made a point of handing it to August F., who had openly objected to the order. In front of the other men, Storm Trooper J. announced that August F. would have to prove his loyalty as a Nazi and his mettle as a Storm Trooper. What kind of example would be set for the younger members of the troop if August F., the senior member of the group and a decorated war veteran, were to shirk from his duty?

Fritz K. now ordered Storm Trooper J., August F., and several of their comrades to dispose of one of the well-known Jewish residents of Lessum, Dr. G. Storm Trooper J. led a column of several dozen SA comrades down one of the main streets of Lessum, the Hindenburgstrasse. As they marched, August F. continued to protest against the order he had been given. He threatened to throw the pistol that Storm Trooper J. had given him into the sewer, but before he could do so the gun had been grabbed away from him. The column turned into the Bremerhavenerstrasse and stopped in front of the home of the Jewish Dr. G. and his wife. Storm Trooper J. called out for August F., who tried to lie low. But the other men forced him to the front, taunting him for his lack of courage.

With August F. standing beside him, Storm Trooper J. began to ring the doorbell repeatedly. A neighbor who lived in the apartment adjacent to the Jewish couple opened the door to the building and was shocked to see the large crowd of men confronting her. Storm Trooper J. pointed his pistol at her chest, shouting, "Are you a Jew?" Before she could respond, Dr. G. appeared at the door.

Dr. G. had once enjoyed a strong local reputation as a physician. He had been admired for his social conscience, having treated poor or unemployed patients free of charge, and having dispensed medications at his own expense. In 1938 Dr. G. was already seventy-eight years old, and he had retired even before the Nazi regime had purged Jews from the medical professions. Dr. G. lived with his wife, who was sixty-five years old at the time of the pogrom.

When Dr. G. appeared at the front door, he was immediately forced back into the building by the Storm Troopers. They treated him as anything but a respected local humanitarian, manhandling him back into his apartment, where his wife had been waiting. Storm Trooper J. turned to August F., pressed the pistol into his hand, and ordered him to shoot the Jewish doctor. August F. resisted the order, but Storm Trooper J. was persistent. When August F. tried to flee, Storm Trooper J. grabbed him, exclaiming in front of the other SA men, "You know the order, now carry it out!" August F. acquiesced. He entered the bedroom where the Jewish couple had in the meantime sought refuge, and pointed his gun at Dr. G. He then announced: "I have been instructed to carry out a difficult assignment." Storm Trooper J. continued to press August F. into action. The wife of Dr. G. then positioned herself between August F. and her husband, exclaiming, "Sir, please aim carefully!" August F. shot the woman twice. As she lay dead or dying, he pointed his pistol at Dr. G., who turned his body away from his assailant. When August F. pulled the trigger, his gun jammed. Dr. G. cowered in fear as August F. adjusted his pistol. August F. then released four shots into Dr. G.'s back. August F.'s impulse was to flee from the scene, but Storm Trooper J. forced him to wait until their comrades could be gathered together for an orderly departure. Storm Trooper J. noticed that August F. was in a state of distress, so he suggested that the two get a drink before they returned home to their families.

Inasmuch as the violence of November 9 and 10, 1938, did not, in most cases, result directly in the killing of Jews, the murders of Dr. and Mrs. G. cannot be cited as typical for the Kristallnacht. But the violence in Lessum did, nonetheless, typify the events of the Kristallnacht in several important ways. The hasty and improvised organization of the pogrom in Lessum, as well as the messiness and miscommunication that were inherent to such an enterprise, conform to a broader pattern of the way the pogrom was initiated in many places around Germany, not only during the night of November 9, but throughout the day on November 10 as well. Because the nationwide pogrom had not been planned in advance, the dissemination of the order to unleash it depended on a network of communication within the Nazi Party that was often less than efficient. This was especially true in smaller communities that were isolated from the main regional offices of the party or the SA.

Also typical was the interplay of motives that lay behind the actions of the perpetrators. While some Storm Troopers could barely disguise their satisfaction that the day of reckoning had finally arrived for Germany's Jews, others, like August F., were badgered or cajoled into action by their comrades. The Lessum case also exemplifies the decisive role played by local officials in determining the form and intensity of the violence. Johann Heinrich Böhmcker's instructions from Munich did not specify that Jews be killed, and it was only locally, in and around Bremen, that the meaning of the directive was distorted as the result of a combination of antisemitic zeal and imprecise communication. The killing of Dr. and Mrs. G. was not the result of a direct order from the leadership of the Nazi regime. But the potential for such brutality already resided in the hearts and minds of some of the SA men in Lessum, and it was precisely this murderous potential that Hitler and Goebbels unleashed on the night of November 9.

Lichtenfels was another provincial town in which violence against the Jews turned deadly during the Kristallnacht.[11] Located in Upper Franconia in northern Bavaria, Lichtenfels had a population in 1938 of about seven thousand. The Jewish community of the town had never been large. In September 1938 it consisted of fifty-three people, having declined from sixty-nine in 1933 at the time of the Nazi takeover. The town had a synagogue, a Jewish cemetery, and a Jewish school that had been founded in 1804. As in many such small towns around the country, the majority of the occupationally active Jews in Lichtenfels made their living from small-scale commerce. Five of the Jews were active as cattle-traders, an occupation that had generated more than its share of antisemitic stereotypes in rural and small-town Germany over the centuries.[12]

The main organizer of the violence in Lichtenfels was forty-four-year-old Lorenz K., a trained engineer who had joined the Nazi Party in 1927 and had served as the chief of the party in the town since 1932.

At about 1:30 AM on November 10, Lorenz K. received the order by telephone from the Nazi regional office in Bayreuth. He assembled his immediate subordinates, among them thirty-six-year-old Wilhelm K., who at the time was the mayor of Lichtenfels and the former head of the local SA. Wilhelm K. was a business clerk who had joined the Nazi Party in 1926, qualifying him as a genuine Nazi "Old Fighter." In the wee hours of November 10, he mobilized a gang of about two dozen SA men. The men wore their SA uniforms as they carried out their tasks; the instruction from Munich to execute the action in plain clothes had not gotten through to Lichtenfels.

Otherwise the pogrom unfolded here much as it did in small towns all over Germany. The violence began at the synagogue, where the Storm Troopers smashed windows, demolished furniture, and threw prayer books and Torah scrolls out onto the street. They then proceeded to attack the Jewish community. It was no secret who the Jews were, where they lived, or where they operated their businesses. The SA men dragged Jews out of their homes and paraded them, most still in their pajamas and nightgowns, through the town. They vandalized Jewish homes and businesses. The forced entry into the home of the Jewish family P. exemplified the intimacy of the pogrom in small communities such as Lichtenfels. The SA men broke down the front door to the cheers of some members of the crowd of onlookers that had formed. Once inside the home, one of the SA men, Franz F., was recognized by Mrs. P., who exclaimed, "Herr F., are you here as well? Please, neighbor, leave us alone!" Franz F. hollered back, "Shut your trap, you old Jewish swine, or we'll strike you dead!" At one business, the textile shop owned by the Jewish family K., systematic plundering took place through the use of a delivery truck, which was loaded up with stolen items at least twice. The same truck was then used to haul away carpets from the synagogue. The arrest of the Jewish men began at around 3:00 AM. The SA men rounded up twenty-two men and threw them into the local jail. One of the Jewish men took his own life with poison in the jail. The police, under orders from the mayor—who happened to be one of the chief organizers of the pogrom—stood by and did nothing. Only at about 4:00 AM did the police begin to intervene, mainly to prevent the looting, which had become widespread, from getting completely out of hand.

What set the otherwise fairly typical case of Lichtenfels apart was the murder of a Jewish woman, Mrs. S., who lived directly adjacent to the synagogue. As she opened a window to see what was happening next door, she was struck hard in the head by a riding crop. The culprit was Franz F., Jr., the twenty-seven-year-old son of the man who had threatened Mrs. P. Mrs. S. was injured, but not badly. This seemed to mark the end of the incident. About twelve hours later, however, on the afternoon of November 10, a mob consisting of both youths and adults formed in front of the synagogue, and the threat to Mrs. S. was renewed. Several members of the mob, including Franz F., Jr., forced their way into her home and abused her physically, throwing eggs into her face and shoving her around until she bled from contact with broken glass. The youths were responsible for much of the brutality, encouraged in their actions by Franz F., Jr., and other adults. Franz F., Jr., seemed to bear some special animus toward Mrs. S. At one point he implored the youths to "strike her dead, the Judensau," echoing some of the language his father had used during the night.

Late on November 10 the body of Mrs. S. was found in a ditch outside of town. Exactly how she was killed and by whom has never been established. In 1949 a German court could not identify the murderer or murderers. It was possible that she had been raped before she was killed, but there was really no way to know. Prosecutors suspected that Franz F., Jr., had followed through on his vendetta against Mrs. S., but this could not be proven, despite the consensus that Franz F., Jr., had been a man of "low instincts." But even though the court could not establish the details of her death, this case was in one respect clearly different from that of the murder of Dr. G. and his wife in Lessum. In Lichtenfels nobody operated under the misconception that an order had been given to kill Jews. Quite to the contrary, the Storm Troopers and their collaborators in Lichtenfels seemed to understand quite fully that their mandate was to terrorize the Jewish community, vandalize their property, and arrest their men—but not kill them. The murder of Mrs. S. was the exception, but one that nonetheless reflected the widely held perception that Jewish life was cheap.[13]

This perception was not restricted to the Storm Troopers of the SA. Several murders during the Kristallnacht were committed by members of the SS, whose role in the pogrom has been underestimated by historians. Whereas the frenetic, at times chaotic, violence associated with the pogrom has been depicted as consistent with the character of the ruffians who populated the SA, it did not seem to correspond to the more methodical and disciplined style of the SS, the organization that in 1941 would take charge of the systematic murder of Europe's Jews. While it is undoubtedly true that the involvement of the SS in the Kristallnacht was eclipsed by that of the SA, its part in the violence was not insignificant.

A unit of SS men perpetrated the cold-blooded murder of the Jewish businessman Alfons V. and the attempted murder of the Jewish businessman Louis L. in Aschaffenburg in the early morning hours of November 10.[14] Aschaffenburg, a city of 40,000 on the border between Bavaria and Hesse, had had a well-established and relatively well-off Jewish community of about 600 at the time of the Nazi takeover in 1933. By November 1938 the number of Jews had declined to 339. A chief source of Jewish prosperity in Aschaffenburg was the manufacture of clothing; in 1935 there were still 20 Jewish-owned clothing factories in the city. Local Nazis resented this continuation of what they regarded as Jewish economic privilege. After 1933 the Jews of Aschaffenburg—like those in most other cities in Germany—had been subjected to various forms of harassment. These had included the desecration of the local Jewish cemetery in 1936.[15]

Early in the morning on November 10, in the middle of the pogrom against the Jews of Aschaffenburg, a small group of local SS men decided to carry out a couple of murders. The group included Heinrich

T., a twenty-seven-year-old grocer who had been a member of the SS since 1933. Heinrich T. had moonlighted as a clerk at his father-in-law's clothing factory, which had placed him in direct economic competition with some of the local Jews. This applied as well to a second member of the group, Georg V., a forty-two-year-old bookkeeper whose main employment was in a clothing factory. Georg V. had joined the Nazi Party and the SS in 1933. Another member of the group was Johann G., a forty-five-year-old machinist who had long been connected with right-wing movements. After fighting in World War One, Johann G. had joined the reactionary Bund Oberland paramilitary organization. He joined the Nazi Party in 1929 and became a member of the SS in 1931. For several years in the mid-thirties he had served on the Aschaffenburg City Council. A further member of the group, Bruno R., had been on the city council as well, serving a term as its secretary. Twenty-nine-year-old Bruno R., an electrician by training, had joined the Nazi Party in 1927 and the SS in 1931.

Although none of the SS men were personally acquainted with either of their Jewish victims, they did select them specifically as targets. A key motive was antisemitism based on economic resentment. This much is certain from the nature of the antisemitic epithets that accompanied the crimes. Upon breaking into the home of the Jewish family L., Heinrich T. exclaimed, "This is for Mr. vom Rath." He then shot his victim and said, "You Jewish swine will exploit German peasants no longer." After leaving Mr. L. to die (in the event, he survived his wounds), the SS men went to watch the burning of the Aschaffenburg synagogue. There Heinrich T. told the others, "Let's get the grain Jew." Of the more than three hundred Jews in Aschaffenburg, Heinrich T. singled out the grain trader Alfons V. for execution. We do not know whether this was an act of retribution for one particular transgression on the part of Alfons V., or whether Alfons V. had more generally come to symbolize Jewish commercial exploitation for the local Nazis. The SS men abducted him from his home and drove him to the edge of town. Heinrich T. lectured the Jewish prisoner, enumerating a catalog of accusations that would have been familiar to any member of the SS. "Now," he said, "you can think about all of your disgraceful deeds, how you've exploited peasants and raped Christian women." One of the other men added, "Think about the most recent disgraceful act of Jewry, think about Herr vom Rath." Alfons V. protested, "I've not done anything," to which one of the SS men responded, "Herr vom Rath was also innocent and was a German. Now it's over for you. You have to pay for the action which your people have perpetrated." Heinrich T. shot the Jewish prisoner repeatedly; then the other SS men dumped him on the road. A milkman on his morning rounds found Alfons V., who was still alive, and drove him to the hospital, where he died six days later.

Many of the Jews who died on November 9 and 10 were not the victims of outright murder. In many instances, barbaric abuse resulted in death. Such was the case when a Jewish woman in Mannheim was seized from her home, locked up in a nearby asylum, and doused with ice-cold water. She died from exposure shortly thereafter.[16] A number of Jews were killed as they defended themselves or their property from attack.[17] Many others committed suicide when they were confronted with situations they found unbearable. These included Dr. Bernhard R., the head of the gynecological clinic in the Jewish hospital in Frankfurt, who took his own life with poison as he was being arrested in front of his own patients in the middle of the night.[18] So while murder was the most heinous of the crimes perpetrated upon the Jews of Germany on November 9 and 10, too sharp a focus on actual cases of premeditated homicide might lead us to underappreciate the depth and breadth of the physical violence during Kristallnacht. The number of Jews who were severely beaten was far greater than the number of those killed, and many were able to survive their wounds only by dint of good fortune. In cases too numerous to count, a frightening viciousness and glee accompanied the beatings.

Although the most memorable images of the Kristallnacht are those of burning synagogues and vandalized Jewish-owned shops, nothing was off-limits for the rioters. The targets included the most vulnerable among Germany's Jews: children and the elderly. The Jewish orphanage in Königsberg was attacked and thoroughly destroyed.[19] In Dinslaken, rioters broke into the orphanage in the middle of the night and forced the children into the courtyard. Then they demolished the interior of the facility, and new housing had to be found for the children.[20] A Jewish old-age home in Werder, near Essen, was invaded and closed down, its elderly residents forced to scramble for lodging elsewhere. The Jewish old-age home in Neustadt was set ablaze and completely demolished. Its seventy-two elderly Jewish residents were hounded out of bed and forced into the street, still in their night clothes. Many of them were later transferred to the already seriously overcrowded old-age home in Mannheim. In Emden, the residents of the Jewish old-age home—all between seventy and eighty years of age—were forced out of bed in the middle of the night and made to march past the burning synagogue. As a form of torture and humiliation, they were forced to stand outside and do knee-bends and other exercises. In Nuremberg, Storm Troopers invaded the Jewish hospital and forced the patients to stand at attention, even those who were in bad shape and those who had just been operated upon. Several died as the result of embolisms and bleeding.[21]

Whereas some Storm Troopers felt pressure to engage in the violence, many others did so with enthusiasm. Amandus D. was a thirty-eight-year-old prison guard. He had joined the Nazi Party in 1932 and had remained fairly active in the SA.[22] His comrade Reinhold P., a financial clerk, was eleven years younger. He had joined the Nazi Party in 1933 and had held a few official positions with the local party. Both men lived in Rockenberg, a small town in Hesse. At the time of the pogrom, Reinhold P. was serving as mayor of the town. In November 1938 there were no Jews in Rockenburg. A pogrom would have been superfluous. But the two men did not want to be left out of the action. On November 10 they decided to help with the attack against the small Jewish communities of the neighboring towns of Gambach, Griedel, and Butzbach. At about 3:30 PM they drove to Gambach, where there were three Jewish families. Local residents directed them to the Jewish homes. The men began to encourage the local population to help with the impending attack. They soon found themselves at the helm of a fairly large group of participants, one that included adults, youths, and even young children. After finishing with the Jewish homes, the mob moved to the town synagogue and continued the vandalism.

Their work in Gambach concluded, the two men got into their car and drove on to Butzbach. Their first stop was a pub, where they fortified themselves with some beer. Amandus D. began to worry that he would miss his evening shift at the prison, which was to begin at 7:00 PM. So the men decided to leave the pogrom in Butzbach to the locals and return home to Rockenberg. On the way they stopped briefly in Griedel to help with the ransacking of a single Jewish home.

The pogrom reached Wölfersheim in Hesse at about 1:00 PM on November 10.[23] A large group of SA men assembled for action in front of the pub that served as their usual meeting place. The leader of the Wölfersheim Nazi Party, Herr E., addressed them, announcing that "the time for revenge has now arrived." Herr E. instructed the local SA commander, Ernst M., to have his men "break everything to bits" and "beat the Jews half to death." As per their orders, they wore civilian clothes, but this fooled no one. They further betrayed their identity as an SA troop as they marched rank-and-file in lockstep. As they advanced, they were joined by a large number of workers from a local business, Hefrag, where Herr E. was employed. Herr E. had already arranged for the workers to be mobilized for the anti-Jewish action. After arriving for work on November 10, the Hefrag workers were told that they would participate in an anti-Jewish action to protest the killing of Ernst vom Rath. Some of the workers were members of the SA, though most were not. Thus reinforced, the group that was about to attack the Jewish community consisted of about 150 men.

The event had taken on the quality of a spectacle. A large throng of onlookers had accompanied the SA column through the streets of the town and had halted with it in front of the two adjacent homes of the Jewish businessmen Julius and Hermann R. The crowd watched as men from the SA and Hefrag broke into the homes, wrecking everything in sight, and physically abused the Jewish families inside. The attackers made a point of finding and burning papers that documented the debts of local Germans to the Jewish businesses. This was by no means the only case in which the pogrom provided the opportunity to erase debts to Jews.[24] As the ledgers burned, the attackers brutally beat both of the Jewish brothers. The terror inside the homes lasted for about an hour. Once the SA and their helpers had finished, many of the onlookers descended on the homes and began looting them. The plunder continued well into the evening.

The pogrom took a particularly brutal form in Bensheim, where the local Nazi leadership encouraged the violence at every turn.[25] The SS set the pogrom in motion early in the morning of November 10, and the violence persisted almost without interruption into the late evening. Members of the local SS, supported by SS comrades from the neighboring town of Auerbach, acted as the initial instigators. The SA, which was more numerous, quickly joined in, as did many townspeople. The judge who presided over the case of twenty-four perpetrators in 1948 expressed shock at the level of spontaneous participation by the residents of Bensheim. They were involved in the desecration and burning of the synagogue, the invasion and vandalism of Jewish homes, the physical beating of Jews, and the extensive looting of Jewish property. As reflected in the list of those convicted in 1948 for their actions ten years earlier, a broad cross-section of Bensheim society played a part in the violence. Rioters ranged in age (in 1938) from twenty-five to sixty-one and were engaged in a wide variety of occupations, including salesman, butcher, locksmith, engineer, building inspector, and automobile mechanic. A key factor accounting for the ugliness of the pogrom and the broad extent of local participation was the role played by the commanding SS officer, Crown Prince Erbach-Schönberg, who throughout the day asserted his authority and personal prestige in inflaming the townspeople against the Jews.

A salient feature of the pogrom in Bensheim was the systematic ritual humiliation of the Jewish community. As the town's synagogue burned, the Jews who had been rounded up were forced to dance around the burning structure. Such scenes were by no means unique to Bensheim; indeed, they were common throughout Germany during the pogrom. But in its totality the Kristallnacht was more than a ritual act of cultural degradation against the Jews of Germany; for many of its perpetrators, it was also an act of collective and individual vengeance against a group who, despite having been persistently demonized, was still present and apparently prosperous.[26] Especially for committed Nazis, the convergence of the death of Ernst vom Rath with the commemoration of Nazi martyrdom intensified the psychological urge not only to inflict violence on the Jews but also to degrade them.

The Nazi leadership had not issued instructions regarding ritual humiliation of the Jews, but such actions nevertheless occurred in a great number of cases. In Laupheim, the decisive events did not occur until late in the night on November 10. SA men forced about two dozen Jews into a market hall next to the Rathaus. The Jews were made to walk continuously in a circle. Not even the elderly were permitted to rest. Meanwhile, the town's synagogue was set ablaze. The SA marched the Jewish men to the synagogue and made them kneel before the burning structure.[27] In Heppenheim, an order came in to the local SA at about 5:00 AM. They were to destroy the synagogue. The Storm Troopers set about their task by 7:00 AM, using fire and explosives. Once the building was in ruins, a large number of local Jews were dragged from their homes and forced to clear the debris. This task required most of the day. When they were finished, the Jews were forced to march through the town toward the jail in a "parade of humiliation."[28]

Similar scenes played out around the country. In Gütersloh, as in many other places, Jews were forced to march through the streets in their night clothes. In Herford, children played in the ruins of the synagogue, tearing Torah scrolls to shreds as they chanted and cheered. In Gailingen, Jews were forced to watch the incineration of the synagogue. In a town in Ostfriesland, Jews were made to stand in their pajamas and sing obscene songs in front of the burning synagogue. In Düsseldorf Jewish men and women had to march barefoot in their pajamas across broken glass littered on the ground. In Lichtenfels, youths played football with Jewish prayer books while Jews were made to look on. In Dortmund, Jews were forced to throw their own furniture and other possessions out the windows of their homes, and then made to carry everything back upstairs. In Vienna, Jews were forced to march through the streets clad in prayer shawls and shredded Torah parchments. In Beuthen Jewish men and women were dragged out of their homes in the middle of the night and forced to watch the synagogue burn. They were made to stand before the burning building for hours. One Jew was forced to kneel before the burning building in order to be photographed. In a city in northern Germany, Jewish men were locked up in a school opposite the burning synagogue and forced to watch as SS men played soccer with a Torah scroll. One of the SS men came into the school, demanding to see the rabbi. He then shaved off the rabbi's beard in front of the other Jewish men and tried to force him into a discussion about religion. When the rabbi refused, the SS man berated him, shouting, "We are stronger than your Jehova."[29]

In Frankfurt, Rabbi H., who was highly regarded for his erudition and decency, was dragged out of the Jewish hospital and forced to watch the burning of the synagogue where both he and his father had taught for many years. Rabbi H. was recovering from a nervous breakdown that he had suffered after having been arrested and held for two weeks by the Gestapo. Given his already weakened condition, the experience was too much to bear. Rabbi H. suffered a seizure and died on the spot.[30]

If the ritual humiliation of Jews was one form of conduct in which rioters engaged without central direction, looting was another. The widespread looting of Jewish homes and shops was, in fact, a nearly universal characteristic of the pogrom, and it occurred despite centrally issued directives prohibiting it.[31] One town in which the looting was especially extreme was Bad Nauheim.[32] The anti-Jewish violence in the town could have been much worse than it was had it not been for the actions of the local Nazi Party leader. Friedrich L. was a genuine Old Fighter, having joined the party in 1923. In addition to his party duties, the thirty-six-year-old Nazi was the chairman of Bad Nauheim's local health insurance board. When the violence began on the morning of November 10, he was at work at his office in a neighboring town. In his absence, Karl S., the leader of the local SA, took the initiative in getting the pogrom started. Friedrich L. rushed back to Bad Nauheim and gathered key members of the party, instructing them to exercise restraint. This did not mean that the pogrom was halted in Bad Nauheim, where Jewish shops were invaded and demolished. But Jewish homes remained largely off-limits, and Jews were not subjected to physical beatings.

Despite this relative restraint, the extent of the looting was especially great in Bad Nauheim. Many of the townspeople who had played no part in the violence engaged in the systematic plundering of the vandalized Jewish shops almost all day long on November 10. The majority of the looters were women. Many had been standing outside the shops as the vandalism unfolded, helping themselves to merchandise that the SA men threw out onto the street. Others who were more bold went into the shops to pick through the spoils. The most popular items were articles of clothing, toys, and small pieces of furniture. When looters coveted bulkier items, they arranged for local youths to do the heavy lifting for them.

Most of the looting on November 9 and 10 was spontaneous. But there were also many examples of premeditated exploitation of the pogrom for personal enrichment. Two especially egregious cases occurred in Munich. The first involved Christian Weber, a prominent local figure in the Nazi Party notorious for financial corruption.[33] Weber had proved adept at manipulating the "Aryanization" of Jewish property for his own financial advantage. On the night of November 9, he led a group of SS men from Munich to the suburb of Planegg, where Baron

Rudolf Hirsch, the scion of a wealthy Jewish family, had his estate.[34] Since the summer of 1938, Hirsch had been involved in negotiations with the city of Munich over the "Aryanization" of his property. Weber's aim on the night of November 9 was to force Hirsch to expedite that process, from which he hoped to profit personally. His group included Hermann Fegelein, who during World War Two would command an SS unit responsible for the murder of thousands of Jews in the Soviet Union (and who would also marry Eva Braun's younger sister). After arriving at the Hirsch estate, the SS men shoved Hirsch around and did some damage to the villa. They burned several rooms, though the building, which Weber hoped to acquire, remained largely intact. On November 10, Baron Hirsch was arrested and sent to Dachau, where he was badly abused, and from which he was eventually released only after promising to sell his property immediately.[35]

No less avaricious than Weber were the members of a group of Hitler Youth leaders in Munich, who on the night of November 9 conspired to exploit the pogrom to extort money from local Jews.[36] The leader of the group, Emil Klein, was a thirty-three-year-old Nazi who had participated in the Beer Hall Putsch in 1923. Much like Christian Weber, Klein was a genuine Nazi "Old Fighter" who found a way to combine authentic ideological commitment with a drive for personal enrichment. In November 1938 Klein was the chief of the Hitler Youth Division "Hochland." On the evening of November 9, he attended the meeting of Nazi leaders in the Munich Old Town Hall, where he heard Goebbels deliver the instructions regarding the pogrom. From there Klein went to a nearby theater, where a number of his subordinates were attending a performance. Klein found them during an intermission and ordered them to assemble later at the Hotel Excelsior. The meeting in the hotel took place at around 1:00 AM. Klein and his men hatched their plan to extort money from wealthy Jews. They targeted in particular members of the Bernheimer family, which over several generations had amassed a fortune through its operation of one of Europe's most successful and prestigious art and antiques dealerships.

The first to be visited was one of the younger members of the family, Paul Bernheimer. Several of Klein's men drove to Bernheimer's villa in the middle of the night. They were admitted into the Bernheimer home after claiming that they were engaging in a "security check." One of the men told Bernheimer that, in view of the death of Ernst vom Rath, Bernheimer would be given an opportunity to express his remorse through a financial contribution to the Hitler Youth. The money, they assured Bernheimer, would be used to educate young Germans. Bernheimer asked how much money was involved. The response was that the amount would be up to him, though the men reminded him that they knew he was very wealthy. After some back and forth, the men named their price: five thousand Reichsmarks. Bernheimer made out a check for that sum and handed it over. He was also compelled to sign a statement condemning the killing of vom Rath and declaring that his payment to the Hitler Youth was voluntary.

The men returned to the Excelsior Hotel and presented the check to their chief, Emil Klein. Although Klein was disappointed in the amount collected from Bernheimer—who, Klein argued, could have paid ten times as much—he was pleased by the success of the tactic, and he ordered his men to repeat it. The next target would be Otto Bernheimer, the owner of the famous business. Klein sent a team to the Bernheimer home with orders to collect 50,000 Reichsmarks. When the men arrived at the home, they were met by Otto's son, Kurt, who explained that the family would need time to arrange payment. He appeased the men temporarily by writing out a check for 800 Reichsmarks. A while later, after some middle-of-the-night scrambling and a telephone conversation with a banker, Bernheimer turned over a money order for 48,000 Reichsmarks.

The operation continued along in this way throughout the night. The Hitler Youth officials extorted 50,000 Reichsmarks from yet another member of the Bernheimer family, in addition to 10,000 from Fritz Kohn, 5,000 from Max Löwenthal, 5,000 from Max Uhlfelder, and 4,000 from Emil Kraemer. The financial extortion was only part of the plan. Emil Klein and his men were also involved in several attempts to force the "Aryanization" of Jewish homes through acts of intimidation. Klein's men occupied two Jewish-owned villas after telling the residents that they would have to leave immediately.

On November 10, Klein dispatched a couple of his men to a branch of the Deutsche Bank to cash the checks that had been collected overnight. In broad terms, the men explained the circumstances in which they had acquired the checks. The bank employees were cautious, claiming that some inquiries would be necessary before they could cash the checks. Klein's men then tried their luck at a second bank, Merk, Fink, and Co. Again they explained that the Hitler Youth had acquired the money during the events of the previous night. As the men haggled with the bank employees, two Gestapo officers arrived to arrest them. The magnitude and audaciousness of the extortion was too much even for the Nazi Party, which later tried and expelled some of the Hitler Youth officials.

Most of the extortion capers that unfolded during the pogrom were more petty. In Nuremberg, Jews were beaten until they signed papers pledging to transfer their property. In Berlin, some Jews were taken to the cellar of the synagogue in Pestalozzistrasse, where they were beaten and then made to stand without a break for a long period of time. Their captors demanded money in return for their release.[37] Like the widespread looting and the elaborate blackmail that was attempted in Munich, these forms of stealing were ultimately predicated on the assumption that Jewish wealth had been acquired illegitimately and was, therefore, fair game.

German youths played a central role in the violence of the Kristallnacht. In many cases the beatings of Jews and the destruction of Jewish property were carried out largely, or even mainly, by teenage boys. Often they were mobilized by school administrators, teachers, or officials of the Hitler Youth. But in many instances they acted spontaneously, goaded on by their friends, their parents, and other adults. The youths at times proved capable of behaving with a brutality on par with that of the older Storm Troopers.

In Büdingen, a mob of adults and schoolchildren terrorized the town's six Jewish families over a period of several hours on November 10. The mob broke into the Jewish homes, smashing dishes and furniture, slitting mattresses, and destroying other personal possessions. In one home, two teenage boys brutally shoved a sixty-year-old Jewish woman, Frau H., and her disabled husband into an alcove under the stairs and beat them. When the woman dashed from her home, she was again seized by a group of youths who beat her up. The group was led by an adult, Georg L., a butcher. A member of neither the Nazi Party nor the SA, Georg L. joined in the violence spontaneously after getting off work in the local slaughterhouse. Ironically, the person who came to the rescue of Frau H. was Karl Albert R., the leader of the Nazi Party in the town. Despite his position, he had not supported the pogrom and had not been involved in carrying it out.[38]

On November 10 at about 11:00 AM, the mayor of the town of Grossen-Linden, who was also the local chief of the Nazi Party, appeared at the town elementary school. He ordered the principal, Wilhelm S., to mobilize the students for an anti-Jewish demonstration. Forty-year-old Wilhelm S. had been a teacher at the school since 1926 and had been promoted to principal in 1933, the same year he joined the Nazi Party. He was not enthusiastic about the order to mobilize the students, but he did as he was instructed. He assembled the students from the four most senior cohorts—about 200 students in all—as well as their teachers. Led by the mayor, the principal, and the teachers, the students walked a few hundred meters to a cluster of Jewish homes, where a large crowd of locals had already gathered. As a group of adults broke into the homes, the students began to throw stones through the windows. Two Jewish children and their aunt were dragged from the home into the street and given over to the students, who battered them with stones and spat on them. Principal Wilhelm S. began to worry that his students were getting out of control. He ordered his teachers to stop them and send them home.[39]

In Jessberg, youths became involved in the violence on the evening of November 9. Even before they received instructions from local Nazi officials, a group of youths assembled in front of the synagogue and began to stone it. As they did so, the local SA leader, Ludwig O., pulled up in his car, stepped out, and announced, "The synagogue must disappear tonight." Some of the SA men under his command soon appeared, equipped with axes and gasoline. Joined by many of the youths, the SA men went to work on the synagogue. After several minutes of vandalism, the Storm Troopers ignited a fire, intending to burn the building down. But three residents of the town—a mason, a railroad worker, and a forester—intervened to extinguish the flames. Later in the evening, the mason, Heinrich S., shouted his disapproval at some members of the mob: "Phooey! Shame on you!"[40]

Late in the night of November 9 the pogrom came to Ober-Mockstadt. A mob consisting mainly of youths formed in front of the home of the Jewish family R. While some broke into the home, others remained outside, lending their support through cheering and chanting. They were egged on by the head of the local SA, Robert L., who assured the boys that "tonight it's a free-for-all, tonight you can all let loose." The sentiment of the crowd was overwhelmingly in favor of the violence, though a number of disapproving onlookers made themselves conspicuous through their silence.[41]

On November 10, students were key participants in the pogrom in Gross-Krotzenburg. Encouraged by their thirty-four-year-old teacher, Werner H., they played a major role in the destruction of the synagogue and the Jewish school. When the county chief of police intervened to end the rioting in the late afternoon, many of the students simply ignored him.[42] The teacher or school administrator in the role of provocateur was a common one on November 10. On that day in Baden-Baden, the director of the Volksschule released students from school and encouraged them to shout, "To Hell with the Jews" as the Jewish population was rounded up around the city. The children were rewarded with candy.[43]

The town of Bad Vilbel had remained quiet through the night of November 9 and well into the evening of November 10. No order to initiate a pogrom had arrived during the night. On the morning of November 10, the local Nazi leader, Ludwig D., had traveled to Frankfurt, where he worked as a business clerk. Only when he arrived in Frankfurt did he find out what had happened overnight. Upon arriving home in Bad Vilbel at around 5:30 PM, he discovered that very little had been undertaken in his absence. A number of locals had broken down the door to the synagogue, but that was the extent of their actions. Ludwig D. held this situation to be unsatisfactory. And so only in the evening of November 10, well after the violence had ended in most other places, did the Nazis mobilize against the small Jewish community in Bad Vilbel. A group of SA men, accompanied by some youths, formed a column and marched through the town. As they advanced, they were spontaneously joined by others. The mob arrived at the home of the Jewish family W. With a great many townspeople looking on, they invaded the house and vandalized it. This process was then repeated at several more Jewish homes. The pogrom ended at the synagogue. A mob composed primarily of youths wrecked the interior of the synagogue and, in the square in front of the building, built a pile of prayer books, Torah scrolls, and other religious objects. They then set fire to it.[44]

It was not only in the smaller communities that youths played a prominent role in the violence. Jewish witnesses to the pogrom in Berlin described a similar phenomenon. Many Jewish shops in the Reich capital were vandalized by gangs of teenage boys on November 10. In one incident, a group of youths stopped a car, dragged out the Jewish driver, and beat him badly. This occurred in the middle of the night in front of the burning synagogue in the Fasanenstrasse. There were similar incidents in Vienna. In the Hietzing district of the city, schoolchildren aged twelve to fourteen were released from school early on November 10 and mobilized for attacks against Jewish homes and shops, which they carried out with great energy and enthusiasm.[45]

The youths who perpetrated violence during the pogrom were, with very few exceptions, never accused of any crime. Postwar German prosecutors focused their attention instead on the teachers and other adults who had provided leadership and encouragement. Thus, despite overwhelming evidence from the trials and from the testimony of Jews that young people had constituted a major class of perpetrators, we have relatively little in the way of concrete information about individual cases. One exception is that of Georg H. Only seventeen years old in November 1938, Georg H. had had a troubled childhood. Never having completed elementary school, he sought training as a mason but failed in that effort as well. He enlisted in the Reich Labor Service and was assigned to work on the system of military fortifications known as the West Wall. He was, by all accounts, an apolitical person.

It so happened that Georg H. arrived at his home outside of Assenheim for a short furlough from the Labor Service on November 10, 1938. Upon bicycling into town, he noticed that a mob had gathered in front of the house of the local Jewish family L. The mob consisted largely of teenage boys and young men. They were being egged on by the leader of the town's Nazi Party. Georg H. had not cycled into town looking for trouble, yet he did not hesitate to join the mob when the opportunity presented itself. He entered the Jewish home, where he saw Herr L. lying on the floor in a corner, using a walking stick to ward off his attackers. Georg H. grabbed the stick away from Herr L., at which point the Jewish man managed to get away and run outside. Georg H. followed him down the street, repeatedly striking him with the stick. After about 100 meters, Herr L. collapsed on the ground. The German youth pounced on him, beating him ferociously with the walking stick. The beating would have continued had it not been for the intervention of a fellow townsperson.[46]

The problematic childhood of Georg H. might well explain his propensity for violence. But how do we explain the violent behavior of so many other youths during the pogrom? The overwhelming majority of them had not dropped out of school, and many came from families that one might characterize as "stable." Groups of teenage boys tend to possess an especially high potential for aggression and mayhem, regardless of culture. In Nazi Germany, however, two factors contributed further to the unleashing of this potential. The first was the presence of adult authority figures who encouraged and rewarded the violent behavior. The second was the steady diet of antisemitic propaganda on which the boys had been nourished in the schools and in their Hitler Youth troops.[47] In the eyes of the thousands of German teenagers who carried out attacks on houses of worship, property, and people during the pogrom, the Jews of Germany had been placed outside the bounds of the community.

The Kristallnacht forced German civil servants, especially policemen and firemen, onto the horns of a dilemma. Trained and sworn to uphold the law and to keep the community safe, they received explicit orders during the pogrom to refrain from doing their jobs. Throughout Germany on November 9 and 10, most German policemen did exactly as they had been ordered, which was to stand by and do nothing. The same held true for firemen, though some of them were called into action only when the flames from a burning synagogue threatened surrounding structures. In at least one case, in Heldenbergen, firemen were called in to dismantle a synagogue because a fire would have been too dangerous.[48] Civil servants responded to their orders with obedience, if not necessarily always with enthusiasm.

One civil servant who did not conform to the general pattern was Wilhelm Krützfeld, a police precinct captain in Berlin. Although the documentation for his actions is scant, Krützfeld is widely credited with having saved the Oranienburgerstrasse Synagogue in Berlin—the city's largest and most architecturally impressive synagogue.[49] As the story goes, Krützfeld and some of the officers under his command faced down

a group of Storm Troopers who were attempting to destroy the building. While holding the SA men at gunpoint, Krützfeld commanded
firefighters to douse the fire that had already been set. Although Krützfeld, like other German policemen, had been ordered to refrain from
intervening against the party-sponsored action, he invoked his responsibility to enforce a law protecting historic buildings. (It is also possible
that he cited the potential danger of the fire spreading to neighboring
buildings. The synagogue in question—like many in Germany—was
integrated into a continuous block of buildings in a densely populated
part of Berlin.) The following day, the head of the Berlin police, Count
Helldorf, an avid Nazi, reprimanded Krützfeld, though he suffered no
formal punishment and was permitted to retire from the police without
incident.

Krützfeld is today regarded in Germany as a hero of the Kristallnacht. To honor his courage, the Berlin police have erected a memorial plaque on the front façade of the building that he saved, which is
now a major tourist attraction. The singular personal quality of Krützfeld's that Germany most celebrates, and to which his "civil courage"
has been attributed, was his professionalism as a policeman—and, more
specifically, the sense of duty and propriety that motivated him as a
Prussian civil servant. He was not a member of the anti-Nazi resistance;
nor was he a philosemite. He merely possessed a healthy sense of right
and wrong, reinforced by a commitment to the rule of law. His story is
compelling not least because Krützfeld's admirable behavior during the
pogrom was fairly exceptional. Most German civil servants lacked the
courage that has been attributed to Krützfeld.

More typical were the police in the town of Gross-Krotzenburg.
On the morning of November 10, they received the order to tolerate
the "actions undertaken by the party against the Jews." They stood by
and looked on as the attacks unfolded. When an order arrived late in
the day to put an end to the violence and prevent looting, they dutifully intervened. Police guards were placed in front of the synagogue to
prevent its incineration. The passivity of the police in the face of what

was clearly a massive violation of law and order remained one of the most powerful memories of Jews who lived through the pogrom in that town.[50] Richard S. of Innsbruck was similarly astonished by the failures of the local police. As SA men began to invade his home at about 3:00 AM, he notified the police station on the telephone. The operator asked whether a Jewish home was involved. When Richard S. answered "yes," the operator replied, "Yes, we know," apologized, and hung up, leaving Richard S. at the mercy of his attackers.[51]

For the majority of civil servants involved in the pogrom, obedience to orders superseded all else. On the morning of November 10, the county government for the region around Giessen assembled all its police officials. The policemen were instructed to expect anti-Jewish actions during the day. They were not to interfere, except to prevent "physical abuse" and looting. Later in the day, the adult male Jews would be arrested and taken into custody. The man who presided at the meeting was Theodor W., the senior official in the local civil service. Theodor W. was fifty-eight years old, a university graduate, a veteran of World War One, the son of a Protestant pastor, and a member of the anti-Nazi Confessing Church. Theodor W.'s own son, a pastor in the Confessing Church, had spent some time in a concentration camp as punishment for dissenting activity. Theodor W. was not a Nazi but rather an essential link in a bureaucratic chain-of-command, the proper functioning of which was essential for the pogrom to succeed. Theodor W. followed his orders on November 10 and expected the civil servants under his authority to do the same.

Present at the meeting to receive his orders from Theodor W. was the head of the police in the small town of Lich, Chief L. We know very little about him, except for the fact that he personally disapproved of the pogrom. By the time he arrived back in Lich from the meeting in Giessen, the violence had already begun. A gang of youths had surrounded the synagogue and were pummeling it with stones. They were being directed and encouraged by Karl K., the leader of the Nazi Party in Lich. The vandalism soon spread to the interior of the build-

ing. Chief L. entered the synagogue and removed the Torah scrolls before they could be desecrated and placed them in the cellar of the town
hall. He did nothing to stop the pogrom, but he did express his dissent
through a small gesture of decency.[52]

Johann W., a fifty-two-year-old policeman in Hungen, was somewhat bolder. Like his fellow policemen, Johann W. had been ordered
not to intervene against the rioters, except to prevent looting. He was
also ordered to arrest adult Jewish men. Given the small size of the police force in Hungen, SA men were deputized to assist with the arrests, a
common practice in Germany on November 10. Johann W. dutifully
carried out the arrests, but he was hardly enthusiastic about the assignment. He tried to rein in the violence of the Storm Troopers who had
been assigned to help him, though with only limited success. He did
manage to prevent the incineration of the synagogue, from which he
collected Torah scrolls and other religious objects, which he later returned to the Jewish community.[53]

Johann W. was not the only German policeman who showed this
kind of respect for sacred Jewish objects. In Cologne, at about 12:30 AM
on November 10, as the pogrom was still in its early phase, the deputy
rabbi of the Orthodox synagogue in the Neumarkt quarter received a
phone call from the local police commander. The rabbi was instructed
to be ready to be picked up by a squad of police in about ten minutes,
and to have the keys to the synagogue with him. The police took the
rabbi to the synagogue, where they collected the Torah scrolls. They
took the scrolls to the office of the police commander and locked them
away—all in the presence of the rabbi. A couple of hours later, the synagogue was devastated in the pogrom. On the following morning, the
rabbi was again brought to the office of the police commander. He was
given the Torah scrolls and told to keep them at his home. The police
commander had acted on his own initiative to save the scrolls, even as
he did nothing to prevent the destruction of the synagogue that housed
them. Saving the Torah scrolls was a small act of respect and decency
that the police commander could afford. Intervening against the de-

struction of the synagogue, by contrast, would have amounted to insubordination, given that the order to stand down had come from the national police leadership.[54]

In many cases, police refrained from abusive behavior toward Jews but acted as accomplices to others who were less scrupulous. Otto L. was a forty-one-year-old policeman in Frankenberg. He had been a member of the Nazi Party since 1933. On November 10 a county official ordered him to arrest the adult male Jews of his precinct. He and several subordinates rounded up the Jews in two cars and delivered them to the jail, which was located in the courthouse. Some time later, three uniformed SS men arrived at the jail carrying a lockbox, which they had found hidden under the floor of the Jewish school. They suspected that the key was in the possession of the Jewish teacher Ferdinand S., who was one of the men held in the jail. The policeman Otto L. removed the Jew from the jail and handed him over to the SS, fully cognizant of where this would lead. The SS men began to beat Ferdinand S. while Otto L. looked on. One of the court employees observed the scene and fetched the presiding judge. The judge took the Jew under his protection, scolding the SS men for their illegal actions, and scolding policeman Otto L. for tolerating them. But the judge neglected to arrange medical care for Ferdinand S., whose injuries from the beating were severe. What was worse, Ferdinand S. was then sent to Buchenwald with the other Jewish men from Frankenberg. He died there four days later from complications arising from a beating administered to him in the immediate presence of a policeman.[55]

For tens of thousands of German Jews, the most horrifying experience during the pogrom was not the frenzied violence on the street but the wave of mass arrests and subsequent deportations to concentration camps. Officially the Jews were not arrested for having committed or attempted any crime. The legal basis for their detention was the fiction of "protective custody," a preposterous notion considering the abuses to which they were subjected. A similar legal fiction undergirded the transfer of some of the arrested Jews to the concentration camps. Authorities relied on the "Labor Mobilization Law," which authorized the German government to order German men between the ages of eighteen and sixty to specific work assignments.[56]

The arrests unfolded in very uneven fashion, differing not only from city to city but also from one police precinct to the next. Beatings, humiliation, and even torture accompanied many of the arrests, though in some cases the arrested Jews were treated more humanely. Much depended on who carried out the arrest. Professional policemen tended to go more by the book and to respect civilized procedures, whereas SA and SS men, many of whom had been spontaneously deputized to help out with the arrests in certain localities, usually behaved more barbarically. In some instances, teenage members of the Hitler Youth participated in the arrests as well.[57]

The arrests were supposed to focus on a specific subset of Jews—prosperous adult Jewish men—but many Jews who did not fit this description were swept up. These included women, the elderly, and even some children.[58] This was the result of confusion about the text of the arrest order, which had been disseminated quickly during the night. It was also the result of the overzealousness of SA and SS men who were not especially concerned with the details of the order. Only gradually did many local police officers achieve a clear understanding of the arrest order and begin to enforce it. As a consequence, many Jews who had been arrested in the initial sweep were released in a matter of hours or after a day or two. Among those who were released—rather than sent to concentration camps—were some men who were veterans of World War One as well as men who could demonstrate that their emigration was imminent. The police exercised a great deal of discretion in such cases, and practices were far from uniform.[59] In Berlin, no Jews were exempted from arrests on November 10, but on November 11 and 12, exceptions were granted to holders of the Iron Cross First Class, those with injuries from World War One, and those with obvious serious illnesses. The Berlin police were also relatively meticulous when it came to identifying the Jews who would be sent to concentration camps. These were men whose assets had been registered at or above 5,000 Reichsmarks. In most other places in Germany, the police were sloppier, and many Jewish men who did not qualify as "affluent" were sent to concentration camps. The practice was also very uneven with regard to exceptions for medical reasons. In some cities and precincts, police physicians were more ready and willing than those elsewhere to declare Jews who were suffering from illnesses or injuries as medically unfit for concentration camps.[60]

Treatment of the arrested Jews was especially cruel in Vienna.[61] One Viennese Jew later reflected that his arrival in Dachau on November 16 actually came as a relief after the horrors he experienced upon his arrest and detention in his home city. The mass roundup began at about 5:00 AM on November 10. Many Jews were arrested in their homes. Others were seized while waiting in line at foreign consulates. During the day, SA men roamed through the city, searching for Jews on the street, in coffee houses, and in hotels. The police and the SA created makeshift jails to hold the arrested Jews. They were held in schools, a church cloister, and an old horse stable. At many of the jails, captors forced the Jews to do physical exercises continuously and beat them when they refused or collapsed. At the stables, Jews were forced to hold their arms high so that as many people as possible could be crammed into the space while they awaited interrogation. Some were made to crawl around on cobblestone pavement on their hands and knees while being forced to spit on and hit one another. Hundreds spent many hours in such conditions, without food or water. The Jews were not allowed to go to the bathroom; many were then punished when they had to relieve themselves. The humiliation took many forms. A class of Jewish schoolchildren, who had been arrested as a group, was forced to march in place while singing. In one jail, an orthodox Jew was made to clean the floor with his beard. While awaiting processing, Jews were continually threatened. They were told they would be shot or sent to Dachau; in the event, only the latter proved to be true. Among the Jewish suicides in Vienna were those of two Jews who threw themselves out of an upper-floor window of the school where they were being held on November 10.

SS guards devised an especially perverse form of terror for several hundred Jews who had been held at the cloister in the Kenyongasse. At around midnight on November 10, the Jews were roused from their sleep and herded into a large hall. The guards asked whether a rabbi was present. When one presented himself, he was placed in the middle of the hall, where SS men pulled his hairs out one by one and carved emblems into his beard. The SS men then ordered the rabbi to recite the Kaddish, the Jewish prayer for the dead. He was forced to repeat the prayer several times, each time louder than the last. The SS men told the Jews in the hall that the prayer was for them, as they would all be shot at 4:00 AM. Given the way they had been treated on November 9 and 10, the threat seemed entirely believable. Many now began to recite the Kaddish along with the rabbi. For several hours, the Jews in the cloister genuinely believed that their murder was imminent.

The sadistic treatment during the arrests in Vienna came largely from the SA and the SS. Treatment at the hands of the police was better. While not especially friendly or helpful, many of the policemen carried out the arrests of Jews politely and in a businesslike manner. Some Jews observed that many of the older policemen were more considerate than their younger colleagues. But the tone and procedures during processing were de facto established not by the police but rather by the SA and the SS. Jews noticed that the police acted much more considerately toward them when SA and SS were not present. The circumstances, therefore, inevitably led many professional policemen to participate in the systematic humiliation and abuse of their prisoners. During the interrogations at one of the collection points, for example, when the police official called out the names of the prisoners, each Jew had to identify himself with the phrase "I am the Jewish swine" preceding his name.

In some towns and cities, the arrests resembled those in Vienna with respect to the sadism exhibited by many of the Nazis involved. In Weimar, arrested Jews were made to stand for long periods, were beaten as they marched, and were not fed for long periods of time. In Erfurt, arrested Jews were tortured and humiliated by the SA in the presence of police. They were forced to remain in a very painful kneeling position for a prolonged period; made to climb ladders while being whipped; and forced to march while SA men sang the Nazi anthem, the "Horst Wessel Song." Several SA men picked out Jews whom they recognized for particular abuse. An SA man identified the Jewish lawyer who had represented his ex-wife in the couple's divorce proceedings. The opportunity for revenge had arrived. In Baden-Baden, a city in which anti-Jewish harassment had remained relatively moderate during the Nazi period, arrested Jews were collected in the vandalized synagogue and told that they would be burned alive in it.[62]

In Berlin, the arrest and processing of Jews was carried out more humanely. More so than in Vienna, the action was dominated by the police, whom many Jews later described as behaving properly or even being "forthcoming" as they executed their orders. One Jewish man later described his experiences. Two plainclothes policemen rang his doorbell at about 5:00 PM on November 10. They explained politely but firmly that they were required to take him into custody. When the Jew requested an explanation—on what grounds was he being arrested, where was he being sent, how long would he be gone—they had no answers. The Jew was allowed to discuss the situation with his wife, though the police demonstrably eavesdropped on the conversation. The policemen then escorted him on an ordinary public bus to the collection point for arrested Jews.[63]

Many of the arrests in Berlin played themselves out in almost exactly this way. The initial arrest was made by one or two policemen who behaved politely and followed normal procedure. But once at the collection point, the situation of the arrested Jew took a turn for the worse. A stricter, more military-like atmosphere prevailed, owing to the presence of men from the SS and the SA, who, unlike the police, shouted antisemitic obscenities. Nevertheless, the systematic terror to which the Jews arrested in Vienna had been subjected was largely absent in Berlin.[64]

More typical for Berlin was the experience of one Jewish man who, after his arrest, was locked in the cellar of a police station with some other Jews. The room was overcrowded and the air was bad, but the Jews did receive some bread and watery soup. They remained in the room overnight and were processed for most of the next day. The processing involved interrogations and a perfunctory medical exam. They spent a second night in the cellar. The next day they were told that they would be sent to the concentration camp at Sachsenhausen.[65]

After the pogrom, it was more common for Jews from Berlin than from most other places to relate stories of assistance received from non-Jews. On November 10, a large number of Jews were arrested in the Dahlem district and held in the police precinct through the day. When no further instruction came regarding what to do with them, the precinct commander released them. Most of the released Jews did not go home, thus managing to avoid a new wave of arrests on the following day. Jews throughout Berlin were able to find refuge in the homes of other Jews who had already been arrested, or in the homes of "Aryans." One non-Jewish businessman quartered eleven Jewish men whom he did not know personally. Two Jews hid for days in a tiny tobacco shop owned by an "Aryan." At a bed-and-breakfast operated by an "Aryan" woman, Jews were allowed to hide in a room that had just been vacated by members of the SA. The sheer size of Berlin was an additional factor that allowed many Jewish men to escape arrest. They simply remained on the move as much as they could, riding busses, trains, and streetcars.[66]

Most of the Jews in Berlin, it should be emphasized, could not escape the dragnet, and elsewhere in Germany the process of arrest, detention, and transfer to concentration camps was even more unrelenting. On November 11, a Jew was arrested in the Hamburg airport while waiting to board a plane for Amsterdam. The fact that he already possessed a valid entry visa for the United States did not persuade the police to let him go. The methods of the Germans who rounded up the Jews ranged from civil to barbaric, very often with one in close proximity to the other. In Munich, where the nationwide pogrom was launched, the mass arrests began as early as 3:00 AM on November 10. While some Munich Jews later reported that their arrests at the hands of Gestapo men were carried out professionally, others recounted the way bedridden Jews were arrested in hospitals and dragged away. In Nuremberg (as in many other places) some Jews received advance warning of their impending arrests from decent citizens with knowledge of the plans, but then the arrests themselves were conducted with great brutality. In Meiningen, some local police openly criticized the brutal actions of the SA, who had attacked the local Jews, rounded them up, and delivered them to the jail. The police acted decently toward the Jewish prisoners, in some cases actually going to their homes to fetch personal possessions that would be needed during their imprisonment.[67]

One German Jew later reported that an embarrassed policeman had explained his role as that of a simple "executing organ," and there is considerable evidence from the testimony of German Jews to support the contention that this sentiment was widespread among German policemen. Nevertheless, the police did not always behave civilly. In Frankfurt, police abused and threatened a rabbi, whom they believed was withholding information about the location of valuable objects from his synagogue. They also accused him—quite preposterously—of having set fire to his own synagogue. In Kiel, a Gestapo officer conspired to turn the arrest of a Jew into an opportunity for murder. While escorting the arrested Jew to the police station, the officer suddenly disappeared, and an SS man who had been trailing them shot the Jew with his pistol. It was clear that the Gestapo man, who was bound by professional police procedures, did not want to kill the Jew himself, so he had arranged for a confederate to pull the trigger. The Jew was left for dead, but some neighbors called an ambulance to take him to the hospital, where he survived.[68]

Jewish men who were arrested and not, for one reason or another, released now faced the dreadful prospect of concentration camp. They were transported to Buchenwald, Dachau, and Sachsenhausen by car, train, or truck. Jews from Munich had a relatively short trip to Dachau; the same applied to Jews from Berlin who were deported to Sachsenhausen. Thousands of others, however, had to endure long and sometimes harrowing journeys to the camps. Jewish men from Breslau were subjected to a grueling ten-hour railway journey to Buchenwald, during which they were viciously abused by SS guards. Jews deported from Vienna to Dachau were forced to remain motionless while staring into the bright lights of their train compartments during the long rail journey to the camp. The Jews from Fuhlsbüttel who were deported to Sachsenhausen by train fared better; they were guarded by policemen who behaved professionally.[69]

We know in retrospect that most of the Jews who were sent to the camps in the wake of the pogrom were released soon thereafter. But the arrested Jews did not know this in advance, and the prospect of being sent to a concentration camp was terrifying.[70] It was common knowledge in Germany that Buchenwald, Dachau, and Sachsenhausen were horrific places where prisoners were subjected to inhumane treatment.[71] The Jewish men in the cars, trucks, and trains that were on their way to these camps did not know when, or whether, they would be released. The pogrom was over, but for these men and their families, a new nightmare was just beginning.

5

"Synagogues Ignited Themselves"

Adolf Hitler spent the night of November 9–10 in his private apartment at the Prinzregentenplatz in Munich. On the morning of November 10, as the violence and arrests continued all over the German Reich, he was kept informed about the course of the pogrom by, among others, Joseph Goebbels.[1] The two men then met for lunch at the Osteria, Hitler's favorite Italian restaurant in Munich. Hitler expressed his satisfaction with the pogrom. The Führer's intentions with regard to the Jews, Goebbels recorded in his diary, were now "entirely radical and aggressive," and Hitler was determined to undertake "very harsh measures against the Jews." These would include, most notably, the definitive "Aryanization" of Jewish property. But, the two men had agreed, the time had now come to put an end to the riots. Hitler reviewed and approved a statement that Goebbels intended to issue to the German nation in which he would call for the violence to cease.[2]

Goebbels issued his statement on the afternoon of November 10. The text was distributed over the DNB wire service at around 4:00 PM and was read aloud over German radio:

> The justified and understandable outrage of the German people against the cowardly Jewish assassination of a German diplomat in Paris vented itself on a large scale last night. In numerous cities and towns of the Reich, measures of retribution were taken against Jewish buildings and businesses. A strict order is now being issued to the entire population to desist from all further demonstrations and actions against Jewry, regardless of what type. The definitive response to the Jewish assassination in Paris will be delivered to Jewry via the route of legislation and edicts.[3]

Twenty minutes later the DNB sent a notice to newspaper editors directing them to print the statement conspicuously on the front page of the next day's editions.[4]

In tandem with this announcement, Goebbels issued a second statement directed specifically at the gauleiter of the Nazi Party. They were to ensure that the "anti-Jewish actions be halted with the same speed with which they originated." The actions, Goebbels claimed, had "fulfilled their desired and expected purpose." An order would soon be issued directing that Jews, and not the insurance companies, would pay for the damages. Goebbels also told the gauleiter to expect a series of legal and administrative measures against the Jews very soon.[5]

Goebbels's statements coincided with a broader effort by the Nazi leadership on November 10 to put a stop to the rioting. Rudolf Hess, the deputy Führer, distributed an urgent message to party offices around the country. "On the explicit order of the very highest authority," he emphasized, "setting fire to Jewish shops or similar actions may not occur in any case or under any circumstances."[6] To anyone associated with the Nazi Party, the identity of "the very highest authority" could not be in doubt.

It proved nonetheless extremely difficult to rein in the destructive energies that the Nazi leadership had unleashed the previous evening. In many places around Germany, violence directed at Jews, their property, and their synagogues continued despite the orders to desist. In many cases, in fact, local Nazi officials had gotten off to such a late start that the pogroms actually began only *after* Goebbels and Hess had called for an end to the pogrom. The apparent lack of discipline was manifest to foreign journalists: on November 11, the British newspaper *Daily Express* ran a banner headline declaring, "Looting Mobs Defy Goebbels."[7]

As Goebbels attempted to dampen the violence, his Ministry of Propaganda instructed the German press about how to report the pogrom. Newspapers were authorized to write about the events as long as they conformed to a certain preferred storyline. They were to emphasize that an "understandably outraged" population had given its "spontaneous answer" to the murder of Ernst vom Rath.[8] There would be no mention of the central role of the Nazi Party as the orchestrator of the violence. Editors were expected to obfuscate the systematic nature of the pogrom by noting that windows were smashed "here and there" and that in some places "synagogues ignited themselves" or had gone up in flames for some other reason. Newspapers were told to focus on local events and avoid any suggestion that an operation had taken place on a Reich-wide scale. The reports were not to be large or prominent, and they were to be relegated to page two or three. There would be no headlines and no pictures related to the violence.[9] The Propaganda Ministry employed its routine procedure for screening press photographs to make sure that no images of the violence were printed in German newspapers or distributed to foreign press agencies.[10]

One manifestly preposterous quality of the official press strategy became evident in the newspapers published on November 11. The prominence accorded to the text of Goebbels's appeal for an end to the violence was conspicuously inconsistent with the unobtrusive coverage accorded to the actual pogrom. In the Munich edition of the *Völkischer Beobachter*, Goebbels's statement dominated page one, but the story about the pogrom took up only one-sixth of a page on the bottom of page two, under the relatively small headline "Outraged Popular Soul Vents." The story focused not on Munich but on Berlin. It referred to the burning of three synagogues but did not explain how they had been ignited or by whom. As Berliners went about their business on November 10, the story explained, they reacted to the sights of the destroyed Jewish businesses with "understandable joy and satisfaction." "It is all too understandable," the newspaper opined, "that the German Volk community defends itself against alien individuals who are, of course, ensnarled with their racial comrades abroad." The Jews of Germany, the story concluded, had suffered the consequences of their "shamelessness." Yet despite their justified outrage, the Berliners had shown a great deal of discipline. No looting had taken place, even though a small amount of goods might have been damaged. And, most important, the action had not disturbed "the hair of a single Jew."[11]

On the evening of November 10, Adolf Hitler held a reception for about 400 German journalists and publishers at his official (though rarely used) Munich headquarters, the so-called Führer Building.[12] Hitler delivered an hour-long address to his guests. He sketched out some of the most important political developments of the year 1938 and thanked the press for its important contribution to maintaining the will and determination of the German people as they confronted the challenges before them. Much of the speech touched on matters of foreign policy. Hitler did not mention the pogrom once. He had most likely decided on the focus and content of his speech days earlier, well before he knew that the pogrom would occur. More important, his assiduous avoidance of the subject reflected his desire to insulate himself from any direct connection with the illegalities arising from the anti-Jewish violence. Hitler had demonstrated the same strategy the previous evening, when he absented himself from the Old Town Hall in Munich before Goebbels rose to deliver his instructions for the pogrom to the Nazi Party elite.

Nevertheless, for Hitler's guests at the Führer Building on November 10, the national pogrom that had unfolded during the preceding twenty-four hours must have been a dominant topic of discussion. When understood in this context, one of Hitler's comments can indeed be interpreted as an indirect reference to the pogrom. Hitler explained to his listeners that much of the rhetoric that he had deployed over the past few years about his desire to preserve peace, though necessary for diplomatic purposes, may actually have created a false impression among the German people. Certain national goals, Hitler explained, required the use of violence, for which the German people needed to be carefully and systematically prepared. It was necessary, he claimed, "gradually to convert the German people psychologically, and slowly to make it clear to them, that there are things which, when they cannot be implemented with peaceful means, must be implemented by means of violence."[13] To be sure, the context for these remarks was foreign policy, and specifically Hitler's understanding that he would not be able to fulfill his long-range territorial ambitions through diplomatic means. But on the evening of November 10, his audience would almost certainly connect his theme of the indispensability of violence to the domestic events of the preceding twenty-four hours.

Among the subjects that Hitler and Goebbels discussed during their lunch at the Osteria on November 10 was the impact of the pogrom on the German insurance industry. Hitler assured Goebbels that the Jews themselves would have to cover the cost of the property damage. "The insurance companies will pay them nothing" was how Goebbels recorded Hitler's statement in his diary.[14] The pogrom was still unfolding even as the two men chatted, but it was already clear to both of them that insurance claims by Jews could pose a potentially large financial problem to German insurance companies.[15] It is quite possible that the issue had been brought to their attention by Hermann Goering, whose consternation at the destruction of property during the pogrom is well documented. For Goering, this particular worry was among a wider set of concerns about potential economic fallout from the widespread vandalism during the pogrom. In his capacity as head of the Four-Year Plan, Goering exercised tremendous influence over the German economy. The seemingly wanton destruction of property clashed dramatically with his frequent exhortations to German workers about productivity. Additionally, Goering worried about the diplomatic consequences of the pogrom.[16] His anger also derived from his having been cut out of the loop when Goebbels and Hitler initiated the pogrom on the evening of November 9, while Goering was already on his way back to Berlin by train.[17]

On November 12, the Saturday after the pogrom, Goering presided over a large meeting of nearly 100 German government and Nazi Party officials, including Joseph Goebbels, at the Reich Air Ministry in Berlin.[18] The main purpose of the meeting was to plan the next wave of legal and bureaucratic measures intended to transfer Jewish property into "Aryan hands," to further marginalize Germany's Jews socially and culturally, and to expedite Jewish emigration. These would be the measures to which Hitler had pledged himself to Goebbels over lunch two days earlier, and which Goebbels had subsequently told the German people to expect very shortly.

Most of the conversation at the nearly four-hour meeting focused on economic, financial, and insurance matters. Goering opened the discussion by noting that Hitler had directly authorized him to coordinate the regime's approach to the Jewish question. Hitler had emphasized his desire that "decisive steps" be taken toward a "settlement" of the Jewish question. This undertaking would require, Goering explained, a wide range of economic, legal, and propagandistic measures. The party must act decisively in the wake of the recent anti-Jewish "demonstrations." Goering did not hold back from sharply criticizing the pogrom and, by implication, Goebbels. "I've had enough of these demonstrations," which, he selfishly observed, "do not harm the Jews, but rather, in the end, me, as I am ultimately responsible for the economy." He underscored the threat confronting the German insurance industry and bemoaned the destruction of consumer goods and "the people's property."

After Goering outlined principles and procedures for the final stage of the "Aryanization" of Jewish property, the discussion moved on to other matters, and Goebbels had his say. He advocated the dissolution of all Jewish synagogues. The Jews should be made to pay for their demolition, and the freed-up space could then be used for parking lots or new buildings. Goebbels claimed that the time had come to prohibit Jews from attending theaters, cinemas, and other entertainment venues. (Later in the day, Goebbels would hand down exactly such a prohibition, relying on his authority as president of the Reich Chamber of Culture.)[19] Jews, Goebbels continued, should be excluded as far as possible from contact with "Aryans" in the public sphere. He suggested measures to prohibit Jews from sharing space with "Aryans" in railroad compartments, public swimming areas, schools, and forests. The discussion turned perversely lighthearted during this phase of the meeting, as Goering responded sarcastically or patronizingly to several of Goebbels's suggestions. In response to Goebbels's recommendation that Jews be banned from entering German forests, for example, Goering joked that the Jews could be restricted to forest areas inhabited by moose, which, like the Jews, were marked by their large, crooked noses. These exchanges should not, however, be interpreted as evidence of a fundamental philosophical disagreement between the two men; rather, they reflect a difference of temperament and emphasis. Despite Goering's unconcealed disapproval of the pogrom, Goebbels emerged from the meeting convinced that Goering was now his ally in the newly radicalized campaign against the Jews. "I'm cooperating with Goering wonderfully," he noted in his diary the next day.[20]

A major part of the meeting was devoted to the insurance question.[21] Goering invited Eduard Hilgard, the director of the insurance giant Allianz and the leader of the Reich Group for Insurance, to address the assembled officials. The pogrom had placed the German insurance industry in a difficult bind. In 1938 the German government had eliminated insurance coverage against damages from domestic disturbances, reasoning that domestic disturbances simply could not and did not occur under Nazi rule. Legally, therefore, the insurance companies were not liable for claims arising from damages incurred during the pogrom. But, as Hilgard explained, the insurance industry worried that a failure to cover the damages would result in lawsuits and ultimately harm its reputation among policyholders living abroad. Hilgard therefore suggested that insurance companies be allowed to honor claims from their policyholders, but then be reimbursed for this huge expenditure by the government. The state, Hilgard probably understood, would not bear the cost itself, but would instead pass it on to the Jews.

Goering now had a different idea: the insurance companies would honor their obligations, but the money paid out to Jews would be confiscated by the state. Having entered the meeting determined to get the insurance industry off the hook, Goering now saw an opportunity to transfer a huge amount of money from the insurance companies into the coffers of the German Reich. After the November 12 meeting, Hilgard and others in the insurance industry moved aggressively—and successfully—to preempt any such plan and to make certain that the cost for repairing the material damages was ultimately borne by the Jews themselves.

In the end, negotiations between the insurance industry and the German government resulted in an elaborate mechanism for transferring the financial liability for Kristallnacht-related damages to the Jewish community. It is in this context that we must understand the notorious order issued by Goering on November 12, within hours of the meeting at the Air Ministry, in which the Jews of Germany were commanded to make a collective "atonement" payment of one billion Reichsmarks to the German government. Although the real reason for the collective fine was the protection of the German insurance industry, the order was cloaked in the rhetoric of moral outrage over the murder of Ernst vom Rath: "The hostile attitude of Jewry toward the German people and Reich, which does not shirk away even from acts of murder, requires decisive and strict atonement."[22]

At no point during the big meeting at the Air Ministry did anybody openly acknowledge the fact that thousands of Jews were either in or on their way to concentration camps. The 30,000 Jewish men who disappeared into Dachau, Buchenwald, and Sachsenhausen in the days after the pogrom constituted about one-tenth of the Jewish population still living in Germany. Their imprisonment transformed an improvised pogrom into an enormous, systematic extortion and blackmail operation conducted by the Gestapo, which determined who would be subject to "protective custody," and by the SS, which ran the camps. The purpose of terrorizing German Jews in this way was to compel them to hasten, first, the transfer of their property into "Aryan" hands, and second, their actual physical departure from Germany. With regard to the first of these goals, the measure proved successful, coupled as it was with the promulgation on November 12 of an "Order for the Exclusion of Jews from German Economic Life." With respect to Jewish emigration from Germany, the mass incarcerations, coming on the heels of the pogrom, produced the desired effect as well. Jewish departures from Germany accelerated dramatically in the weeks and months after the pogrom. Tragically, however, many German Jews who were now determined to leave the country ran up against severe immigration restrictions in the United States and elsewhere, and they found themselves stranded in Germany when war broke out in September 1939.

The Nazi concentration camps had held only a small number of Jews before 1938. The vast majority of camp prisoners had been Communists or others arrested for political reasons, as well as so-called asocials. In Dachau, for example, Jewish prisoners had rarely numbered more than 100 before 1938. In May 1938, in the aftermath of the annexation of Austria, a significant number of Austrian Jews were arrested and sent to Dachau. They were joined there a couple of months later by

Jewish prisoners who had been picked up in a wider dragnet of supposedly "work-averse" Germans. By the autumn of 1938, therefore, Dachau
housed about 2,000 Jews. In late September, most of them were transferred to Buchenwald,[23] which had previously held Jews only in exceptional cases.[24] As for Sachsenhausen, there were about 800–900 Jews
there on the eve of the pogrom, most having been swept up during the
campaign against the "work-averse."[25]

The mass detention of Jews in concentration camps after the pogrom, therefore, marked a new strategy in the Nazi regime's antisemitic
campaign. Tens of thousands of Jews were now thrown at the mercy of
the SS personnel who ran and manned the camps, giving them an opportunity to translate their virulently racist antisemitism into practice
behind electrified fences and barbed wire, where they could act with
impunity. The result was a prolonged terror not only for the prisoners
but for their loved ones as well. The Jewish men were cut off from their
wives and families. Direct communication was impossible, and the authorities withheld information about the condition of the detainees. In
contrast to the relatively brief horror of the pogrom that preceded it,
this terror could last for days, weeks, and, in some cases, even months.

The flood of new prisoners began on November 10 and continued
through November 16, when Reinhard Heydrich declared the "arrest
action" complete.[26] All told, about 31,000 Jewish men had been imprisoned: 11,000 in Dachau, 9,800 in Buchenwald, and 10,000 in Sachsenhausen.[27] In most cases, the men were simply sent to the nearest of the
three camps, but sometimes the Gestapo abruptly diverted a transport
to a more distant camp in order to spread out the burden posed by the
new prisoners.[28] Many of the transports were small, consisting of fewer
than 10 prisoners. But Jews from the major cities arrived in sizable
transports. At Buchenwald, for example, most of the new prisoners arrived between November 10 and November 13 in a total of 103 transports. They arrived at Buchenwald from Frankfurt/Main in transports
numbering 338, 581, 450, 451, 32, 432, 243, and 94. The two transports
from Breslau contained 963 and 811 Jews, respectively. Other large trans-

ports arrived in Buchenwald from Hannover (316), Kassel (435 and 258), Oppeln (388 and 258), Magdeburg (375), and Bielefeld (249 and 157).[29]

Even though the camp system had been expanded in the late 1930s, the camps were not prepared to absorb such large numbers of new prisoners so quickly.[30] Upon arrival, many of the Jews had to sleep outside and in the open, despite mid-November cold, on improvised straw beds. There were serious shortages of food, water, latrines, showers, and other facilities related to hygiene. The situation was especially bad at Buchenwald, the newest and still most primitive of the three camps, where the camp commander decided in the wee hours of November 10 to create a Sonderlager—or special camp—for the thousands of new Jewish prisoners he was told to expect. Separated from the main camp by barbed wire, the Sonderlager consisted of five very large but flimsy barracks that were hastily constructed by inmates even as the masses of new Jewish prisoners were arriving. Conditions in the improvised barracks were considerably worse than those in the regular camp. There were no toilets or washbasins, no heat, and no windows. Toilet facilities consisted of two open-air latrines.[31]

For many of the Jewish prisoners, arrival at the camp was especially traumatic. Over the years, the SS had developed fairly standardized procedures for initiating new inmates into the camps. These were intended to shock the prisoners into understanding that the camp personnel exercised absolute power over them. Survival depended on acknowledging this power and conforming to discipline.[32] The methods employed by the SS guards upon receiving new prisoners included forcing them to run a gauntlet while being kicked and beaten, ordering them to stand for exceedingly long periods of time, and depriving them of food, water, and permission to use the latrine. This physical abuse was accompanied by a great deal of verbal abuse and humiliation. In one unusual case, a member of the Gestapo escorting a group of Jews to Dachau briefed the prisoners on the welcome that awaited them.[33] Most of the newly arriving Jews, however, did not have the benefit of such information.

At each camp, the SS guards introduced their own variations into the standard operating procedure for receiving the new inmates. At Sachsenhausen, prisoners who arrived by train were forced to run the two-kilometer distance from the railway station to the camp entrance. This was especially difficult for older or less fit men, some of whom died before reaching the camp. When a prisoner collapsed from the exertion, the others were forced to trample him. All the while, the men were kicked and punched by the guards. At Dachau, as new Jewish inmates tried to answer the questions put to them during processing, the guards forced water into their mouths with garden hoses. Some of the Jews entering Dachau were told that they had been sentenced to five years in the camp, and that their term would be extended to twenty years if they failed to follow camp discipline.[34]

At Buchenwald, the reception and first few days at the camp came to be known among former prisoners as "Murder Week."[35] The primitive conditions in the Sonderlager were compounded by the viciousness of the SS guards. The commander of Buchenwald, Karl-Otto Koch, made it quite clear to his camp personnel that brutal treatment of Jews would be regarded as career-promoting conduct. New Jewish inmates went twenty-four hours without food. When food finally arrived, it was not necessarily a relief. In one case, a meal of potatoes induced a mass outbreak of diarrhea, and the prisoners suspected that the food had been laced with a laxative. A humiliation that became a favorite of the Buchenwald guards was "carrying the shit," which involved forcing inmates to transfer human feces from the primitive latrine to the garden. They forced Jewish prisoners to clean the latrines with kitchen utensils and with their bare hands. The guards nicknamed the Jewish unit that carried out this task "Commando 4711," in reference to the trademark number of Eau de Cologne.[36] Treatment at the hands of SS guards was no more humane at Dachau and Sachsenhausen.[37] At Sachsenhausen, prisoners were put to work moving stones, sacks of cement, and sand. The work was actually a form of torture, as the men were forced to carry their burdens with outstretched arms at a brisk pace. Old men were not exempted from the backbreaking tasks. Some of the prisoners were forced to drink water containing dust from the cement. The prisoners were fortunate that there were not enough SS guards to be present at all times. When guards were absent, the Jewish prisoners were under the supervision of other inmates, usually Communist political prisoners, whose behavior was much more humane.

In all the camps, SS guards commonly singled out for special abuse Jews who were overweight, wealthy, or particularly "Jewish-looking." The overweight prisoners were subjected to beatings and ridicule when they could not perform physical exercises. The SS guards were usually very young men—in their early twenties—and they added to the humiliation of the older prisoners by addressing them in the familiar "Du" form. Many of the guards tended to pick on older prisoners and on those who were well educated, such as lawyers and doctors. The antisemitism of the SS guards was intensified by class envy. At Buchenwald, a favorite ploy among the guards was to ask prisoners what their occupations were. They followed up with questions about the size of bank accounts, monthly pensions, apartments, and so on. The more education and wealth involved, the more brutal the reaction. One prisoner was beaten to death after giving his occupation, somewhat sarcastically, as "millionaire." Notably, the guards never asked the Jewish prisoners about their military experience in the German army during World War One—a subject that would have been inconsistent with the stereotype of the parasitical, treacherous Jew.

The guards were obsessed with depriving the Jewish prisoners of their dignity. Ritual forms of humiliation were the norm. In one instance, a group of rabbis was forced to stand outside the apartment of a camp officer and serenade him to sleep. In another, Jewish prisoners were made to pick up crumbs of bread from the ground and eat them. Jews were often forced to sing obscene songs, or to walk around carrying signs with slogans such as "We are the Destroyers of German Culture." When Jews refused to recite aloud phrases like "I am a shit Jew," they were subjected to severe beatings. Like all prisoners in the camps, Jews who were judged to have violated discipline were subject to public

flogging and other severe punishments. After their release and emigration, quite a few of the Jewish prisoners claimed that the guards derived
genuine sadistic enjoyment from these punishments. One former prisoner speculated that the young SS guards were engaging in a form of
"pathological-erotic unloading."[38]

Several hundred Jewish prisoners died in the camps under these
conditions between November 1938 and early 1939.[39] Many of the deaths
were murders at the hands of SS guards. Quite a few Jews took their
own lives, sacrificing themselves on the electric fence rather than endure
the horrors of the camp. Many of the deaths resulted from heart attacks
induced by hard labor or other forms of extreme physical exertion. Others were the consequence of exposure to the increasingly cold late autumn and winter weather. Yet another cause of death was the absence of
vital medications, such as insulin for men suffering from diabetes. More
generally, the camp administration did not bother to provide medical
care to the Jewish prisoners.

Terrifying as it was, for most of the Jewish prisoners, the stay in the
concentration camp was relatively brief. The gradual release of the Jews
arrested in connection with the pogrom began in late November and
continued for several months into the spring. Most were released in a
matter of weeks after their arrest. From the regime's point of view, the
purpose of their captivity was to leverage the transfer of their property
and their expeditious departure from Germany. The authorities issued
a flurry of orders to ensure that the blackmail operation would function
smoothly. On November 16, Reinhard Heydrich told the commandants
of the concentration camps that the detention of Jews should not be allowed to interfere with negotiations over the "Aryanization" of their property.[40] In cases where the presence of the Jewish prisoner was needed
to conclude such a negotiation, he should be released from the camp
immediately. In the same order, Heydrich stipulated that Jews already
in possession of emigration papers should be released from camps to
expedite their departure from Germany. He also issued a blanket order
for the release of Jewish prisoners over the age of sixty, who were not
supposed to be in the camps in the first place. The administrations of

the concentration camps were slow to implement this last instruction. On November 24, Heydrich sent an additional urgent message to the camp commanders, scolding them for not yet having released the elderly Jews.[41] In the meantime, many of the Jews in question had already died. It has been estimated that of the Jews who died in Buchenwald in the weeks after the pogrom, 20 percent were over sixty years of age.[42]

On November 25, Heydrich ordered the release of Jewish attorneys whose services were needed in "Aryanization" proceedings.[43] Three days later he directed the camp commandants to release Jewish prisoners who had seen combat, or, in the parlance of the time, "fought at the front," during the First World War.[44] Heydrich did not explain the logic behind the release of these prisoners, but he did note that he was acting at the request of Hermann Goering. Negative reactions to the Kristallnacht had been especially pronounced in German military circles, and the summary imprisonment of Jewish combat veterans in concentration camps must have been an additional irritant. So it might well be that the release of the veterans was the result of an effort at damage control on the part of Goering, himself a veteran of the war as well as a severe critic, on tactical grounds, of the pogrom. The veterans —or, more likely, their families—would be allowed to confirm their military record either by producing their Honor Cross for Service at the Front or by submitting other documentation.

Producing the paperwork necessary to secure the release of the Jewish men was a task left, in a great many cases, to their wives. The Jewish women engaged in a desperate scramble to collect documents demonstrating that they and their husbands had sold, or were preparing to sell, their property, and that their emigration was in process. The women in many cases took it upon themselves to sell homes or businesses even while their husbands languished in the camps. They waited in long lines for days at foreign consulates, attempting to obtain visas, and then had to deal with the Gestapo and other German authorities to arrange for the release of the men.[45] For many of the women, securing information about the condition, and sometimes even the location, of their husbands was a major struggle. Uncertainty surrounding the fate of the men placed tremendous stress on wives as well as on other family members.[46]

The gradual discharge of the Jewish camp prisoners continued into December and January. On December 2, camp commandants were directed to release Jewish prisoners over the age of fifty.[47] On January 21, 1939, the order came to release the small number of Jewish prisoners who were under the age of eighteen.[48] By the spring of 1939, only several hundred of the 30,000 Jewish men arrested in November were still in the camps. They consisted, for the most part, of men who were suspected of trying to dodge "Aryanization," who had difficulty demonstrating their preparations to emigrate, or whose "protective custody" was extended for some reason other than simply being Jewish.[49]

Upon their release from the camps, the Jewish men were warned not to talk about their experiences. These threats were part of the standard operating procedure for the release of the Jews. Heydrich had specifically ordered camp personnel to issue the warnings.[50] The prisoners were told that Nazi agents kept tabs on émigrés, so that even North America would not provide a refuge. Those who talked would end up in a concentration camp for the rest of their lives, or measures would be taken against their families still in Germany. Given what they had just experienced, many of the released prisoners took these threats to heart. They were reluctant to discuss the details of their experiences in the camps, even with their wives. When Hertha Nathorff's husband returned home to Berlin from Sachsenhausen on December 16, he told her, "I am OK, and I was OK. Please don't inquire any further."[51] Many Jews who emigrated shortly after their release from the camps were willing to give detailed accounts of their imprisonment to the Jewish Central Information Office based in Amsterdam, but most of their reports remained anonymous out of a very legitimate fear of German reprisal.[52]

The efforts of the Propaganda Ministry and the German press and radio to convince the German people that the pogrom had been a justifiable and legitimate expression of contempt for the Jews could not negate the inconvenient fact that a massive number of illegal acts had been committed. These ranged from relatively petty transgressions, such as looting, to serious crimes, such as murder, battery, and rape. The Nazi leadership, therefore, faced a dilemma. On the one hand, if it acted as though no laws had been broken, it risked losing its credibility with Germans who still valued a sense of order and a functioning system of justice. On the other hand, pursuing justice against persons who had committed crimes during the pogrom—especially members of the Nazi Party—could potentially prove highly embarrassing to the party and its leaders. How could one prosecute and punish individual acts committed in connection with the pogrom without discrediting the entire action and the people who were ultimately responsible for it?

The party, the Gestapo, and the Reich Ministry of Justice began to confront this dilemma even before the pogrom had come to an end. On November 10, the Ministry of Justice agreed to let the Gestapo and the party take the lead in any investigations that might ensue from the violence. State prosecutors, who were subordinate to the Ministry of Justice, were allowed to proceed with investigations only after cases had been assessed by the local Gestapo. The Gestapo, therefore, played the lead role and, in consultation with local party leaders, turned cases over to prosecutors only when they were deemed not to be politically sensitive. Many of these cases involved looting. Heydrich had been critical of the massive looting even as it was unfolding on November 10, and he had repeatedly ordered police to intervene against it.[53] Immediately after the pogrom, local police and Gestapo tracked down several hundred looters throughout the country, usually sparing them from prosecution in exchange for their turning the stolen goods over to the police.[54] The de facto amnesty for looters was only partially successful, however. Weeks after the pogrom, authorities were still imploring Germans to come forth with the looted goods.[55] Ironically, the information the Gestapo compiled about looters in November 1938 would serve as the basis for the prosecution of some of the same looters a decade later, in Allied-occupied Germany.

In early December 1938 it became clear to Nazi Party officials that even cases involving looting and other relatively minor offenses had the potential to generate embarrassment. The party therefore moved to seize greater control over the legal process, excluding state prosecutors altogether in cases involving party members. On December 7, acting for the party (and presumably with Hitler's approval), Deputy Führer Rudolf Hess decreed that all cases against members of the Nazi Party would be handled entirely by the Gestapo and the Nazi Party Court.[56] The professional jurists in the Justice Ministry complained but did not prevail. The new procedure marked a substantial transfer of authority over the legal system from traditional institutions of German justice—police, state prosecutors, and the courts—to extralegal enforcement organs of the Nazi dictatorship—the Gestapo and the Nazi Party itself.[57]

On December 10, Heydrich instructed Gestapo offices about how they should proceed.[58] All cases involving killing of Jews, serious battery, blackmail, looting, embezzlement, and sexual offenses were to be investigated by local Gestapo offices. The investigations, Heydrich emphasized, were to proceed inconspicuously so as to "arouse as little notice as possible." The local office of the Nazi Party Court was to be consulted at every stage of the process. The Gestapo could also receive information from criminal police and prosecutors who may have investigated a case at an earlier stage. The investigators were to aspire to an "objective and accurate reconstruction" of each case; they were to gather information with regard to the facts of each case, as well as the background and motivation of the suspects. Heydrich laid particular emphasis on establishing the actual motive for the crime. He instructed the local Gestapo offices not to be unduly strict toward suspects who were deemed to have acted out of "idealistic" motives. In the context of the pogrom, Heydrich employed the term "idealistic" to describe people who believed that they were pursuing the wishes and interests of the Nazi movement. In contrast, motives that were not considered "idealistic" included greed, sadism, and the urge for sexual gratification. Suspects who acted out of these impulses were to be investigated more thoroughly.

Even in cases where the motive was "idealistic," suspects who acted in an "inhuman" way were to be subject to disciplinary action of some sort. In determining motive, it would be particularly important for the Gestapo to establish what orders a suspect had received from his superiors. Heydrich ordered automatic arrest and trial before party courts for two categories of suspects: blackmailers and looters who acted out of greed and who had previous records of such behaviors; and sexual offenders. He was also very clear about which actions should not be cause for discipline: "Arson, damage to property, and destruction of synagogues and Jewish cemeteries are in principle not to be prosecuted."

Despite this perversion of justice, members and officials of the party were not necessarily forthcoming with the investigators. They remained inclined to protect themselves, their comrades, and their underlings. When their resistance to the investigations became apparent, Rudolf Hess circulated a strongly worded admonition to party offices, ordering them to cooperate with the Gestapo.[59] As the investigations proceeded during December 1938, ordinary German citizens caught wind of the legal double-standard that was being applied for the benefit of party members, and they were not happy about it. One judge in Bavaria informed the Reich Ministry of Justice that exempting party members from the normal legal process had led people in his district to question "whether we still live in a Rechtsstaat"—this being the German term for "rule of law," a tradition to which many Germans continued to cling even as the Nazi regime rapidly dismantled it.[60]

The manner in which the Gestapo and the Nazi Party Court ultimately disposed of the cases they investigated did little to appease such critics; quite the contrary. While most of the cases were handled, and dismissed, by local Nazi Party courts, thirty defendants were tried before the Supreme Party Court in Munich between late December 1938 and early February 1939. These were the cases that appeared to have been especially egregious. The court expelled four Storm Troopers for having raped or molested Jewish girls during the pogrom. It condemned the immorality of these acts but also underscored the violation of Nazi racial principles. The court convicted Heinrich Frey, a Nazi since 1932, of having sexually abused a thirteen-year-old Jewish girl in Duisburg.

The court ruled that Frey's actions had "sullied" the Nazi struggle against Jewish influence "in order to satisfy his lower instincts."[61] The court's reasoning was similar in the case of two SA men from Linz, Friedrich Schmidinger and Johann Hintersteiner. Schmidinger had joined the Nazi Party in 1929. The court concluded that the two men had "sullied the honor of the movement" by forcing a Jewish woman to undress and then molesting her during an invasion of her home.[62] A fourth SA man, Gustav Gerstner from Niederwerrn, was convicted for theft as well as for sexual misconduct during the pogrom. After expulsion from the party, all four of these men were turned over to the state for prosecution under the Nazi regime's miscegenation laws—but, notably, not for battery or rape. Although only these four cases of sexual abuse in connection with the Kristallnacht made their way to the Supreme Nazi Court, there is good reason to assume that a larger number of similar crimes had been committed but were never investigated or entered into the official record.

The Supreme Nazi Court was far more lenient in its adjudication of cases involving the murder of Jews. The vast majority of the party members who were investigated for murder either got off scot-free or were subjected to relatively mild disciplinary measures. None were expelled from the party. The court ruled that these man had followed orders, acted in good faith on the basis of garbled or confused orders, believed that their actions were in keeping with the intentions of the Nazi leadership, or had been motivated by an understandable outrage at the murder of Ernst vom Rath.[63]

After the court had handed down these judgments, it asked Hitler to pardon the defendants in order to shield them from future indictment by state prosecutors. The Führer obliged.[64] The pardons were a gesture of solidarity with Germans who had carried out the party's wishes, as well as a tactic for disposing of a political nuisance. It was also, even if only implicitly, a claim by Hitler to ownership of the pogrom, for it was he who, in the final analysis, had authorized the very crimes that he now pardoned.

6

"A Tempest in a Teapot"

The majority of Germans had not participated directly in the pogrom, but they could not escape the magnitude of the event. Hundreds of thousands had witnessed acts of violence against people and property. In Vienna, the burning of the synagogue in the Leopoldstrasse was reported live and in vivid detail on local radio.[1] Throughout Germany, in large cities and small towns, synagogues lay in ruins, shattered glass littered the sidewalks in front of Jewish shops, and plundered Jewish property had been snatched up into a great many homes. The mass arrest of Jews and their subsequent banishment to concentration camps had taken place largely in the open. The way Germans reacted to these developments must be an issue of central importance for scholars of the Holocaust, as it goes to the question of how much anti-Jewish violence the ordinary citizens of the Third Reich were prepared to condone on the eve of World War Two.

Before this became an important question for historians, it was a matter of some urgency for the Nazi regime itself. Germany at that time did not possess the kind of modern opinion polling that is now taken for granted. In the Third Reich, public opinion was gauged mainly by keeping an ear to the ground. One agency, the Security Service (SD), employed a wide network of informants stationed throughout German society. Other agencies went about the same business less systematically. The results were far from what contemporary survey specialists would regard as "scientific." Opinion reports prepared for official use in the Nazi regime pose a couple of significant challenges to the historian. The officials responsible for preparing them operated in an authoritarian and ideologically saturated environment. They had any number of reasons to distort their reporting, consciously or otherwise. Some mayors and other local officials were not eager to admit that significant segments of the population under their authority dissented from a major action on the part of the Nazi regime. On the other hand, some officials who were zealous Nazis may have been led by ideologically induced para- noia to exaggerate the breadth and depth of popular dissent. Despite these problems, when used with care, the information collected through this process enables the historian to achieve a nuanced understanding of German public opinion toward the pogrom.

The complexity of the public response can be illustrated by an ex- ample drawn from around the city of Bielefeld in northwestern Ger- many. On November 14, the Gestapo station in Bielefeld circulated a memorandum to government offices in the surrounding region. It con- tained a request for information concerning the consequences of the pogrom.[2] It divided the request into fourteen specific categories of in- formation, mostly having to do with the material and economic dam- ages wrought by the violence. Question 14, however, went to a more fundamental issue: the response of the German public. In addition to a general assessment of public opinion, the Gestapo requested detailed information about disapproving comments and the people who made them.

The reports that trickled in over the next two weeks reflected a wide range of responses. The mayor of Bielefeld reported that the people of his city most definitely sympathized with the "struggle against Jewry" and understood the need to employ "extraordinarily sharp measures" in the effort to render the Jews "harmless." The people of the city were not especially offended by the destruction of the synagogue. What did offend them, however, was the senseless destruction of property that would have "sooner or later gone over to Aryan ownership." The mayor reported that many witnesses shook their heads in disapproval or looked on in "icy silence" as the destruction ran its course.[3] This theme was expressed almost universally in the responses to the Gestapo office. A county official in Halle/Westphalia reported that the citizens of his region acknowledged the need for "measures of revenge for the cowardly murder" of vom Rath, but that they disapproved of the destruction of "people's property." They shared with the people of Bielefeld—and of other communities in the region—the assumption that the Jewish-owned property destroyed in the pogrom would have soon been transferred to the German people, and therefore should not have been destroyed.[4] Moreover, they could not comprehend how the willful and organized destruction of property could be consistent with the goals of the Four-Year Plan, which had placed on the shoulders of every German the responsibility to increase economic productivity.[5] In several communities, including Peckelsheim and Bega, citizens demonstrated their objection to the cavalier destruction of property by withholding contributions to the Winter Assistance charity.[6]

The report from the county commissioner of Höxter struck a different chord. As in almost every other location, the population was upset at the needless destruction of property. But here, many Germans were also upset at the way the Jews had been treated. While the majority had initially been supportive of the anti-Jewish action, many had then turned against it, repelled as they were by the physical abuse and mass arrest of Jews. The sight of battered and bedraggled Jews being dragged away to a concentration camp had created sympathy for them among the locals. In the end, most of the people in Höxter had concluded that the pogrom had damaged Germany's reputation and had been a violation of "German dignity."[7] The mayor of Borgentreich asserted that about 60 percent of the citizens of his town were critical of the pogrom, in part because of the destruction of property, but also because of the removal of Jews to concentration camps. The implicit suggestion was that the other 40 percent of the townspeople had had no objection to what had transpired.[8]

In Minden, the public had by and large applauded the pogrom.[9] A similar response came from the town of Atteln.[10] An official from Neuhaus reported that the residents of his town greeted the pogrom with "satisfaction."[11] The mayor of Detmold went further, characterizing the reaction among his citizens as one of "genuine satisfaction."[12] The mayor of Bad Oeynhausen assured the Gestapo that the people of his town had reacted to the pogrom "with understanding" and that there had been no complaints.[13] The mayor of Bückeburg characterized opinion in his community as "very divided." In this case, however, the criticism stemmed entirely from the damage to property and the breakdown of public order, whereas sympathy for the Jewish victims of the pogrom was not a factor.[14]

Quite a few of the reports that flowed into the Gestapo office in Bielefeld noted that the pogrom had generated significant discomfort because of the attack on houses of worship and the destruction of sacred religious objects. This was especially true among the Catholic inhabitants of the region.[15] As many Catholics regarded their own faith and religious organizations as objects of Nazi persecution, they feared that their own churches might be next. This sentiment among the Catholics in the Bielefeld area was duplicated on a larger scale in the mostly Catholic province of Bavaria.[16] In the city of Bielefeld itself, strong disapproval of the destruction of Jewish houses of worship was also present in Protestant circles, especially among Germans who were sympathetic to the anti-Nazi "Confessing Church."[17] In other circles, the tone was quite different. At a Protestant church in Munich, the pastor sermon-

ized that the violence against the Jews had fulfilled the prophesy of Mat-
thew 27:25, according to which the blood of Christ would forever be on
the hands of the Jews. The pogrom, the pastor claimed, had been the
result of God's will.[18]

A Gestapo official reading all these reports in Bielefeld could have
reached only one logical conclusion: opinion about the pogrom was divided, even polarized. A majority of the population had not approved
of the action, but a significant portion either supported it or did not
object to it. Catholics tended to be more alarmed than Protestants. Disapproval focused mainly on damage to property and the general breakdown of order; less concern was expressed over the treatment or fate
of the Jews themselves. In all these respects, the reports for the region
around Bielefeld were fairly representative of the divisions within German public opinion that scholars have described for other regions of
Germany in November 1938.[19]

It has been suggested that many Germans who were morally outraged by the barbaric treatment of the Jews during the pogrom were too
afraid to express their true feelings, and so they expressed their protest
in terms of economic concerns.[20] By November 1938, the Nazi regime
had developed a broad array of mechanisms to repress opposition and
to punish open dissent. Prosecution was one method among many for
retaliating against critics of the regime. Ordinary Germans were subject to the influence of the Nazi Party, and the state apparatus it had
come to dominate, on many levels, and they knew that the regime did
not take kindly to criticisms of its policies targeted at the Jews. People
who might, under other circumstances, have been inclined to condemn
the Kristallnacht on moral or humanitarian (as opposed to material)
grounds had good reason to think twice before doing so. Thus the con-
temporaneous evidence on which historians must base their assessment
of Germans' reactions to the pogrom may very well underrepresent the
breadth and depth of moral rejection.

When trying to measure the level of moral disapproval of the pogrom, therefore, we must bear in mind the Nazi regime's willingness to

punish its citizens for such gestures of defiance. Germans who voiced such criticism ran the risk of arrest and prosecution for violation of the 1934 law against maligning the leaders of the party or the government.[21] In Munich alone between November 1938 and March 1939, prosecutors brought thirty-two such cases arising from the pogrom and its aftermath.[22] Germans throughout the Reich faced the same potential fate. One case involved Hermann B., a fifty-eight-year-old laborer in Wuppertal. One day at work, he expressed the view to a colleague that, after the burning of the synagogues, Germany could no longer be considered a land of culture. Either overheard by a third person or denounced by his coworker, Hermann B. was prosecuted in 1939 and sentenced to five months in prison. Another case involved Franz H., a twenty-seven-year-old teacher of Catholic religion at the vocational school in Bad Kissingen. On November 10, he was scheduled to speak to his students about the Immaculate Conception. But after being provoked by one of his students, he lost his temper and denounced the pogrom in front of the class. He compared the burning of German synagogues to the antireligious campaign in the Soviet Union. The school administration did not take long to react. The next day, all the members of the class—thirty-four students in all—were systematically interviewed about Franz H.'s outburst. Several days later, the case was turned over to the prosecutor. The Ministry of Justice in Berlin ultimately recommended against an indictment, but the chilling effect intended by the investigation had been achieved.[23]

Members of the clergy were not exempt from this kind of treatment. Two Protestant pastors in Rosswälden, a town in southwest Germany, found themselves in trouble with the authorities after preaching against the pogrom. On November 13, in a sermon on the Sunday after the Kristallnacht, Julius von Jan condemned the violence on biblical grounds. He was subsequently attacked by a Nazi mob and taken into "protective custody" by the Gestapo. A few days later, Jan's colleague, Paul Veil, condemned Jan's treatment at the hands of the authorities and, for good measure, reinforced Jan's condemnation of the pogrom. Veil had already been under some suspicion in local party circles. He had been a member of the Nazi Party as late as 1932, but had then turned against the movement. In a sermon delivered on November 16, Veil declared that the burning of houses of worship could only happen in a country in which "the people no longer hear God's word." As a result, the state prosecutor in Stuttgart indicted Veil for his negative comments about "leading personalities of the state and the Nazi Party." Preparations for prosecution moved forward in 1939 but were suspended after the beginning of the war.[24]

German prosecutors and courts proved especially strict in cases where the criticism emanated from Jews themselves. Henriette S. was a fifty-six-year-old Jewish woman in Frankfurt who was married to an "Aryan." Shortly after the pogrom, she asked a non-Jewish shopkeeper about the latter's opinion regarding the violence. The shopkeeper defended the pogrom, arguing, with respect to Herschel Grynszpan's attack on Ernst vom Rath, that "it's not right when a guy goes and shoots a defenseless, harmless person." Henriette S. responded by calling the perpetrators of the pogrom "rascals, rogues, and criminals." Hitler was "the biggest thief," she said, adding, "if I could, I would poison all of them." In the indictment of Henriette S., the state prosecutor characterized her as "impudent and impertinent." Convicted of maligning the national leadership, she was sentenced to six months in prison. A similarly harsh punishment was meted out to Elsa C., a twenty-three-year-old "half-Jew" from Munich. Elsa C. had been forcibly sterilized in 1935 owing to "moral feeblemindedness." In November 1938 she was employed in the kitchen of the Löwenbräukeller restaurant. On November 12, in a discussion with a coworker, she denounced the pogrom, in the process uttering the phrase, "I could vomit in the face of the Führer." The local prosecutor preferred to issue a warning to Elsa C., but he was overruled by the Ministry of Justice in Berlin, which ordered a full prosecution. After a trial, Elsa C. was convicted and sentenced to four months in prison.[25]

Even when prosecutors did not act, party activists managed to impose serious consequences on Germans whose utterances or behaviors could be interpreted as critical of Nazi policy or as sympathetic toward the Jewish victims of the Kristallnacht. A good case in point is that of Paul Kahle, the head of the seminar for Oriental Studies at the University of Bonn. Together with his wife and sons, Kahle helped Jewish acquaintances clean up the mess left in the wake of the vandalism. On November 17, the local Nazi newspaper, the *Westdeutscher Beobachter,* accused Kahle of treason. This kind of journalistic denunciation was not the same as a formal indictment by a state prosecutor, but it was enough to provoke Nazi activists in the faculty and the student body to go after the professor. Kahle was subjected to serious harassment at the university and was then informed by the administration that his dismissal would follow. Kahle and his family fled to Britain in February 1939.[26]

An assessment of German attitudes toward the pogrom must also take into account private or discreet expressions of morally motivated condemnation. These were common in certain aristocratic and professional military circles, for example, where an old-fashioned sense of honor still prevailed.[27] Such critics of anti-Jewish violence often continued to cling to traditional antisemitic prejudices. For some of the participants in the military-aristocratic anti-Hitler resistance, for example, doubts about the Nazi regime were reinforced as a result of the pogrom. Although they had believed in the propriety of anti-Jewish legislation and the necessity of "Aryanizing" Jewish property, they were critical of the violent methods employed during the Kristallnacht, which they regarded as a national embarrassment and as a violation of German honor.[28] Claus Schenk von Stauffenberg, the central figure in the July 20, 1944, plot to assassinate Hitler, reportedly turned white with shame when he learned of the events of the pogrom. The violence reinforced his belief that the masses required the leadership of aristocrats who operated with nobility and dignity.[29] Another figure associated with the July 20 plot, Ulrich von Hassell, entrusted to his diary on November 25, 1938, his belief that the pogrom had been a "genuine disgrace." Never before, in his estimation, had Germany "lost so much credit in the world." He not only feared for Germany's international reputation but also dreaded the implications of the pogrom for life inside Germany. It did not bode well for Germany's future that the country was increasingly in the grip of a "system" that had been capable of doing such a thing.[30]

Another member of the resistance, Helmuth James Graf von Moltke, noted in a letter written on November 20, 1938, that "what we must hope is that public opinion in the world is finally roused to the worldwide threat to the foundations of our civilization."[31] Shortly after the pogrom, Helmuth Groscurth, a counterintelligence officer, wrote in his diary that "one must be ashamed to remain a German."[32] Later, while serving with the German Army in occupied Ukraine in 1941, Groscurth would attempt, unsuccessfully, to block the massacre of ninety Jewish children by the SS.[33] Even Adolf Hitler's own army adjutant, Major Gerhard Engel, was angered and embarrassed by the pogrom.[34] The sentiments of these men must have certainly reflected those of a great many Germans who did not keep private diaries or otherwise have their private thoughts recorded for posterity.

The depth and breadth of the moral indignation at the pogrom, therefore, may very well have been a good deal greater than even the leaders of the Nazi regime came to realize. This having been said, there is another point on which the evidence is entirely clear. Objections to the barbarism of the Kristallnacht were not tantamount to a general critique of the Nazi regime's anti-Jewish policies. The opinion reports make abundantly clear that the overwhelming majority of the German public—including those who were critical of the pogrom—had approved of the legal and bureaucratic measures implemented against the Jews since 1933. When, in the weeks after the Kristallnacht, the Nazi regime implemented a host of measures to accelerate the "Aryanization" of Jewish property and to hasten the emigration of Jews from the country, criticism remained muted.[35]

Officials at the Ministry of Propaganda recognized that many Germans had been unhappy about the pogrom for one reason or another.

To counteract this discontent they launched a major propaganda campaign in the days after November 10. Another reason for the campaign was to neutralize the profound condemnation of the pogrom that was emanating from abroad, especially from Great Britain, France, and the United States.[36] The propaganda offensive, which began on November 11 and extended into December, proceeded on several tracks simultaneously. First, it tried to reassure the German people that the pogrom had been an exceptional event, and that anti-Jewish policy would once again follow a legal and bureaucratic path. Second, it underscored the whole panoply of supposed dangers that the Jews posed to Germany, historically and in the present. An important element of this line of propaganda was the characterization of Herschel Grynszpan's killing of Ernst vom Rath as an attempt by "World Jewry" to foment war between Germany and France. Third, it tried to deflect criticism from Britain and the United States by pointing to the racist and colonialist practices of these countries. And fourth, it hurled accusations of hypocrisy at countries that bemoaned the treatment of Jews in Germany even while refusing to open their doors to Jewish refugees. The Ministry of Propaganda coordinated the campaign, issuing frequent instructions to German newspaper editors, who, notwithstanding an occasional exception, followed the guidelines they received from Berlin.[37]

Several of the press directives underscored the need to convince the German population that the pogrom would not be repeated. This emphasis was most certainly a reaction to internal criticism of the pogrom and was closely linked to the high-level decision to shift back to a legal-bureaucratic approach to anti-Jewish policy now that, as Goebbels had claimed on November 10, the violent actions had "fulfilled their desired and expected purpose."[38] On November 12, the Propaganda Ministry instructed German newspapers to combat certain rumors that were running rampant in the aftermath of the pogrom. Among these was the prospect that all German Jews would now be locked up in a ghetto, or that all Jews under age sixty would be sent to a labor camp. The ministry blamed the foreign press for spreading these rumors. With regard to the chief basis for this rumor—the fact that thousands of Jews were at that moment languishing in concentration camps—the German press was ordered to deny that any mass arrest of Jews had actually taken place. The authorities had, instead, carried out only "isolated arrests for specific reasons."[39] The press was to assure the German people that the "Jewish question" was now going to be "definitively resolved" once and for all, but not through violence.[40]

No room could be left for doubt when it came to the necessity of new anti-Jewish measures. On November 15, the Propaganda Ministry instructed German editors to run articles emphasizing the criminal nature of the Jews as a people. These stories would coincide with a press campaign targeted specifically against Herschel Grynszpan, who was portrayed as the latest in a long list of Jews who were prepared to commit crimes to further Jewish interests. On November 17 the ministry ordered the press to emphasize the disproportionately great wealth of German Jews, in a clear attempt to provide cover for the huge collective fine that had been imposed on the Jews to pay for damages resulting from the pogrom, and for the newly accelerated process of "Aryanization."[41]

Also on November 17, the Propaganda Ministry informed editors about a major new effort to enlighten the German people about the detrimental effects of the Jewish presence in Germany over the course of centuries: "Every German newspaper" would be expected to participate. According to the directive, "the influence of the Jews in Germany should be demonstrated in the labor movement, in liberalism, in culture, in finance, at the princely courts, during the war, in the strike of the munitions workers, in the last year of the war, in the November revolt, in the first governments of the Republic, in corruption, etc."[42] Special emphasis should be given to the key role Jews played in Germany's defeat in 1918, and in the revolution that brought the hated Weimar Republic into being. This particular effort, the ministry explained, was designed to silence German "fuddy-duddies" who sympathized with the Jews and opposed the Nazi regime's policies to marginalize them. The ministry distributed a list of arguments to be included in the newspaper articles and recommended books that could serve as sources for journalists. The volumes included *The Jews in Germany*, an antisemitic handbook published by the Institute for the Study of the Jewish Question, which was itself a Propaganda Ministry front operation, and *Immorality in the Talmud*, an antisemitic tract by Alfred Rosenberg, the Nazi Party's chief ideologist.[43] The ministry also recommended works that had been published by antisemitic scholars whose "scientific" approach to the "Jewish question" brought with them a special intellectual cachet. The recommended works of scholarship included books by the historian Walther Frank, who was the director of the pro-Nazi Institute for History of the New Germany, as well as articles from the journal *Research on the Jewish Question*, which was published by the Jewish Research Department of Frank's institute.[44]

With respect to foreign criticism of the pogrom, Goebbels considered the problem to be just temporary, "a tempest in a teapot."[45] Clever propaganda, he believed, would suffice to avert any major foreign policy consequences that might result from the pogrom. This element of the propaganda campaign was also reflected in guidelines the Propaganda Ministry issued to the German press. Taking its cue from remarks Goebbels made to foreign correspondents in Berlin on November 11, the campaign initially targeted critical comments about the pogrom that had been made in the British House of Commons. To neutralize this criticism, German journalists were instructed to emphasize the harshness of measures that the British had recently taken against Arabs in Palestine. These had included the destruction of Arab homes, executions, and life-long prison sentences. If the British Commons considered it important to debate the Jewish question in Germany, the Propaganda Ministry suggested, then perhaps the German Reichstag would have to debate British atrocities in Palestine.[46] Hitler was especially gratified by this clever exploitation of the Palestine question.[47]

To reinforce such arguments, the ministry provided the German press with a steady flow of what today would be called "talking points."

"Where," one should ask, "is the world's conscience with regard to the atrocities in Palestine, while in Germany a few windows are broken or a few synagogues burned?" Were the homes of Arabs destroyed by British forces no less important than Jewish synagogues? In addition to underscoring British hypocrisy, the goal of this kind of propaganda was to depict the British as stooges of the Zionists in Palestine. The ministry also directed newspapers to publish details about British atrocities in the Boer War and in India.[48] In that conflict, the ministry pointed out, the British had systematically starved to death 20,000 Boers, who were a "people of culture" and "not simple negroes." In light of this record of barbarism, who were the British to lecture the Germans about morality? The Germany of 1938 was not the Germany of 1918, and it would no longer tolerate British condescension and "English educational methods." The ministry further instructed editors that British criticism of Germany was the result of Jewish influence over the British government and press. The criticism, therefore, was the product of a particular "clique" and did not reflect the sentiments of the entire British population.[49] The Propaganda Ministry employed an essentially similar approach in its attempts to neutralize criticism from the United States. It ordered German newspapers to discredit the Americans as hypocrites by emphasizing two points. First, the Americans themselves had been guilty of exterminating the Indians of North America, and second, the tone of the American press was controlled by Jewish publishers and editors.[50]

German propaganda reinforced the accusation of Anglo-American hypocrisy by noting that neither England nor the United States was prepared to admit German Jews who were attempting to emigrate. The simple message to be conveyed by the German press was that "nobody wants the Jews." The reason for this, the Propaganda Ministry explained, was that these countries recognized full well that the Jews "constitute a national danger." They preferred, therefore, that Germany "keep these parasites within its own borders."[51] The Propaganda Ministry ignored the contradiction inherent in this argument, namely, that Jews, despite their alleged control over much of British and American society, were somehow unable to secure a pro-Jewish immigration policy.

The antisemitic press campaign after Kristallnacht was not limited to newspapers. German radio broadcast a barrage of relevant programming as well. Two news programs, "Midday Echo" and "Evening Echo," focused heavily on Jews and the "Jewish question" inside Germany. In the days and weeks leading up to the pogrom, such programming had by and large been absent from German radio. But the broadcast schedule for the last three weeks of November reflected the new emphasis the Propaganda Ministry placed on Jewish-related programming after the Kristallnacht:

November 11, Evening: Report on "The Eternal Jew" exhibition
November 15, Evening: Report on "The Eternal Jew" exhibition
November 17, Midday: Live coverage, funeral of E. vom Rath
November 19, Evening: Institute for Study of the Jewish Question
November 22, Midday: The Jewish Question
November 23, Midday: The Jews in Soviet Russia
November 23, Evening: International Jewish Criminals
November 24, Evening: Against Jewish Megalomania
November 25, Evening: The Emancipation of the Jews
November 26, Midday: Rothschild's Gold
November 26, Evening: The Jew as Warmonger
November 28, Midday: The Jews in Soviet Russia
November 28, Evening: America and the Jews
November 29, Midday: Jewish Superstitions
November 29, Evening: World Criminal Judah
November 30, Evening: The Jewish Offensive

The Jewish-related radio programming trailed off after November 30, but it did not end. Thirteen such programs aired during the month of December.[52]

By late November 1938, Joseph Goebbels was convinced that the propaganda campaign had worked. On November 27 he wrote in his diary, "The agitation over the Jews has run itself out. We have achieved our goal. The world has other problems at this point."[53] Goebbels, however, sorely underestimated the degree of damage the pogrom had done to Germany's international standing. Especially in Great Britain and the United States, the Kristallnacht—which had been reported upon and condemned very widely—had reinforced the belief that Nazi Germany was a regime of exceptional barbarity rather than a traditional power with which one could negotiate normally. British and American advocates of a long-term peaceful coexistence with the Third Reich now had a much more difficult time making their case. Blinded by ideology and arrogance, Goebbels was unable to recognize this shift, but German diplomats stationed on the ground in London and Washington could not ignore it.

The German ambassador in London, Herbert von Dirksen, reported the bad news to Berlin on November 17. The pogrom had made it much easier for "anti-German circles" to attack Prime Minister Neville Chamberlain's plan for achieving a *modus vivendi* with Germany. Dirksen pointed to the "pessimism that has overtaken just those sections of the British public who actively supported Anglo-German friendship"; the effectiveness of these "pro-German circles" had been "crippled."[54] The news from Washington was not any better. On November 14, the German ambassador, Hans Dieckhoff, reported a similar swing in American opinion. "Until November 10," he wrote, "large and powerful sections of the American people had still remained aloof" from anti-German sentiment. "Today this is no longer the case." Dieckhoff continued, "The outcry comes not only from Jews but in equal strength from all camps and classes, including the German-American camp." Elements of American society that had "maintained a comparative reserve" or had even "expressed sympathy toward Germany" were now turning away. This was, Dieckhoff emphasized, a "serious matter."[55] On the same day that Dieckhoff filed his report, the United States underscored its protest over the pogrom by withdrawing its ambassa-

dor in Berlin, Hugh Wilson, "for consultations." The Germans reciprocated, removing Dieckhoff from Washington, a gesture Goebbels
praised as an appropriate response to the American "twaddle."[56] The
two countries would not again exchange ambassadors until 1949.

The demonization of Herschel Grynszpan as an instrument of "World
Jewry" constituted a central element of the Nazi regime's propaganda
strategy after the Kristallnacht. In the aftermath of the pogrom, Herschel Grynszpan became the focus of international attention. The
American journalist Dorothy Thompson championed his cause, pub-
lishing an article about him in the New York *Herald-Tribune* on November 16. Jewish organizations in France and elsewhere collected
money to hire high-powered attorneys for Grynszpan's legal defense.
They included the famous antifascist lawyer Vincent de Moro-Giafferi.
Grynszpan himself was at times overwhelmed and confused as the members of his defense team argued over legal strategy. Some preferred to
downplay political motivations and emphasize instead Grynszpan's volatile emotional state at the time of the shooting, while others wanted to
use the case to highlight German atrocities against the Jews. For his
part, Grynszpan did not deviate from the explanation he had first given
to the French interrogators: he had shot Ernst vom Rath to avenge the
brutal treatment of his family and of other Jews at the hands of the Germans.[57]

On November 11, Wolfgang Diewerge convened a meeting of officials from the Propaganda Ministry and the Foreign Office to discuss
how to exploit the Grynszpan case for anti-Jewish propaganda. Diewerge had coordinated the Propaganda Ministry's news coverage of the
shooting in Paris starting on November 7. It was clear that no extradi-
tion of Grynszpan from France to Germany would be possible, even
though the shooting had taken place inside the German Embassy.
French law did, however, allow the family of Ernst vom Rath to partici-

pate in the trial as a civil party, and to appoint a representative to the court. The person chosen for this task, probably by Hitler himself, was Friedrich Grimm, a professor of international law at the University of Münster and a prominent Nazi attorney.[58] Grimm had represented German defendants before French courts in the 1920s and possessed excellent connections in the German Propaganda Ministry and Foreign Office.[59] He had known Diewerge since the "Cairo Jew Trial" of 1934, and in 1936 the two men had collaborated on German propaganda related to the Wilhelm Gustloff shooting.[60] The Grynszpan case provided the men with an opportunity to renew their earlier partnership in the same roles.[61]

As is evident from internal Propaganda Ministry documentation that was not intended for external consumption, Diewerge was genuinely convinced that Grynszpan had killed vom Rath as the instrument of an international Jewish conspiracy. He told his colleagues that it was his own "personal conviction" that the conspirators behind Grynszpan had also set up David Frankfurter to kill Wilhelm Gustloff in 1936. Diewerge's paranoia about Jewish violence manifested itself in further ways. He gave credence, for example, to the preposterous rumor that Jews in South Africa had been planning to assassinate members of the German community and to burn down their homes.[62]

While Diewerge coordinated the German approach to the Grynszpan case in Berlin, Friedrich Grimm traveled to Paris to keep abreast of the French investigation. His status as the vom Rath family's representative enabled him to keep close tabs on the interrogations of Grynszpan and on the thinking of the French police. In effect, if not officially, Grimm operated as an agent of the German government, sending detailed reports about his findings and impressions back to Berlin. Fearing that the French would be all too ready to treat Grynszpan as a lone killer, he believed that it was particularly important to keep pressure on French police to search for the Jewish conspirators behind the murder. Like Diewerge, Grimm was deluded by his own ideology and sincerely believed that such conspirators actually existed.[63] He continued to cling to this illusion as late as 1953, when he expressed it in his apologetic memoir.[64]

Neither Diewerge nor Grimm could ever make up his mind exactly how the relationship between Grynszpan and the supposed Jewish conspirators had actually functioned, but the main thrust of their narrative was that a desperate and angry Grynszpan had been a willing pawn of diabolical Parisian Jews and their foreign confederates. Both men entertained speculative scenarios for how Grynszpan's actions might have been instigated by Jewish conspirators, but they found no concrete evidence for any of them. Neither man considered the possibility that the conspiracy was difficult to explain because it did not actually exist.[65]

One idea Diewerge advanced was to ask the German Foreign Office to pressure the Poles into preventing Grynszpan's parents from traveling to Paris for the trial. Diewerge feared that they would be asked to testify about the conditions of their deportation from Hannover and, furthermore, about the miserable conditions of their existence in the no-man's-land between Germany and Poland.[66] Grimm was confident that the Poles would cooperate on this matter, given that, as he saw it, "Poland is indeed known around the world as an antisemitic country." Grimm may well have been encouraged in this regard by coverage of the pogrom in the Polish nationalist and Catholic press, which had expressed understanding for German outrage at the machinations of "World Jewry."[67] But Grimm also thought that it might be advantageous to let the parents appear at the trial, as it was almost certain that they would unintentionally assist the German cause by projecting a very poor impression of East European Jewry.[68]

Attempts to influence the legal process in France were not limited to those of Grimm. In February 1939, the Gestapo sent its own investigator, Kriminalrat Bömelburg, to Paris to "assist" with the French investigation. Bömelburg agreed with Grimm that the French seemed to be dragging their feet in the search for the Jewish conspirators. Not long after his arrival in Paris, Bömelburg informed Berlin that he suspected that the lead French investigator, Criminal Commissar Roche, was a Jew. Bömelburg based his suspicion on "the appearance of this man." The Gestapo, however, was not able to confirm whether Bömelburg's supposition was correct.[69]

In the early months of 1939, Diewerge developed a plan for a multi-faceted propaganda campaign that would be launched to accompany Grynszpan's trial by the French. Its goals would be, first, to demonstrate that Grynszpan had acted as a lackey for "World Jewry"; second, retro-actively to justify the November pogrom to the German people and to the world; third, to shift attention away from international criticism of ongoing anti-Jewish measures in Germany; and fourth, to discredit anti-German sentiment in France by branding those who were sympa-thetic to Grynszpan—especially the "Jewish-controlled press"—as war-mongers.[70] This last goal had taken on additional importance since November. In late 1938 and early 1939, the pro-Munich faction in the French government found itself increasingly on the defensive, and the Germans wanted to buttress it. They pursued this aim in part through a systematic propaganda campaign about Grynszpan inside France itself. The plan was to distribute pamphlets and to plant articles in friendly French newspapers.[71] This propaganda campaign, in Diewerge's eyes, became all the more urgent after the German-led dismantling of Czechoslovakia in March 1939, which dealt a major blow to the "ap-peasement" faction in France. Diewerge was now convinced that "Jew-ish propaganda has succeeded in creating a general hysteria among the French population."[72] That Germany's destruction of the sovereign state of Czechoslovakia might have played some role in fueling the fears of the French did not seem to have occurred to him.

One way to counteract Jewish influence over French politics would be to publish a book setting out the case against Grynszpan and his Jewish co-conspirators. The book, *Attack against Peace,* was edited by Diewerge himself and was produced in consultation with the Foreign Office, the Foreign Organization of the Nazi Party, and the Gestapo. Intended to highlight the "connection between the murder and Jewish warmongering around the world," the book would, it was hoped, enable readers to "correctly understand" the forthcoming French trial of Grynszpan. Readers in both Germany and France had to know that the trial was not about a confrontation between the two countries, but rather about "a Jewish attack against Germany, exploiting French hospitality." The book was published in Germany in the spring of 1939.[73] Initially, the German Embassy in Paris recommended against its translation and distribution in France, fearing that this approach would be too heavy-handed and would backfire.[74] But the German Foreign Office decided in the end to distribute the German-language volume in France in order to counter anti-Nazi brochures that Jewish organizations had put into circulation.[75]

Preparations for the trial in Paris dragged on through the summer of 1939, only to be overtaken by more momentous events. With France and Germany at war as of early September, the prospects of a trial now seemed very distant, though Grynszpan remained in France in pretrial custody. The situation was altered dramatically as a result of the German army's conquest of France in the spring of 1940. Grynszpan fell into German hands, as did the files of his defense attorneys and his French police interrogators.[76] In July 1940 the Germans were careful to ensure that the new Vichy government in France acceded officially to the transfer of Grynszpan to Germany so that it would not appear like a kidnapping.[77] Grynszpan was interrogated by the Gestapo in Berlin and then later transferred to the Sachsenhausen concentration camp. Friedrich Grimm, meanwhile, worked his way systematically through the captured French documents, interpreting what he read through his own ideological filter. Evidence of Jewish organizations coming to the assistance of vom Rath simply proved, in his mind, that a conspiracy of "World Jewry" had been behind Grynszpan and his actions from the beginning. As for Dorothy Thompson, who was not Jewish, Grimm concluded that she was really an anti-German in "Christian-humanitarian disguise."[78]

The Germans now began preparations for their own trial of Grynszpan. In the autumn of 1941, the Ministry of Justice instructed the state prosecutor to indict Grynszpan for high treason and murder. The indictment, which was issued on October 16, claimed that Grynszpan had killed Ernst vom Rath in order to "call the world's attention to the supposed persecution of the Jews in Germany, and to place pressure on the Reich government to abstain from measures intended to eliminate Jewish influence over the life of the German people."[79] Two weeks later, Hitler gave his personal consent for the trial preparations to move forward.[80] Roland Freisler, the state secretary in the Ministry of Justice, was at first chosen to serve as the chief prosecutor. Freisler was an old Nazi who was known for his toughness and ideological fanaticism. At the request of Goebbels, however, Hitler decided in the spring of 1942 to replace Freisler with Otto Georg Thierack, the president of the People's Court (and the future minister of justice), whom Goebbels judged to be more politically astute than Freisler and more sensitive to the needs of the Propaganda Ministry.[81]

Wolfgang Diewerge reviewed guidelines for the trial preparations in a series of memoranda generated between October 1941 and May 1942. The trial would be held before the People's Court and would be broadcast nationally on radio. The court, by prior arrangement, would sentence Grynszpan to death. "The murderer," Diewerge emphasized, "is in himself not interesting. The murderer is interesting only as a type of tool employed by World Jewry. World Jewry sits in the defendant's seat." The killing of Ernst vom Rath, Diewerge pointed out, should be seen as "a signal of World Jewry for the beginning of a war against National Socialist Germany. The French people were incited into a war by World Jewry against its own interests." Diewerge concluded: "The struggle of Germany against Jewry before the war both domestically and internationally was a struggle for peace. The extermination of Jewry is a precondition for the coming New Order in Europe."[82]

Nazi plans for the mass deportation and murder of European Jews were, in fact, gradually shifting into high gear as the trial preparations went forward. As the German state prosecutor issued his indictment against Grynszpan on October 16, 1941, German mobile commando units had already been murdering Jews in the Soviet Union for several months. The first of hundreds of transports carrying Jews from the German Reich "to the east" had actually departed from Vienna on October 15, just a day before the indictment.[83] At the Wannsee Conference of January 20, 1942, German officials outlined an ambitious plan for the forced transfer of Jews from around Europe to Poland, where they would perish from the hardships of slave labor or be executed. Construction of the camps in Poland where Jews would be murdered commenced shortly thereafter, while Nazi officials spread out across German-occupied Europe to organize the roundup and deportation of Jews for delivery to the killing centers.

Against this background, the trial planners clearly understood their project as a method for legitimizing the "Final Solution." In a "Führer Information" memorandum prepared for Hitler in March 1942, the Justice Ministry explained that a primary goal of the Grynszpan trial would be to "neutralize foreign sympathy actions for the Jews."[84] Joseph Goebbels, for his part, knew exactly what was happening to the Jews in "the east" at precisely that moment, and it was no coincidence that preparations for the Grynszpan trial in March 1942 coincided with a broader antisemitic propaganda offensive inside Germany, the central theme of which was Jewish responsibility for the war.[85] Goebbels, who oversaw this propaganda campaign, was, it should be emphasized, one of Hitler's chief sources for information about preparations for the trial.[86] The trial "will be very interesting," the Führer mentioned to some members of his entourage in late March 1942.[87] There can be little doubt, then, that at the very highest levels of the Nazi regime, the planning for the Grynszpan trial was understood in connection with the unfolding mass murder of the Jews.

By April 1942, Diewerge and his colleagues had produced a day-by-day outline for a week-long show trial.[88] Day One would be devoted to presenting the facts of the shooting in Paris on November 7, 1938. During Day Two, which was to focus on the motives of the defendant,

Friedrich Grimm would provide expert testimony about how Jewish conspirators in Paris had manipulated Grynszpan to commit the murder. Days Three through Five would constitute the heart of the trial. Here, the prosecution would establish "the Political Background of the Crime." The prosecution planned to deploy German academics as expert witnesses, invoking the intellectual authority deriving from their university affiliations, professorial titles, and publications. One of these would be Professor Gerhard Kittel from the University of Tübingen. Kittel was a distinguished scholar of the New Testament who, after 1933, had emerged as one of Germany's leading antisemitic academic intellectuals. Kittel's task would be to explain to the court how Jewish law, as interpreted specifically in the Talmud, granted Jews permission to murder Gentiles.[89] Grynszpan's shooting of vom Rath could thus be presented to the court, and to the world, as a religiously sanctioned murder.

During this segment of the trial, the prosecution would also focus on the role of the United States in the anti-German alliance. It would demonstrate that the Jewish warmongers who had arranged for Grynszpan to murder vom Rath had also been in league with Franklin Roosevelt. The American president's supposed connivance with international Jewry had for some time already been a major theme in Nazi propaganda. In September 1941—before the entry of the United States into the war—Diewerge himself had published a pamphlet about Roosevelt's relationship to the Jewish-dominated "world plutocracy."[90] The prosecution planned to buttress its case by calling Professor Friedrich Schönemann of the University of Berlin as an expert witness. Recognized as "the father of American Studies in Germany," Schönemann had previously held visiting positions at Harvard and at the University of Nebraska.[91] Although he could not be counted among the hard-core academic antisemites in the Third Reich, his lectures and publications often noted the influence of Jews over American culture and politics. He had argued, for example, that Jews had allied with African-Americans to undermine the legitimacy of "racial theory," and that propaganda organized and financed by American Jews had been instrumental in turning public opinion in the United States against Nazi Germany.[92] Schönemann's assignment at the Grynszpan trial would be to describe the overweening influence of Jews over American foreign policy, thus providing a connection between Grynszpan's actions, the warmongering of "World Jewry," and American hostility to Nazism.

On Day Six of the trial, the prosecution would summarize its case. The trial would conclude on Day Seven, when the court would hand down its ruling and its death sentence against Grynszpan. There would be no appeal, and the sentence would be executed expeditiously.

One obstacle to moving forward with the trial emerged from the complicated nature of the relationship between Germany and the Vichy government in France. Vichy France was, technically, an independent state, and officials in the Vichy Interior and Justice Ministries had let it be known that they would consider a trial of Grynszpan on German soil to be a violation of French sovereignty.[93] It was not until early 1942 that these objections could be overcome, in part through the diplomatic efforts of Friedrich Grimm. The Vichy government, in the words of a German diplomat, would now welcome the trial as an opportunity to focus attention on "international Jewry as the real enemy and originator of the war."[94] The Vichy government also decided to permit Georges Bonnet, who had been the French foreign minister in November 1938, to appear at the trial as a star witness for the prosecution. Before the war, Bonnet had been a leading advocate within the French government for a soft line vis-à-vis Germany.[95] Bonnet had now agreed, albeit reluctantly, to testify to the effect that his diplomatic efforts had been torpedoed by Jewish interests inside France and elsewhere.[96] In Diewerge's plan for the trial, the subject of Bonnet's testimony would be the "influence of Jewry on the French government toward preventing a rapprochement with Germany."[97]

In addition to all the potential external obstacles, Herschel Grynszpan threw a wrench into the works himself. In the autumn of 1941 he told his Gestapo interrogator that the shooting in Paris had actually been related to a homosexual liaison that he had had with Ernst vom Rath.[98] In the immediate aftermath of the shooting in 1938, rumors about vom Rath's alleged homosexuality had circulated in Paris, but both Grynszpan and his lawyers had insisted to the French investigators that Grynszpan had not known his victim previously. Most historians who have written about Grynszpan have tended to regard the homosexuality story as a clever defense tactic concocted either by Grynszpan or by his lawyer. One respected scholar, the German diplomatic historian Hans-Jürgen Döscher, however, has dissented from this consensus. Döscher has contended that Grynszpan and vom Rath had indeed been involved in some kind of sexual relationship in 1938. Döscher bases his argument on Ernst vom Rath's medical records and on documents suggesting that officials in the German Foreign Office tried to impede planning for the Grynszpan trial and bury evidence. Döscher also argues that the German Embassy in Paris had covered up the fact that Grynszpan and vom Rath had known each other before November 7, 1938. The embassy, Döscher claims, simply fabricated the now oft-repeated story that Grynszpan had arrived at the embassy demanding to see the ambassador, but was then escorted to the office of the low-ranking Ernst vom Rath, who just happened to be available.[99]

There is a compelling irony in Döscher's version of events. After the shooting in November 1938, Döscher maintains, both Grynszpan and the German government deliberately imposed a political spin on a crime that they knew had really been motivated by personal factors. According to this interpretation, it lay in the interests of both sides to elevate the killer into something much larger than he had actually been. Grynszpan's initial decision to portray himself as a champion of the Jewish people, Döscher claims, was reciprocated by the German government's decision to cast him as an agent of "World Jewry." Only later did Grynszpan recognize that he could undermine the propaganda aims of his coming show trial by actually telling the truth about his relationship with vom Rath. We will probably never know for certain what, if anything, actually happened between Grynszpan and vom Rath in Paris before November 7, 1938.

In Berlin, the officials in charge of planning the trial were caught very much off guard by Grynszpan's new story.[100] They firmly believed that Grynszpan was lying. Joseph Goebbels wrote in his diary: "Grynszpan has invented the obnoxious argument that he had had a homosexual relationship with the murdered Legation Counselor Ernst vom Rath. This is, naturally, a shameless lie." Even though Goebbels dismissed the new story as a fabrication, he recognized immediately that it could undermine the desired propagandistic effect of the coming trial.[101] The propaganda minister wanted the trial to focus on Jewish warmongering and not on a possible sordid homosexual relationship between a Jewish teenager and a fallen German diplomat and Nazi Party member. In January 1942 Hitler, after considering opinions from the Propaganda and Justice Ministries, decided that the problem did not justify halting preparations for the trial.[102]

At the Propaganda Ministry, Diewerge remained confident that the homosexuality issue would not pose a major problem. If Grynszpan were to raise the subject in his testimony, he argued, it would be plain for all to see that this was a "dirty Jewish maneuver," a "typical characteristic of Jewish squalidness."[103] The Ministry of Justice reacted to Grynszpan's new claim by adding a sodomy charge to its indictment of him, a tactic which Goebbels rejected as stupid and almost certain to backfire with respect to the propagandistic goals of the proceedings.[104] Goebbels, for his part, continued to dismiss any possibility that Grynszpan's claim could be true: "One can here once again recognize with what infamous perfidy the Jews operate."[105] But the minister continued to worry about what this new development might mean for the trial. The antisemitic narrative of the trial, he believed, would become completely obscured by scandalous rumors of vom Rath's homosexuality, regardless of how carefully the proceedings could be choreographed and stage-managed.[106]

As doubts about the project mounted, the planners made one last attempt to save the trial. In a proposal the Ministry of Justice delivered to Hitler on April 17, 1942, they suggested that the presiding judge at the trial could cut Grynszpan off as soon as the defendant referred to the homosexuality issue. The judge would announce that such a "typical Jewish insult to a victim of murder" would not be allowed in the courtroom. Moreover, they suggested, the French investigators who had originally interrogated Grynszpan would be held at the court and, if necessary, be produced to confirm that Grynszpan had never mentioned a relationship with vom Rath during the many months that he had been in French custody.[107]

Hitler's specific response to this proposal has disappeared from the historical record, but it was most likely not enthusiastic. Plans for the trial were placed on hold shortly thereafter. At the time, both Diewerge and Grimm were given to understand that Hitler had made the decision himself.[108] By the middle of May 1942, Goebbels had also turned definitively against the project. The propaganda minister could never overcome his fears that the homosexuality issue would overshadow the intended message of the trial. And there were other problems as well. Germany's relations with Vichy France had recently entered a sensitive phase. The first transport of Jews from France to Auschwitz had departed on March 27, and preparations were in full swing for many more.[109] On April 26, Pierre Laval had returned to the French cabinet, with responsibility for the Interior, Foreign Affairs, and Information. In addition to the mounting German pressure for the handover of French Jews, Laval also faced German demands for increased French support for the war against the Soviet Union.[110] Further complicating matters were several successful attacks by French partisans against radio broadcasting facilities, to which the Germans were responding with severe "expiation measures." This convergence of developments may well have been why Joachim von Ribbentrop, the German foreign minister, now informed Goebbels that an appearance at a Grynszpan trial by former French Foreign Minister Georges Bonnet no longer "lay in the interests of German foreign policy." Goebbels evidently agreed that the time was no longer auspicious for a heavy-handed propaganda extravaganza involving France.[111]

Although the trial had, theoretically, only been postponed until late 1942, the project was now effectively tabled forever. The final reference to the subject extant in the documentary record is a "Führer Information" memorandum that the Ministry of Justice prepared for Hitler at the beginning of July 1942. According to the ministry, Grynszpan had retracted his claim of having had a sexual relationship with vom Rath. He continued to maintain, however, that he possessed knowledge of homosexual relationships that vom Rath had had with others. The Ministry of Justice added the observation that vom Rath's brother had recently been convicted of sodomy by a military field court.[112] The insinuation inherent in this last point must have been obvious to Hitler.

Postwar testimony from survivors of Sachsenhausen points to the probability that Herschel Grynszpan was executed in the summer of 1942, shortly after his life had been rendered dispensable by the decision to abandon the show trial.[113] After the war, a rumor circulated that he had survived and was living in Paris under a false identity. Most historians have rejected this story as unfounded.[114] Grynszpan's father, however, did survive the war, and in 1960 he secured a death certificate for his son from a West German court in Hannover. The date assigned by the court to Herschel Grynszpan's death was May 8, 1945, the day of the German surrender.[115]

At no stage during the preparations of the show trial did anybody involved in the planning question the proposition that Grynszpan had acted as part of a larger Jewish conspiracy, and at no stage did anyone question whether such a story would seem credible to the German people. The decision to abandon the project was based, as we have seen, on an altogether different set of considerations. The narrative that was to be propagated at the trial corresponded perfectly to the broader effort undertaken by Nazi propagandists to pin the guilt for the war on the Jews. Joseph Goebbels, Wolfgang Diewerge, and Friedrich Grimm, among others, were deluded by antisemitism to the point where they could sincerely attribute the act of a volatile teenager to the supposed warmongering conspiracies of "World Jewry" or "International Jewry." Hitler, for his part, went to his death in April 1945 convinced that—in the words of his Political Testament—"the truly guilty party of this murderous struggle is Jewry."[116]

7

"Defendants and Witnesses Openly Hold Back with the Truth"

In 1945 the Third Reich lay in ruins, the full extent of its atrocities clear for all to see. The Germans now began the long and difficult process of coming to terms with the catastrophe. National Socialism had already been discredited in the eyes of many Germans, either by virtue of its crimes or because of the physical destruction the Nazi regime had wrought within Germany itself. This repudiation was by no means universal, however, and it was with good reason that the victorious Allies perceived a need to subject German society to a systematic program of "denazification" and political reeducation. Bringing the perpetrators of Nazi crimes to justice would be a central component of this effort. From the perspective of 1945, after many millions of Jews and others had been murdered, the Kristallnacht no longer seemed like a transgression of great magnitude. Nonetheless, the events of November 1938 featured prominently in the postwar adjudication of Nazi crimes. The manner in which the courts dealt with the pogrom, mainly between 1945 and 1949, influenced the way the Kristallnacht would be remembered—and, in certain respects, forgotten—in postwar Germany.

Initially, Allied and German courts shared the responsibility for adjudicating Nazi crimes.[1] Trials were regulated by the provisions of Allied Control Council Law No. 10, which stipulated that though the occupying powers remained in charge of prosecutions in principle, they could delegate to German courts cases involving crimes committed by Germans against German nationals. As a general rule, German courts assumed responsibility for prosecuting Nazi crimes that had been committed inside Germany before the outbreak of war in 1939. These included cases arising from the Kristallnacht. The perpetrators of the pogrom had regarded their Jewish victims as foreign parasites, and not as a legitimate constitutive element of the German people. But it was the nationality of the pogrom's victims, and not the alien identity ascribed to them by Nazi ideology and propaganda, that determined which courts would have jurisdiction. So German prosecutors and judges were entrusted with the administration of justice to the perpetrators of the pogrom. The German courts did, however, operate under the watchful eye of Allied occupation authorities.

The first arrests of Germans suspected of having participated in the Kristallnacht took place in the summer of 1945.[2] By the end of the year, prosecutors in the American and British zones had opened many investigations, and this pattern continued during much of 1946.[3] From late 1946 to early 1947, Kristallnacht-related prosecutions accounted for a significant proportion of the cases heard before German courts in the American zone. All told, more than 7,000 Germans were indicted for Kristallnacht-related crimes in about 1,200 separate trials before West German courts in the decades after 1945.[4] These figures do not apply to the Soviet zone, East Germany, or Austria. Despite the aggressiveness with which Soviet and East German authorities moved against certain categories of Nazi criminals, the number of cases arising from the Kristallnacht in the Communist area was insignificant compared with that in the west.[5] In contrast, several hundred people were prosecuted for Kristallnacht-related cases in postwar Austria, the vast majority in Vienna, where the pogrom had been especially widespread and violent.[6]

Usually prosecutors targeted multiple defendants who had participated in the pogrom in the same town or neighborhood. Most of the trials had fewer than ten defendants, but several had many. The largest trial was launched in 1946 against thirty-four men accused of involvement in the pogrom in Hamburg. In some communities, prosecutors investigated multiple suspects but proceeded to trial with only a few defendants owing to inadequate evidence.[7]

The Kristallnacht had paled in comparison with the genocide and other atrocities committed by the Nazi regime between 1939 and 1945. It was, nevertheless, the most significant antisemitic measure adjudicated by German—as opposed to Allied—courts in the immediate postwar period. How well, or how poorly, the German justice system carried out this responsibility is a matter of perspective. The challenges were formidable. Perhaps chief among them was the sheer size of the event and the vast number of Germans who had participated in it. Although more Germans were prosecuted for their role in the pogrom than is often recognized, they represented only a fraction of the people who had been involved in the violence in one way or another. The defendants, moreover, did not constitute a representative sample of the Germans who had participated in the pogrom. In accordance with standard practice in German criminal justice, perpetrators who had been youths at the time of the pogrom were generally exempted from prosecution. Although many of the trials clearly established that young people had played a significant role in the violence, whether as members of Hitler Youth units or as students, they almost never counted among the accused. Prosecutors focused instead on the adults who had recruited and encouraged the young rioters.

Prosecutors often targeted the local Nazi officials who had acted as the ringleaders of the violence in their communities. In cases where it was impossible to pin specific major offenses, such as murder or battery, on these leaders, prosecutors pursued charges of "disturbing the peace." Rank-and-file SA men and other lower-level participants in the pogrom were subject to prosecution mainly in cases involving murder and battery. Prosecutors generally did not pursue charges against looters, thus excluding from postwar justice a significant number of "ordinary" Germans who had stolen from their Jewish neighbors in November 1938. In a few exceptional cases, however, looters were charged, almost as if to remind the German public that such behavior had been widespread during the pogrom.[8] That only a small percentage of the perpetrators of the pogrom were ever placed on trial reinforced the dominant, albeit erroneous, belief in postwar Germany that only a tiny segment of German society had actually been responsible for the Kristallnacht.

A shortage of judges proved another challenge for prosecutors. The German legal profession and judiciary had become Nazified between 1933 and 1945, making it difficult to identify prosecutors and judges who could be relied upon to carry out their responsibilities fairly and professionally.[9] Nor could trials for Nazi crimes appear to be a form of "victor's justice," as many Germans had perceived the Nuremberg trial and other Allied-led prosecutions. To establish the rule of law and create a judicial system that would enjoy popular legitimacy, courts had to avoid show trials with predetermined outcomes. This became especially important in the western zones of occupation once the impression became widespread that German tribunals in the Soviet zone were operating as kangaroo courts. The desire to bring the perpetrators of Nazi crimes to justice, therefore, had to be weighed against the need to erect a legal system worthy of a nascent democratic society, one in which defendants would be judged fairly, according to the weight of the evidence against them.

An additional challenge derived from the fact that neither German courts in the western occupation zones nor Austrian courts employed the legal innovations, including the indictment for "crimes against humanity," that the Allies had introduced at the Nuremberg trial. Instead, even when adjudicating crimes related to Nazi antisemitic and racial policy, these courts operated on the basis of existing German criminal law. During the Nazi years, murder, battery, disturbing the peace, and other familiar crimes had remained illegal, and many German jurists preferred to prosecute Nazi crimes on the basis of the existing criminal statutes rather than to depend on novel legal constructions like "crimes against humanity," which many German jurists (and not a few American ones) had denounced as unacceptable examples of ex post facto law. The situation was different in the Soviet zone, where courts followed procedures and legal definitions established by the Soviet military administration.

In the western zones and in Austria, then, the perpetrators of the Kristallnacht were tried using traditional German definitions of criminal behavior and long-standing practices for ordinary criminal prosecutions. The Kristallnacht, however, had not been an ordinary crime. It had been a quasi-official act, encouraged and sanctioned by the nation's political leadership. The majority of the perpetrators had believed that they were acting at the very least with the government's consent, when not in accordance with explicit orders from above.

Yet another challenge arose from the massive dislocations that prevailed in Germany immediately after the war. Many of the people who had been involved in the pogrom were no longer physically present in the same place they had been in November 1938. A large percentage of the Jewish victims had either been killed during the war or had emigrated from Europe. Tracking them down and deposing them for the trial was an expensive and time-consuming process. As a result, at many of the trials, the voice and the perspective of the Jewish victims were quite often entirely absent.

Many of the perpetrators had also been killed in the war, either in combat or in Allied bombing raids. Moreover, many of the former local Nazi Party officials who had been interned by the Allies for interrogation had played an especially important role in organizing the pogrom in their communities in 1938. Locating them and making them available to a local court could be a time-consuming and bureaucratically burdensome process. In addition, a sizable number of German men who had participated in the pogrom found themselves in Soviet captivity after the war. Many would not be repatriated to Germany for years. Finally, given that a substantial segment of prewar German territory had been ceded to Poland after the war, prosecutors found it next to impossible to investigate and try Kristallnacht-related crimes in cities like Breslau, which were now part of Poland.[10]

All these obstacles to justice were compounded by the prosecutors' dependence on oral testimony. Prosecutors were sometimes able to rely on the investigative files of the Gestapo from late 1938, when the suspects had actually confessed their crimes with the expectation that the party would protect them.[11] One trial in 1948 even featured a former Gestapo agent as a key witness for the prosecution.[12] The archives of the Nazi Party High Court also fell into American hands, enabling occupation officials in the U.S. zone to prompt German prosecutors to reopen cases against Nazis whose crimes the party had swept under the rug in 1938 and 1939.[13] In most Kristallnacht-related cases in the late 1940s, however, oral testimony was decisive. The crimes under investigation had occurred almost a decade earlier, and the intervening period had hardly been an uneventful one. Many of the cases would turn on the ability of victims or witnesses to testify convincingly about events that were no longer fresh in their memories. While they might have been able to describe the major contours of the pogrom as they experienced it, they could not always provide persuasive testimony about the specific actions of a particular defendant. Prosecutors and judges also discovered that defendants and witnesses were often very selective in what they could and could not remember. In the absence of documentary or other concrete forms of evidence, many defendants were confident that they could lie to the court with impunity, and witnesses often proved unwilling to testify against friends and neighbors.[14]

Courts strove to establish the motives of the defendants before them. This was especially true in cases related to the killing of Jews, as

German criminal law required proof of a "base motive" in order to obtain a conviction for murder. One such base motive was antisemitism. Obviously this meant that defendants faced with a murder indictment had a very good reason to deny any antisemitic motive. Nonetheless, in some cases prosecutors were able to demonstrate antisemitic motives on the basis of comments the defendants made at the time of the crime. This also held true for the trials of SS men and local party officials of long-standing, who had a clear record of anti-Jewish statements and actions before November 1938. In one case, a court in Aschaffenburg ruled that "racial hatred was especially pronounced" among SS men, and that their crimes during the pogrom had been motivated by "ideologically fueled bloodlust." In some trials involving defendants who had not been hardened members of the party, the SS, or the SA, courts recognized antisemitic motives but ruled that guilt was mitigated by exposure to Nazi propaganda and indoctrination. A court in Hanau noted the "intellectual poisoning and sickness of great magnitude" that had been created by Nazi rule. The court showed leniency to a convicted defendant because his decision to join the Nazi Party was born of desperation caused by unemployment.[15]

Many judges were frustrated by the lack of cooperation they perceived among defendants and witnesses. A judgment from Giessen in 1948 noted that it had been very difficult to reconstruct details of the crime because of "the reticence of the witnesses in view of the political character of the trial." Judges often criticized the selective memories of witnesses and defendants. In many cases, witnesses were able to recall vivid details of the violence even while claiming that they could not remember who had committed it. In one such case, tried before the court in Marburg, witnesses testified in great detail about the pogrom in the small town of Falkenburg but claimed not to remember whom they had recognized among the mob. The judge did not find this testimony to be credible, given the small size of the community, but there was nothing he could do. It was not uncommon for witnesses to finger defendants during pretrial investigations, only to recant once on the witness stand.

After such a recantation was made before a court in Giessen, the judge announced that "defendants and witnesses openly hold back with the truth." In some cases, the accused ringleaders got off scot-free because witnesses could not place them at the scene of the crime, even while their former subordinates, whose participation could be better documented, were convicted.[16]

Judges were also often exasperated by the tendency of many defendants to shift blame onto the shoulders of comrades who had died in the war, or who were unavailable for the trial because they found themselves in Soviet prison camps.[17] It was obvious that a huge discrepancy existed between the magnitude of the crime, which was amply documented, and the ability of the legal system to bring the guilty parties to justice.

When evidence against defendants was ironclad, they sometimes invoked the "superior orders" defense, portraying themselves as the hapless instruments of a coercive regime. In cases involving former members of the SA, prosecutors attempted to undermine this defense by calling attention to the SA's own regulations from the 1930s, according to which Storm Troopers were supposed to disobey orders that were clearly illegal.[18] When defendants then claimed that they had considered an order to have been legal precisely because it had been issued by the party, the courts were not sympathetic. As a judgment passed down by a court in Hanau stated, "the illegality of the order to unleash pogroms against Jews [was] objectively obvious."[19]

The "superior orders" defense proved more effective in the cases of policemen who had arrested Jews or who had failed to intervene against anti-Jewish violence. The courts were more ready to sympathize with the predicament of policemen than with those of SA men, given that hierarchy, discipline, and obedience to civil authority had been considered central tenets of professional conduct. Moreover, policemen, generally speaking, did not receive orders to harm Jews themselves, and, in carrying out orders to arrest Jews, they themselves were not responsible for the crimes committed by members of the SA and the SS once the

Jews were in custody. Some courts were even willing to accept the argument that the police believed that arrest would protect Jews from further violence.[20]

Courts showed a similar leniency to firemen who had obeyed orders to let synagogues burn in November 1938. Although it would have been within their rights to refuse such an order, it would be unjust to punish a civil servant for having lacked the personal and civic courage to do so in the oppressive environment of Nazi Germany. In the opinion of one court, most firemen were "simplethinking people" from whom such an act of disobedience would have been too much to expect.[21]

Precise statistics on rates of conviction and severity of sentences have yet to be compiled for the hundreds of Kristallnacht trials conducted in the occupation zones of Germany. Several of the trials certainly did yield convictions for major crimes and correspondingly serious punishments. As early as September 1945 a German court in Mosbach sentenced Alfred G. to five years in prison for his role in the destruction of the synagogue and Jewish property in the town of Strümpfelbrunn. In 1946 a court in Bamberg convicted four men for their role in the destruction of the local synagogue, imposing prison sentences ranging from five to seven years. Several cases ended with notable sentences in 1948. These included a murder case in Bremen, in which two men were sentenced to ten and fifteen years in prison, respectively. Another case of murder, in Aschaffenburg, led to the conviction and fifteen-year prison sentence for Heinrich T. Two men were sentenced to five- and six-year sentences, respectively, for their role in the destruction of the synagogue in Bremerhaven. In a case tried in Dortmund, two men were sentenced to twelve years each in prison for their role in destroying the synagogue in Lünen, as well as violence committed against Jews in that town. In 1949, Friedrich P. was sentenced to ten years in prison by a court in Frankenthal for his role in destroying the synagogue in Neustadt and in setting ablaze an old-age home, which resulted in several deaths. In 1950, a court in Düsseldorf sentenced Josef

B. to life in prison for his role in killing a Jew in the town of Hilden. As late as 1953, a court in Munich sentenced Guido I. to six years in prison for his role in the killing of a Jew in Chemnitz on November 10, 1938.[22]

Even though some of these sentences were later reduced, these examples suggest that German prosecutors and courts did succeed in bringing some perpetrators of the Kristallnacht to justice. It was also true, however, that in many cases trials ended in acquittals or with defendants' receiving lenient sentences after being convicted. This stemmed in part from the common judicial practice of taking the biographical details of a convicted defendant into consideration during sentencing. Courts tended to show mercy to convicted defendants who had fought in either or both of the two world wars, or who were experiencing problems stemming from poor health or advanced age at the time of their conviction. A court in Bremen, for example, convicted a defendant of killing a Jew but reduced his sentence from fifteen to ten years on account of both his courageous service in the First World War and his age: at sixty-five, the court ruled, the defendant was "approaching the end of his life."[23]

As the prosecutions unfolded, attorneys in the legal division of the United States Military Government were initially troubled by the rate of acquittals and the leniency of many of the sentences, though by mid-1947 they had become satisfied that the German courts were conducting the trials properly.[24] Complaints about lax justice were often registered by representatives of the small Jewish community that was present in Germany after the war. To them it seemed obvious that the great majority of Germans had not owned up to their responsibility for the catastrophe of November 1938.[25]

In contrast to the situation in Germany, reliable statistics have been compiled for the results of the postwar Kristallnacht trials conducted in Austria. The court in Vienna convicted 200 out of 304 defendants charged with crimes related to the pogrom. The average prison sentence was about 17 months. The court in Innsbruck convicted 33 out of 34 defendants, while the court in Linz convicted 2 defendants out of 18, and the court in Graz convicted 10 out of 14. Although the conviction rate in Austria (excepting Linz) was relatively high, the number of defendants who were actually charged was low when one considers the magnitude and viciousness of the pogrom in Vienna.[26]

From the very beginning, Germans had been ambivalent, at best, toward Allied efforts at reeducation, denazification, and prosecutions for Nazi crimes. In the western occupation zones, opinion gradually shifted decisively against these programs. Once the Federal Republic had achieved independence in 1949, all the political parties supported granting a blanket amnesty for a wide array of Nazi crimes that they did not consider major. Such a measure would help integrate a large number of petty Nazi criminals and fellow travelers into the new, democratic (West) Germany, underscoring the end of the occupation and the return of German self-determination. It would also reinforce the break with the Nazi period and the Second World War. Germany would be able to look to the future rather than dwell on the past.[27]

The result of this sentiment was the "Law for Granting Exemption from Punishment," which took effect on December 31, 1949. This amnesty law stipulated that sentences of less than six months in prison as the result of conviction for a Nazi crime would not be executed. The effect of this measure was to discourage prosecutors from pursuing cases against relatively minor offenders. During the internal German debate over the wisdom of the law, one of its leading opponents was the Bavarian minister of justice, Josef Müller, who had been a member of the anti-Nazi resistance before 1945. Müller, who was known among his admirers as "Joe the Ox Man" (*Ochsensepp*), argued that the amnesty would let many "pronounced criminals" off the hook. He pointed specifically to criminals "either already sentenced or facing sentencing for grave acts of Nazi violence, particularly for serious breaches of public peace and similar offenses resulting from the anti-Jewish measures of 1938." Müller regarded the amnesty as "legally and politically untenable." This position proved highly unpopular in Müller's own party, the conservative Christian Social Union, and contributed to his dismissal as party chairman in 1949.[28] In the environment of the time, it was Müller's objection, and not the amnesty, that proved politically untenable.

The 1949 amnesty, which was approved by the western occupying powers, did not put an end to all Kristallnacht prosecutions. But it did, as Müller had predicted, introduce a major obstacle in many cases. German prosecutors had depended heavily on indictments for disturbing the peace when evidence was lacking for more serious charges, and convictions for disturbing the peace rarely brought with them prison sentences of more than six months. It no longer made sense to pursue cases against Germans whose roles in the pogrom had amounted merely to damaging property, looting, or verbally encouraging vandalism. Although the vast majority of Germans who had participated in the Kristallnacht would probably never have been identified and prosecuted, the effect of the amnesty was to let them off the hook legally as well.

As was the case with denazification more generally, the pursuit of justice for the crimes of Kristallnacht was ultimately subordinated to the desire to integrate former Nazis into the new postwar order. The justice that had been achieved was real, but it was also selective, uneven, and gravely incomplete. This record should not, however, hide from view an indispensable service performed by the Kristallnacht trials in another respect. Despite all their problems, the trials generated an immense body of testimony and other documentation allowing for a detailed historical reconstruction of the events of November 1938 at the local level. Many of the judgments relating to the pogrom in smaller communities emphasized the widespread participation of the local population in the violence, even if the individual culprits could not be definitively identified and brought to justice. This reality was emphasized in several judgments issued by the court in Giessen. In a ruling on a case concerning the pogrom in Wölfersheim, the court observed that SA men had invaded and vandalized Jewish homes "in the presence of a large portion" of the town's population. The Storm Troopers committed the bulk of the vandalism, but participation in the subsequent looting was far more democratic.[29] The same court, in a judgment relating to the pogrom in Gedern, also underscored the widespread nature of the participation of the townspeople as enthusiastic spectators in a "theater" of violence. The SA had received "welcome support" from large numbers of civilians. The court concluded that in Reichenberg the crowd's support for the SA and Hitler Youth during the pogrom had clearly reflected an "internal" sympathy for the rioters. In the case of sixteen residents of Bad Nauheim who had been accused of looting, the court emphasized the point that looting should be considered an essential element of the pogrom and not merely a trivial element of the aftermath.[30] This was a damning verdict, but its essential message has never really been thoroughly absorbed in German society.

The Kristallnacht has, in the meantime, become an important element in the German culture of ritualized commemoration. But German collective memory of the event has tended to be selective, uneven, and incomplete, very much like the administration of justice to the perpetrators of the pogrom. Some early historical research had suggested the existence of widespread participation by ordinary Germans in the pogrom.[31] But the narrative of the pogrom that took hold in German society during the postwar period was a sanitized one. Spontaneous anti-Jewish violence and mass participation in the brutality were forgotten in favor of a self-exculpatory narrative in which responsibility for the pogrom was attributed to Hitler, Goebbels, and the SA. Psychologically comforting and politically convenient in both halves of divided Germany during the Cold War, this narrative has persisted in Germany since unification. It has helped to underscore a sense of discontinuity from the predecessor criminal regime, and to project responsibility for the pogrom onto "Nazis" who are no longer present in German society.

In the western occupation zones of Germany, commemoration of the Kristallnacht began soon after the war.[32] It took various forms, including solemn ceremonies, speeches, and marches. Initially these commemorative activities were carried out mainly by Jewish groups and by organizations of Nazi victims. They were also organized primarily as local events. Over time, ever more German communities and institutions, such as churches and labor unions, initiated their own commemorations of the pogrom. These events tended to attract the most attention on round-numbered anniversaries of the Kristallnacht. A watershed year was 1978, on the fortieth anniversary of the pogrom, when, for the first time, a large number of high-profile ceremonies took place all over the Federal Republic. Much attention was also given to the annual commemoration in years when widely publicized antisemitic incidents occurred in Germany.

The commemorations often took the form of powerful, emotion-laden ceremonies that lacked concrete historical content. They fulfilled the ritualistic purpose of signaling recognition of the suffering inflicted on Germany's Jews during and after the pogrom, but they evoked the actual events of November 1938 only in the most general way. The dominant representation of the pogrom was vague and nonthreatening to the mass of ordinary Germans. It underscored the role of the Nazi regime in the planning and execution of the pogrom, while pointing to the negative reactions of the German people. This view of the pogrom reflected a more general tendency in postwar Germany to magnify the distinction between "the Nazis" and German society. Although dominant for much of the postwar period, this interpretation of the Kristallnacht, it should be emphasized, was not universal. The contrary view—that the German people had participated in the crimes of the Kristallnacht in large numbers—was rare but nonetheless present. As one German observer put it in 1959, during the pogrom "hundreds of thousands danced through the streets in a wild frenzy, while millions watched the horrible drama unfold approvingly."[33] This kind of remembrance, however, was repressed in the service of a new and forward-looking political order.

The high-point of Kristallnacht commemoration in West Germany occurred in 1988, in connection with the fiftieth anniversary of the pogrom. The occasion was marked by ceremonies all over the country. The main event was a ceremony held in the Bundestag in Bonn on November 10. During the event Philipp Jenninger, a member of the Christian Democratic Party and the president of the Bundestag, delivered what would become one of the most controversial speeches in postwar German history. Several dozen members of the parliament protested Jenninger's remarks by walking out in the middle of his talk. Within hours of the speech, Jenninger resigned from his position. The West German commemoration of the fiftieth anniversary of the Kristallnacht, it seemed, had been sullied by a scandal.

What had Jenninger done wrong? For one thing, he had insisted on delivering the commemorative speech himself, rather than inviting Heinz Galinski, the chairman of the Central Council of Jews in Germany, to speak. Many members of the Bundestag, especially those in the Green Party, claimed to be outraged by this slight against the representative of Germany's Jews. In addition, Jenninger's critics at the time claimed that the delivery of the speech had been clumsy to the point of insensitive. Some sections of the speech had been intended to describe antisemitic sentiments and stereotypes that had been common during the Nazi era. According to his critics, Jenninger had not been careful enough to distance himself from the sentiments that he was describing. There is, however, good reason to suspect that at least some of this criticism was disingenuous and politically motivated.[34]

The actual content of Jenninger's speech, as opposed to the mode of its delivery, contained one of the bluntest and most nationally self-critical descriptions of Nazi anti-Jewish policy articulated by a major German politician up to that time.[35] Instead of the vagaries characteristic of most commemorative speeches, Jenninger's conveyed a substantive and detailed account of how the Nazi regime had implemented its antisemitic program in the face of little domestic opposition in a society that had a long and deeply rooted tradition of antisemitism. When it came to the Kristallnacht, however, even Jenninger's otherwise courageous speech conformed to a familiar pattern. After claiming, accurately enough, that the Nazi regime had been the instigator and chief organizer of the pogrom, Jenninger lapsed into a well-established narrative when describing the reaction of the German population. The German people, he claimed, had remained by and large "passive" during the pogrom. "Only a few," he continued, had joined in the violence carried out by the "organized mob" of SA and SS. It would be unfair to characterize Jenninger's speech as entirely exculpatory of German society, as he did emphatically condemn the "silence" of the churches and of most onlookers. But with regard to the question of popular participation in the pogrom, Jenninger's speech was hardly controversial. To the contrary, it may be taken as evidence that a tradition of denial persisted after half a century.

In East Germany, little attention was given to the memory of the Kristallnacht for the first three decades after the war.[36] This pattern was not fundamentally dissimilar from that in the west, but the reasons for it were different. The Communist regime did not ignore the pogrom but preferred to emphasize other aspects of Nazi terror, such as the oppression of the working class and the persecution of Communists. East German memory of the Kristallnacht, as of the Nazi persecution of the Jews more generally, was shaped by Marxist theory, which characterized Nazism as the German form of Fascism. This understanding of history left little room for a serious consideration of Nazi racism, giving priority instead to a view of Fascism as an instrument of the capitalist elite in the struggle against the working classes.

In the absence of official support or even attention, the small Jewish community in East Germany commemorated the pogrom quietly. The autocratic nature of the East German system generally did not allow for independent Kristallnacht commemorations of the sort that occurred with gradually increasing frequency in the west. The one significant exception to this was the commemoration by the Protestant Church, which managed to exercise a certain degree of autonomy from the Communist state. When in 1978 the East German regime for the first time sponsored a major Kristallnacht commemoration, it was motivated at least in part by the desire to keep up with the church. Increased official recognition of Nazi atrocities committed specifically against Jews was part of a strategy to enhance the legitimacy (and economic position) of East Germany in Western Europe and the United States. In 1988, on the fiftieth anniversary, the East German regime sponsored several high-profile events, not least in order to compete with West Germany for the mantle of the most antifascist of the two post-1945 German states. One year later, East German authorities announced that their citizens could travel freely to the west. It was entirely coincidental that this announcement came on the fifty-first anniversary of the Kristallnacht. But the dramatic opening of the Berlin Wall introduced a new and serious complication into the place of November 9 on the calendar of historical commemoration in Germany.

With regard to their historical content, the official East German Kristallnacht commemorations tended to be vague and formulaic. Agency for the pogrom was simply attributed to "Hitler-Fascism," the vestiges of which, it was claimed, had been thoroughly expunged from East Germany. Speakers avoided genuinely critical confrontation with the real history of the pogrom, restricting themselves to platitudes about "warnings for the future." Not infrequently commemorations were instrumentalized for the purpose of supporting official positions in conflicts related to the Cold War. At a commemoration in Dresden in 1978, Gerhard Schill, the mayor of that city, connected the need to honor the memory of the Jews killed in the pogrom to the necessity of condemning American research on a neutron bomb.[37] The readiness of the East German regime to exploit the memory of the Kristallnacht in this way, it should be emphasized, does not necessarily mean that East Germans who participated in the commemoration were not sincere in their "antifascism" or in their desire to recognize Jewish suffering under the Nazis.[38]

Since 1989, commemorations of the Kristallnacht have become, in the words of one expert observer, a "crucial component in the reconstruction of German national identity." They are a form of "negative celebration" that underscores a national commitment to oppose not only antisemitism but racism and xenophobia more generally.[39] At the same time, Germany has seen a dramatic efflorescence in scholarship about Nazism and the Holocaust. This has been made possible by the emergence of a younger generation of scholars determined to revisit established orthodoxies about the darkest chapter of the German past. The social and cultural climate in which they have operated has been conducive to their work. Having overcome the division of the country with the conclusion of the Cold War, many Germans sensed a need to address the other major obstacle to the normalization of their society: the failure to have confronted the Nazi past adequately.

One consequence of the explosion of such scholarship has been the emergence of a more candid and emphatically critical assessment of the role of ordinary Germans in the Kristallnacht. This reexamination has profited immensely from work produced by practitioners of local and regional history, whose sharply focused research has reconstructed events on the ground during the pogrom in unprecedented detail.[40] They and other German historians have challenged the dominant narrative of a pogrom that was perpetrated by a small segment of the population in the face of popular passivity and disapproval. They have, instead, portrayed the Kristallnacht as a combination of centrally directed violence and the cathartic release of antisemitic passions that were widespread—though by no means universal—in German society.[41] It takes time for the conclusions of scholarship to inform popular perceptions of the past, but one can be hopeful that the uncomfortable truth about the Kristallnacht will be absorbed into the vibrant, confident, and self-critical democratic culture of contemporary Germany.

Note on Sources

This fresh look at a familiar event is based in large part on primary sources that have recently been made more easily accessible than they had previously been. These include the records from post-1945 trials of Kristallnacht perpetrators. It is not commonly known that thousands of Germans who were involved in the Kristallnacht were prosecuted in German courts after 1945. These trials produced a rich and valuable body of material for historians. In the past these records had been distributed in local archives around Germany, with access complicated by privacy restrictions. Happily, the Institute for Contemporary History in Munich, in tandem with Yad Vashem in Jerusalem, has undertaken an ambitious project to make this documentation more easily available to historians.[1]

Another important source for this study has been the collection of several hundred Jewish testimonies deposited in the Wiener Library in London. These were given by German Jews in late 1938 or early 1939, when the memories of the pogrom were still very fresh. Their chief advantage to the historian is their unedited and unprocessed quality. They originated as an effort to chronicle the event rather than to interpret it historically or philosophically. They do not reflect narratives that may have been imposed on the event by historians or memoirists in later years. These testimonies have been available to researchers for decades, but few historians have made extensive use of them.[2]

Historians wishing to examine German popular responses and attitudes toward the Nazi regime's Jewish policies have traditionally depended on a very limited universe of documents. The two most important collections have been, first, the so-called Reports from the Reich, which were compiled by the Nazi Security Service; and second, the reports compiled by the Social Democratic Party of Germany, which had been officially banned in 1933 but continued to function clandestinely.[3] Historians have supplemented information from these collections with observations culled from the memoirs and diaries of Germans—both Jewish and non-Jewish—and from reports prepared by foreign diplomats stationed in Germany. An important new body of source material has been made available to historians desiring to explore this question. A German-Israeli–sponsored team of scholars has combed through the archives of Germany—including many smaller archives at the local level—in search of any documents that might have some bearing on German attitudes toward Nazi Jewish policy. This ambitious project resulted in a CD-ROM containing almost 4,000 documents, many of which had been previously unknown to historians. A good number of these relate directly to the Kristallnacht.[4]

Sharply focused local studies constitute a final category of source materials that have facilitated a new interpretation of the pogrom. As Germans have abandoned earlier self-imposed constraints on intensive research into the Nazi past, they have produced a formidable literature about the course of the Kristallnacht in individual communities. This phenomenon began with the commemoration of the fiftieth anniversary of the pogrom in 1988. Although these local studies, by their very nature, tend to have a narrow geographic focus, they contain a wealth of information that would otherwise be attainable only through visits to dozens of archives.[5]

Notes

Introduction

1. For a discussion of the controversies surrounding the term, see Harald Schmid, *Erinnern an den "Tag der Schuld": Der Novemberpogrom von 1938 in der deutschen Geschichtspolitik* (Hamburg: Ergebnisse, 2001), pp. 81–84. A useful collection of statements about the controversy is contained in Heinz Lauber, *Judenpogrom: "Reichskristallnacht" November 1938 in Großdeutschland* (Gerlingen: Bleicher, 1981), pp. 41–46.

2. It was long a matter of consensus that the Russian government had played an active role in initiating the pogroms. This view has been challenged by scholarship that began to appear in the early 1990s. Few historians doubt, however, that the Russian authorities at the very least condoned antisemitic violence when it suited their needs. See, e.g., John D. Klier and Shlomo Lambroza, eds., *Pogroms: Anti-Jewish Violence in Modern Russian History* (Cambridge: Cambridge University Press, 1992).

3. Hitler to Gemlich, 16 December 1919, in Eberhard Jäckel, ed., *Hitler: Sämtliche Aufzeichnungen, 1905–1924* (Stuttgart: Deutsche Verlags-Anstalt, 1980), pp. 88–90.

4. Raul Hilberg, *The Destruction of the European Jews,* third edition (New Haven: Yale University Press, 2003), vol. I, p. 50.

5. Notable studies include Hans-Jürgen Döscher, *"Reichskristallnacht": Die Novemberpogrome 1938* (Munich: Propyläen, 2000); Martin Gilbert, *Kristallnacht: Prelude to Destruction* (New York: HarperCollins, 2006); Hermann Graml, *Reichskristallnacht: Antisemitismus und Judenverfolgung im Dritten Reich* (Munich: DTV, 1998); Lionel Kochan, *Pogrom, 10 November 1938* (London: Deutsch, 1957); Wolf-Arno Kropat, *"Reichskristallnacht": Der Judenpogrom vom 7. bis 10. November 1938—Urheber, Täter, Hintergründe* (Wiesbaden: Kommission für die Geschichte der Juden in Hessen, 1997); Dieter Obst, *"Reichskristallnacht": Ursachen und Verlauf des antisemitischen Pogroms vom November 1938* (Frankfurt: Lang, 1991); and Anthony Read and David Fisher, *Kristallnacht: The Nazi Night of Terror* (New York: Random House, 1989).

6. Among the best short treatments of the Kristallnacht in works on anti-Jewish policy are Wolfgang Benz, "Der Novemberpogrom 1938," in Wolfgang Benz, ed., *Die Juden in Deutschland 1933–1945: Leben unter nationalsozialistischer Herrschaft* (Munich: Beck, 1988), pp. 499–544; Saul Friedländer, *Nazi Germany and the Jews,* vol. 1: *The Years of Persecution, 1933–1939* (New York: HarperCollins, 1997), pp. 269–293; Peter Longerich, *Politik der Vernichtung: Eine Gesamtdarstellung der nationalsozialistischen Judenverfolgung* (Munich: Piper, 1998), pp. 198–207; and Michael Wildt, *Volksgemeinschaft als Selbstermächtigung: Gewalt gegen Juden in der deutschen Provinz 1919 bis 1939* (Hamburg: Hamburger Edition, 2007), pp. 319–335. Notable examples of anthologies and journals include Walter H. Pehle, ed., *Der Judenpogrom 1938: Von der "Reichskristallnacht" zum Völkermord* (Frankfurt: Fischer, 1988); and the special issue of *Zeitschrift für Geschichtswissenschaft* 46 (1998).

7. Kropat, *Reichskristallnacht,* pp. 56–78.

8. The first scholar to emphasize this point was Wolfgang Benz, "Applaus, Beteiligung, Missbilligung: Zum Verhalten des Publikums in der 'Reichskristallnacht,'" *Zeitschrift für Geschichtswissenschaft* 46 (1998), pp. 961–971.

1. "Our Path Is the Right One"

1. Michael Wildt, *Volksgemeinschaft als Selbstermächtigung: Gewalt gegen Juden in der deutschen Provinz 1919 bis 1939* (Hamburg: Hamburger Edition, 2007).

2. Marion A. Kaplan, *Between Dignity and Despair: Jewish Life in Nazi Germany* (New York: Oxford University Press, 1998); Claudia Koonz, *The Nazi Conscience* (Cambridge, Mass.: Harvard University Press, 2003).

3. Wildt, *Volksgemeinschaft als Selbstermächtigung*, pp. 108–111; Peter Longerich, *Politik der Vernichtung: Eine Gesamtdarstellung der nationalsozialistischen Judenverfolgung* (Munich: Piper, 1998), pp. 26–30.

4. Wildt, *Volksgemeinschaft als Selbstermächtigung*, pp. 176–218; Longerich, *Politik der Vernichtung*, pp. 70–101.

5. Wildt, *Volksgemeinschaft als Selbstermächtigung*, pp. 301–311; Longerich, *Politik der Vernichtung*, pp. 172–185, 190–195.

6. Gerhard Botz, *Nationalsozialismus in Wien: Machtübernahme, Herrschaftssicherung, Radikalisierung 1938/39* (Vienna: Mandelbaum, 2008), pp. 126–136.

7. *Die Tagebücher von Joseph Goebbels*, ed. Elke Fröhlich, 30 vols. (Munich: Saur, 1993–2007), part I, vol. 6, entry for 19 June 1938.

8. Wildt, *Volksgemeinschaft als Selbstermächtigung*, pp. 308–310.

9. Longerich, *Politik der Vernichtung*, pp. 190–195.

10. Botz, *Nationalsozialismus in Wien*, pp. 502–504.

2. "This Bloody Jewish Deed"

1. Peter Longerich, *Politik der Vernichtung: Eine Gesamtdarstellung der nationalsozialistischen Judenverfolgung* (Munich: Piper, 1998), pp. 195–197; Bettina Goldberg, "Die Zwangsausweisung der polnischen Juden aus dem Deutschen Reich im Oktober 1938 und die Folgen," *Zeitschrift für Geschichtswissenschaft* 46 (1998), pp. 971–984.

2. Michael Marrus, "The Strange Story of Herschel Grynszpan," *American Scholar* 57, no. 1 (Winter 1988), pp. 69–91; Hans-Jürgen Döscher, *"Reichskristallnacht": Die Novemberpogrome 1938* (Munich: Propyläen, 2000), pp. 63–65.

3. Wolf-Arno Kropat, *"Reichskristallnacht": Der Judenpogrom vom 7. bis 10.*

November 1938—Urheber, Täter, Hintergründe (Wiesbaden: Kommission für die Geschichte der Juden in Hessen, 1997), p. 9.

4. Ibid., p. 8.

5. See *NS-Presseanweisungen der Vorkriegszeit: Edition und Dokumentation*, vol. 6/III: 1938, ed. Karen Peter (Munich: Saur, 1999), as well as program summaries of the Reichsrundfunkgesellschaft in Bundesarchiv Berlin, R78/1309–1310.

6. *Die Tagebücher von Joseph Goebbels*, ed. Elke Fröhlich, 30 vols. (Munich: Saur, 1993–2007) (hereafter *Goebbels-Tagebücher*), entries for October and first week of November 1938 in part I, vol. 6.

7. Jürgen Hagemann, *Die Presselenkung im Dritten Reich* (Bonn: Bouvier, 1970), pp. 38–40.

8. Wolfgang Diewerge, *Als Sonderberichterstatter zum Kairoer Judenprozess: Gerichtlich erhärtetes Material zur Judenfrage* (Munich: Eher, 1935).

9. Wolfgang Diewerge, *Der Fall Gustloff: Vorgeschichte und Hintergründe der Bluttat von Davos* (Munich: Eher, 1936).

10. Institut für Zeitgeschichte, Munich (hereafter IfZ), Zeugenschrift Wolfgang Diewerge, ZS 593.

11. Norbert Frei, *Vergangenheitspolitik: Die Anfänge der Bundesrepublik und die NS-Vergangenheit* (Munich: Beck, 1996), pp. 366–368, 380; Ulrich Herbert, *Best: Biographische Studien über Radikalismus, Weltanschauung und Vernunft 1903–1989*, 3rd ed. (Bonn: Dietz, 1996), pp. 461–465. The central figure in the group, Werner Naumann, had been the state secretary in Goebbels's Ministry of Propaganda, where he had worked together with Diewerge. See also Zeugenschrift Wolfgang Diewerge, ZS 593, IfZ.

12. DNB-Rundruf (20:37), in *NS-Presseanweisungen*, vol. 6/III: 1938, no. 3176.

13. Even on the following day, November 8, the embassy's communications to Berlin were objective and devoid of any such accusations. See Welczek to Auswärtiges Amt, 8 November 1938, reproduced in Döscher, *"Reichskristallnacht,"* pp. 77–79.

14. "Jüdische Mordbanditen," DNB Dienstblatt, Vienna, 7 November 1938, 21:45, IfZ.

15. These were the possible measures about which the *New York Times* speculated in its first article about the vom Rath shooting and the German propaganda campaign. "Nazis Ask Reprisal in Attack in Envoy," *New York Times,* 9 November 1938 (the dateline on the article is 8 November).

16. This account of events in Kassel is based on the following sources: Kro-

pat, *Reichskristallnacht*, pp. 56–59, as well as documents printed on pp. 204–211; Wilhelm Frenz, Jörg Kammler, and Dietfried Krause-Vilmar, eds., *Volksgemeinschaft und Volksfeinde: Kassel, 1933–1945*, 2 vols. (Fuldabrück: Hesse, 1984, 1987), vol. 1 (documents), pp. 248–255, and vol. 2, pp. 193–198.

17. Frenz et al., *Volksgemeinschaft und Volksfeinde*, vol. 2, pp. 149–150.

18. "Wie Mauschel nach der Flöte tanzen musste," *Kasseler Post*, 13 August 1937, reproduced in Frenz et al., *Volksgemeinschaft und Volksfeinde*, vol. 1, pp. 200–201.

19. Frenz et al., *Volksgemeinschaft und Volksfeinde*, pp. 190–191. "Spontane Kurhessen-Demonstration," *Kurhessische Landeszeitung*, 8 November 1938, printed in Kropat, *Reichskristallnacht*, pp. 204–205, calls attention to the "unbeirrbare Abneigung gegen das Judentum" in Kurhessen. See also Rudolf Euler, "Zur Frage der jüdischen Durchsetzung innerhalb der ländlichen Bezirke Kurhessens," *Archiv für Rassen- und Gesellschaftsbiologie* 29, 1 (1935), pp. 73–82.

20. Kropat, *Reichskristallnacht*, p. 59, and statement by Karl Ehser, 27 May 1947, printed in Kropat, *Reichskristallnacht*, pp. 208–210.

21. Kropat, *Reichskristallnacht*, p. 59.

22. Ibid., p. 79.

23. Heydrich to Lammers, 9 November 1938 (containing text of report from Staatspolizeistelle Kassel), and Chef d. Sicherheitspolizei to Chef d. Ordnungspolizei, 9 November 1938, printed in Kropat, *Reichskristallnacht*, pp. 206–208.

24. Frenz et al., *Volksgemeinschaft und Volksfeinde*, vol. 1, p. 248.

25. Ibid., vol. 2, p. 193.

26. Urteil, Landgericht Kassel, 3 K Ls 16/46, 17 December 1946, IfZ.

27. "Spontane Kurhessen-Demonstration," *Kurhessische Landeszeitung*, 8 November 1938, printed in Kropat, *Reichskristallnacht*, pp. 204–205.

28. News of the violence in Electoral Hesse was not carried on the DNB newswire until late in the afternoon on November 8. The single report that came over the DNB wire was on November 8 at about 5:00 PM.

29. Döscher, *"Reichskristallnacht,"* pp. 71, 79, 81.

30. DNB Dienstblatt for 8 and 9 November, IfZ.

31. Mitteilungen an die Schriftleitungen, 9 November 1938, 18.55, bound with DNB Dienstblatt, IfZ.

32. Kropat, *Reichskristallnacht*, pp. 59–66.

33. Regierungspräsident Kassel to Ortspolizeibehörde, 8 November 1938, 16.35 Uhr, printed in Kropat, *Reichskristallnacht*, p. 207.

34. Urteil, Landgericht Kassel, 3 K Ls 2/49, 22 April 1949, IfZ.

35. Urteil, Landgericht Kassel, 3 Ks 4/48, 5 May 1948; 3 K Ls 3/49, IfZ.
36. Urteil, Landgericht Kassel, 3 K Ls 20/47, 7 July 1947, IfZ.

3. "Now the People Shall Act"

1. DNB Dienstblatt, Vienna, 9 November 1938, 21:45, Institut für Zeitge-schichte, Munich (hereafter IfZ).
2. The implied connection was registered in London. See, for example, Halifax to Ogilvie-Forbes, 11 November 1938, *Documents on British Foreign Policy 1919–1939* (hereafter DBFP), third series, vol. III (London: HMPO, 1950), p. 268.
3. This point was common in the testimony of many German Jews arriving in Britain in late 1938 or early 1939. See, e.g., Private Reports on Jews in Germany, Wiener Library, London (hereafter Wiener Library Reports), testimony of Heinz Nassau, no date (late 1938 or early 1939), no. 6. Nassau, who lived in southern Germany, received a fairly accurate description of the pogrom in Bebra through his personal grapevine.
4. Lionel Kochan, *Pogrom: 10 November 1938* (London: Andre Deutsch, 1957), p. 44; Ogilvie-Forbes to Halifax, 8 November 1938, DBFP, third series, vol. III (London: HMPO, 1950), p. 262.
5. Halifax to Ogilvie-Forbes, 9 November 1938, DBFP, third series, vol. III (London: HMPO, 1950), p. 264.
6. Statement of Herr Oppermann, 22 November 1938, Wiener Library Reports, no. 1.
7. "Umfangreiche Waffenfunde bei Berliner Juden," DNB Dienstblatt, 8 November 1938, IfZ.
8. Statement of Herr Oppermann, 22 November 1938, Wiener Library Reports, no. 1.
9. See, for example, Wiener Library Reports, nos. 37, 55, and 60.
10. Statement of Herr Oppermann, 22 November 1938, Wiener Library Reports, no. 1.
11. Herbert Freeden, *Die jüdische Presse im Dritten Reich* (Frankfurt: Athenäum, 1987), pp. 170–171; Katrin Diehl, *Die jüdische Presse im Dritten Reich: Zwischen Selbstbehauptung und Fremdbestimmung* (Tübingen: Niemeyer, 1997), p. 233.
12. This observation is from Paul Connerton, *How Societies Remember* (New York: Cambridge University Press, 1989), p. 42. On the Nazi martyr cult see Jay Baird, *To Die for Germany: Heroes in the Nazi Pantheon* (Bloomington:

Indiana University Press, 1990), pp. 41–72; Sabine Behrenbeck, *Der Kult um die toten Helden: Nationalsozialistische Mythen, Riten und Symbole* (Vierow: SH-Verlag, 1996), pp. 299–313. For details on the 1938 commemoration see Andreas Heusler and Tobias Weber, *Kristallnacht: Gewalt gegen die Münchner Juden im November 1938* (Munich: Buchendorfer, 1998), pp. 42–44.

13. Dr. Karl Brandt, whom Hitler had sent to Paris to keep an eye on vom Rath's condition, was one of the chief architects of the euthanasia program that would begin in Germany less than a year later. Brandt was actually present in vom Rath's hospital room at the time of his death. There is no evidence, however, that Brandt intervened medically to facilitate or accelerate vom Rath's death. The French autopsy established that his death resulted from damage to the spleen, stomach, and pancreas caused by one of the bullets. Alain Cuenot, *The Herschel Grynszpan Case*, trans. Joan Redmont (Beverly Hills, Calif.: David Rome, 1982), pp. 58–59.

14. The most thorough analysis of this question is Frank Maciejewski, "Der Novemberpogrom in ritualgeschichtlicher Perspektive," *Jahrbuch für Antisemitismusforschung* 15 (2006), pp. 65–84.

15. *Die Tagebücher von Joseph Goebbels,* ed. Elke Fröhlich, 30 vols. (Munich: Saur, 1993–2007) (hereafter *Goebbels-Tagebücher*), part 1, vol. 6, entry for 10 November 1938.

16. Nicolaus von Below, *Als Hitlers Adjutant* (Mainz: Hase und Koehler, 1980), p. 136.

17. Report by Bernhard Heese, "Der Judenpogrom in Dessau am 9. November 1938," Stadtarchiv Dessau. The writer was the former city archivist of Dessau. The document is also cited in Wolf-Arno Kropat, *"Reichskristallnacht": Der Judenpogrom vom 7. bis 10. November 1938—Urheber, Täter, Hintergründe* (Wiesbaden: Kommission für die Geschichte der Juden in Hessen, 1997), p. 79. Kropat dates the document from 1953, though some of the phraseology suggests that it was actually written before the end of the Nazi regime.

18. DNB Dienstblatt, Vienna, 9 November 1938, 20:35, IfZ.

19. France was on Greenwich Meridian Time in 1938.

20. Brandt to Hitler, 9 November 1938, 16:45, reproduced in Hans-Jürgen Döscher, *"Reichskristallnacht": Die Novemberpogrome 1938* (Munich: Propyläen, 2000), p. 81.

21. DNB Dienstblatt, Vienna, 9 November 1938, 18:15, IfZ.

22. Aktenvermerk by Siegler, 2 October 1952, Zeugenschrift Heinrich Heim, Zs 243, IfZ. The SA witness in question was Max Jüttner.

23. *Goebbels-Tagebücher,* part 1, vol. 6, 10 November 1938.

24. Ibid.

25. Karl Freiherr von Eberstein, the Polizeipräsident of Munich, testified to this effect at Nuremberg; see *Der Prozess gegen die Hauptkriegsverbrecher vor dem Internationalen Militärgerichtshof* (Nuremberg: [s.n.], 1947–1949) (hereafter IMT), vol. 20, p. 320, session of 6 August 1946. A second witness was Nazi Youth Leader Baldur von Schirach, who described the scene in his memoir, *Ich glaubte an Hitler* (Hamburg: Mosaik, 1967), p. 243. See also related reminiscences by Rudolf Jordan, the gauleiter of Halle-Merseburg, *Erlebt und Erlitten: Weg eines Gauleiters von München bis Moskau* (Leoni am Starnberger See: Druffel-Verlag), pp. 180–181.

26. Gerhard L. Weinberg, *The Foreign Policy of Hitler's Germany: Starting World War Two, 1937–1939* (Chicago: University of Chicago Press, 1980), pp. 467–470. On the connection between the pogrom and Hitler's understanding of German foreign policy see also Stefan Kley, "Hitler and the Pogrom of November 9/10, 1938," *Yad Vashem Studies* 28 (2000), pp. 87–113.

27. "Besprechung bei Generalfeldmarschall Goering am 14.10.38," 1301-PS, IMT, vol. 27, pp. 160–164.

28. Saul Friedländer, *Nazi Germany and the Jews,* vol. 1: *The Years of Persecution, 1933–1939* (New York: HarperCollins, 1997), pp. 270–271.

29. *Goebbels-Tagebücher,* part I, vol. 6, 9 November 1938. Below, *Als Hitlers Adjutant,* p. 135.

30. "Stenographische Niederschrift von einem Teil der Besprechung über die Judenfrage unter Vorsitz von Feldmarschall Goering im RLM am 12. November 1938, 11:00 Uhr," IMT, document 1816-PS, vol. 28, pp. 499–540.

31. *Das Tagebuch der Hertha Nathorff: Berlin-New York, Aufzeichnungen 1933 bis 1945,* ed. Wolfgang Benz (Munich: Oldenbourg, 1987), pp. 132–133.

32. "Who Started the Jewish Pogrom?" *Sunday Times* (London), 13 November 1938.

33. Dieter Obst, *"Reichskristallnacht": Ursachen und Verlauf des antisemitischen Pogroms vom November 1938* (Frankfurt: Lang, 1991), p. 75. Obst reconstructs the attendance at the Kameradschaftsabend from the seating plan that survives in the Munich city archive. The total attendance at the event was almost 480 persons. Many, however, used Hitler's departure as an opportunity to leave as well, and they were therefore not present to hear Goebbels's instructions.

34. Hermann Graml places the time of the address at 10:00 PM. Graml, *Reichskristallnacht: Antisemitismus und Judenverfolgung im Dritten Reich* (Mu-

nich: DTV, 1998), p. 17. Baldur von Schirach claimed that it was sometime after 9:00 PM. Schirach, *Ich glaubte an Hitler,* p. 243. Max Jüttner, who was deputy chief of staff of the SA in 1938, remembered it being after 10:30. Zeugenschrift Max Jüttner, Zs 251, IfZ.

35. NSDAP Oberstes Parteigericht, Bericht (Geheim), 13 February 1939, IMT, document 3063-PS, vol. 32, pp. 20–29.

36. Schirach, *Ich glaubte an Hitler,* p. 244; Zeugenschrift Max Jüttner, Zs 251, IfZ.

37. NSDAP Oberstes Parteigericht, Bericht (Geheim), 13 February 1939, IMT, document 3063-PS, vol. 32, pp. 20–29. The report states that at 1:40 AM a telex (Fernschreiben) was sent out to the Gaupropagandaämter. Furthermore, the report refers to an appendix containing the telex. This appendix, however, was missing when the document was published in the record of the International Military Tribunal in 1946, and it has never been found subsequently.

38. This point is emphasized in Zeugenschrift Max Jüttner, Zs 251, IfZ. Even though Jüttner's postwar statements were intended to exculpate the SA, this specific assertion is supported by evidence that will be discussed in Chapter 4.

39. Himmler speech of 8 November 1938, printed in Bradley F. Smith and Agnes F. Peterson, eds., *Heinrich Himmler: Geheimreden 1933 bis 1945* (Frankfurt: Propyläen, 1974), pp. 25–49. The section on Jews is on pp. 37–38.

40. "Das fehlt noch," *Das Schwarze Korps,* 3 November 1938. Excerpts are printed in Kropat, *Reichskristallnacht,* pp. 202–204.

41. Michael Wildt, ed., *Die Judenpolitik des SD 1935 bis 1938: Eine Dokumentation* (Munich: Oldenbourg, 1995).

42. "Zum Judenproblem," January 1937, in Wildt, *Die Judenpolitik des SD,* pp. 95–105.

43. Geheimes Feldschreiben, Müller to Staatspolizeileitstellen, 9 November 1938, 23:55, in Kropat, *Reichskristallnacht,* pp. 213–214.

44. Blitz-Fernschreiben, Heydrich to Staatspolizeileitstellen, SD-Oberabschnitte, SD-Unterabschnitte, 10 November 1938, 1:20, in Kropat, *Reichskristallnacht,* pp. 214–216.

45. Kropat, *Reichskristallnacht,* pp. 87–89.

46. Funkspruch from Daluege, 10 November 1938, printed in Kropat, *Reichskristallnacht,* pp. 216–217.

47. Obst, *"Reichskristallnacht,"* pp. 75–83. Rudolf Jordan later claimed to

have seen Goebbels speaking with Heydrich in the hall shortly before Goebbels's speech; he even contended that Heydrich addressed the Nazi officials after Goebbels had finished speaking. Jordan, *Erlebt und Erlitten,* p. 181. But had Heydrich actually done this, the Nazi High Court would probably have mentioned it in its report of February 1939.

48. "Eidesstattliche Erklärung vom 5. Juli 1946 des SS-Hauptsturmführers Luitpold Schallermeier," IMT, Affidavit SS-5, vol. 43, pp. 510–513.

49. Richard J. Evans, *Lying about Hitler: History, Holocaust, and the David Irving Trial* (New York: Basic Books, 2001), pp. 56–57.

50. After the war, Karl Wolff also placed Himmler in Hitler's apartment at the time. "Meine Kenntnis über die im Nürnberger Urteil festgestellte Behandlung der Juden," Zeugenschrift Karl Wolff, Zs 317, folder 2, IfZ.

51. DNB Dienstblatt, Vienna, 10 November 1938, IfZ.

52. *Goebbels-Tagebücher,* part I, vol. 6, 10 November 1938.

53. DNB Dienstblatt, Vienna, 10 November 1938, IfZ.

54. Below, *Als Hitlers Adjutant,* p. 136.

55. Heusler and Weber, *Kristallnacht,* pp. 49–50.

56. *Goebbels-Tagebücher,* part I, vol. 6, 10 November 1938.

57. Wagner's reticence on November 9 was also documented in an investigation undertaken by the Hitler Youth. See Michael Buddrus, "'Wir fahren zum Juden Geld holen!' Hitlerjugend, Antisemitismus, Reichskristallnacht," *Jahrbuch des Archivs der deutschen Jugendbewegung* 18, 1993–1998, p. 79.

58. *Goebbels-Tagebücher,* part I, vol. 6, 10 November 1938; Below, *Als Hitlers Adjutant,* p. 136.

59. Angela Hermann, "Hitler und sein Stosstrupp in der 'Reichskristallnacht,'" *Vierteljahrshefte für Zeitgeschichte* 56, no. 4 (2008), pp. 603–619.

60. See, for example, Martin Gilbert, *Kristallnacht: Prelude to Destruction* (New York: HarperCollins, 2006), p. 26: "A violent mass action against the Jews had been in the minds of the Nazi leaders for some time. As vom Rath lay gravely wounded, the moment seemed to have come to bring existing plans into instant readiness." Gilbert provides no further evidence for the existence of such plans.

4. "The Time for Revenge Has Now Arrived"

1. Weather report from *Völkischer Beobachter,* 10 November 1938.

2. On the delayed pogrom in Danzig, which possessed a special status under the League of Nations, see Herbert S. Levine, *Hitler's Free City: A History of*

the Nazi Party in Danzig, 1925–39 (Chicago: University of Chicago Press, 1973), p. 134; Samuel Echt, *Die Geschichte der Juden in Danzig* (Leer/Ostfriesland: Rautenberg, 1972), pp. 185–186; and Erwin Lichtenstein, *Die Juden der freien Stadt Danzig unter der Herrschaft des Nationalsozialismus* (Tübingen: Mohr, 1973), pp. 76–83.

3. This point is emphasized in Dieter Obst, *"Reichskristallnacht": Ursachen und Verlauf des antisemitischen Pogroms vom November 1938* (Frankfurt: Lang, 1991).

4. Ibid., pp. 119–138. Obst's sample is that of 170 men who were prosecuted after 1945 for crimes perpetrated during the pogrom. While the data provide useful background for gaining insight into the SA men, they do not suffice for the kind of precise, empirical, quantitative conclusions that Obst himself draws from them. Obst's methodology is predicated on the very questionable assumption that this sample of men who were prosecuted after 1945 is representative of those who actually participated in the pogrom. It ignores, for example, the fact that many of the younger men who were involved in the pogrom later perished in World War Two at a higher frequency than their older comrades. This oversight may account for an upward skewing of Obst's conclusions for both age distribution and distribution by seniority in the Nazi Party.

5. Report by NSDAP Oberstes Parteigericht to Goering, 13 February 1939, *Der Prozess gegen die Hauptkriegsverbrecher vor dem Internationalen Militärgerichtshof* (Nuremberg: [s.n.], 1947–1949) (hereafter IMT), vol. 32, document 3063-PS, pp. 20–29.

6. We have no reliable figure for Jewish suicides in connection with the events of November 1938, but it was certainly several hundred. Christian Goeschel, "Suicides of German Jews in the Third Reich," *German History* 25, no. 1 (2007), pp. 27–31.

7. Report by NSDAP Oberstes Parteigericht to Goering, 13 February 1939, IMT, document 3063-PS, vol. 32, p. 28.

8. Ibid. See also Donald McKale, "A Case of Nazi 'Justice'—The Punishment of Party Members Involved in the Kristallnacht, 1938," *Jewish Social Studies* 35 (1973), nos. 3–4 (July–October), pp. 228–238.

9. Institut für Zeitgeschichte, Munich (hereafter IfZ), Urteil, SG Bremen, 11 February 1948, Gb 11.06.

10. The terms used, according to the trial record, were *umgelegt, ausgerottet,* and *vernichtet.*

11. Urteil, LG Coburg, 8 September 1949, IfZ, Gc 02.01/2.

12. Baruch Z. Ophir and Falk Wiesemann, *Die jüdischen Gemeinden in Bayern, 1918–1945: Geschichte und Zerstörung* (Munich: Oldenbourg, 1979), pp. 141–142.

13. Urteil, LG Coburg, 8 September 1949, IfZ, Gc 02.01/2.

14. Urteil, LG Aschaffenburg, 19 November 1948, IfZ, Ga 05.01.

15. Ophir and Wiesemann, *Die jüdischen Gemeinden in Bayern,* pp. 255–260.

16. Private Reports on Jews in Germany, Wiener Library, London (hereafter Wiener Library Reports), no. 157.

17. See Wiener Library Reports no. 72, for an example in Wiesbaden.

18. Wiener Library Reports no. 88.

19. Wiener Library Reports no. 19.

20. Wiener Library Reports no. 20; Yitzhak S. Herz, "Kristallnacht at the Dinslaken Orphanage: Reminiscences," *Yad Vashem Studies* 11 (1976), pp. 344–368.

21. Wiener Library Reports nos. 19 (Werder), 240 (Neustadt), 241 (Emden), 37 (Nuremberg).

22. Urteil, LG Giessen, 30 September 1948, IfZ, Gg 01.29.

23. Urteil, LG Giessen, 18 November 1949, IfZ, Gg 01.21.

24. See also Wiener Library Reports no. 36 for a description of an incident in Oderwald.

25. Urteil, LG Darmstadt, 16 July 1948, IfZ, Gd 01.25.

26. Peter Loewenberg, "The Kristallnacht as Public Degradation Ritual," *Leo Baeck Institute Yearbook* 32 (1987), pp. 309–323; Frank Maciejewski, "Der Novemberpogrom in ritualgeschichtlicher Perspektive," *Jahrbuch für Antisemitismusforschung* 15 (2006), pp. 65–84.

27. Urteil, LG Ravensburg, 5 March 1948, IfZ, Gr 01.01.

28. Anklageschrift, Oberstaatsanwalt LG Darmstadt, 9 September 1949, IfZ, Gd 01.26.

29. Wiener Library Reports nos. 4 (Gütersloh, Herford), 17 (Gailingen), 36 (Ostfriesland), 65 (Lichtenfels), 101 (Dortmund), 123 (Vienna), 618 (Beuthen), 193.

30. Wiener Library Reports no. 4.

31. During the day on November 10, for example, Reinhard Heydrich, in an "urgent" message to police offices around Germany, had to reiterate the prohibition against looting that had been included in the original instructions distributed in the middle of the night. Fernschreiben (Blitz), Heydrich to

Staatspolizeistellen and SD-Oberabschnitte, 10 November 1938, Bundesarchiv Berlin, R 58/276.

32. Urteil, LG Giessen, 12 April 1950, IfZ, Gg 01.33.

33. Thomas von Berg, *Korruption und Bereicherung: Politische Biographie des Münchner NSDAP-Fraktionsvorsitzenden Christian Weber (1883–1945)* (Munich: M. Press, 2003), pp. 48–52.

34. Urteil, Landgericht Munich, 14 June 1946, IfZ, Gm 07.94/6. Some details of the case appear in Andreas Heusler and Tobias Weger, *"Kristallnacht": Gewalt gegen die Münchner Juden im November 1938* (Munich: Buchendorfer, 1998).

35. For an account of Hirsch's abuse in Dachau, see Wiener Library Reports no. 69.

36. For a collection of documents relating to this case see Michael Buddrus, "'Wir fahren zum Juden Geld holen!' Hitlerjugend, Antisemitismus, Reichskristallnacht," *Jahrbuch des Archivs der deutschen Jugendbewegung* 18 (1993–1998), pp. 13–156.

37. Wiener Library Reports nos. 65 (Nuremberg), 100 (Berlin).

38. Urteil, LG Giessen, January 1949, IfZ, Gg 01.08.

39. Urteil, LG Giessen, 24 February 1949, IfZ, Gg 01.23.

40. Urteil, LG Marburg, 1950, IfZ, Gm 03.09.

41. Urteil, LG Giessen, 13 November 1947, IfZ, Gg 01.27.

42. Urteil, LG Hanau, 14 February 1949, IfZ, Gh 04.03.

43. Wiener Library Reports no. 93.

44. Urteil, LG Giessen, 28 July 1948, IfZ, Gg 01.28.

45. Wiener Library Reports nos. 31 (Berlin), 60 (Vienna).

46. Urteil, LG Giessen, 17 September 1946, IfZ, Gg 01.47.

47. Michael Kater, *Hitler Youth* (Cambridge, Mass.: Harvard University Press, 2004), pp. 62–63, understates the extent to which the Hitler Youth participated in the pogrom, though he more generally emphasizes the ideological indoctrination of German youth into antisemitic and racist ideology.

48. Urteil, LG Giessen, 3 November 1948, IfZ, Gg 01.37.

49. Heinz Knobloch, *Der beherzte Reviervorsteher: Ungewöhnliche Zivilcourage am Hackeschen Markt* (Berlin: Jaron, 2005). The story of Krützfeld's exploits during Kristallnacht is based to a large extent on the reminiscences of his son, who was very young in 1938.

50. Urteil, LG Hanau, 14 February 1949, IfZ, Gh 04.03.

51. Wiener Library Reports no. 751.

52. Urteil, LG Giessen, 12 September 1949, IfZ, Gg 01.30.

53. Urteil, LG Giessen, 8 April 1948, IfZ, Gg 01.41.

54. Wiener Library Reports no. 92.

55. Urteil, LG Marburg, March 1953, IfZ, Gm 03.08.

56. Wiener Library Reports no. 49.

57. Wiener Library Reports no. 298.

58. Harry Stein, "Das Sonderlager im Konzentrationslager Buchenwald nach den Pogromen 1938," in Monica Kingreen, ed., *"Nach der Kristallnacht": Jüdisches Leben und antijüdische Politik in Frankfurt am Main 1938–1945* (Frankfurt: Campus, 1999), p. 26.

59. For a good summary of these points see Wiener Library Reports no. 172.

60. Wiener Library Reports no. 618.

61. The following discussion is based on Wiener Library Reports nos. 24, 60, 62, 63, 179, 190, 213, 216, 219, and 304.

62. Wiener Library Reports nos. 168 (Weimar), 2 (Erfurt), 48 (Baden-Baden).

63. Wiener Library Reports nos. 323, 340.

64. Wiener Library Reports no. 340.

65. Wiener Library Reports no. 528.

66. Wiener Library Reports no. 618.

67. Wiener Library Reports nos. 75 (Hamburg), 67 (Munich), 239 (Nuremberg), 123 (Meiningen).

68. Wiener Library Reports nos. 216, 50 (Frankfurt), 8 (Kiel).

69. Wiener Library Reports nos. 52 (Breslau), 219 and 228 (Vienna), 305 (Fuhlsbüttel).

70. Wiener Library Reports no. 528.

71. Robert Gellately, *Backing Hitler: Consent and Coercion in Nazi Germany* (New York: Oxford University Press, 2002).

5. "Synagogues Ignited Themselves"

1. *Die Tagebücher von Joseph Goebbels,* ed. Elke Fröhlich, 30 vols. (Munich: Saur, 1993–2007) (hereafter *Goebbels-Tagebücher*), part I, vol. 6, entry for 10 November 1938. Rochus Misch, who served as Hitler's telephonist, courier, and bodyguard, claimed that, many years after the pogrom, Karl Wilhelm Krause, who had been Hitler's personal servant in 1938, had told him that Hitler had

observed the burning of a Munich synagogue during the night. This story appears in no other source. Rochus Misch, *Der letzte Zeuge. "Ich war Hitlers Telefonist, Kurier und Leibwächter"* (Zurich: Pendo, 2008), pp. 56–57.

2. *Goebbels-Tagebücher,* part I, vol. 6, 11 November 1938.

3. Institut für Zeitgeschichte (hereafter IfZ), DNB Dienstblatt, Vienna, 10 November 1938, 16:00. For evidence that the message was broadcast and widely noted on the afternoon of 10 November, see Bürgermeister Bückeburg, "Bericht für den 10.11.1938," 17 November 1938, in Otto Dov Kulka and Eberhard Jäckel, eds., *Die Juden in den geheimen NS-Stimmungsberichten, 1933–1945* (Düsseldorf: Droste, 2004), document 2626.

4. Nr. 3213, DNB-Rundruf (16.20 Uhr), 10 November 1938, in *NS-Presseanweisungen der Vorkriegszeit: Edition und Dokumentation* (Munich: Saur, 1999), vol. 6, p. 1061.

5. Anordnung, Goebbels to Gauleiter, 10 November 1938, reproduced in Wolf-Arno Kropat, *"Reichskristallnacht": Der Judenpogrom vom 7. bis 10. November 1938—Urheber, Täter, Hintergründe* (Wiesbaden: Kommission für die Geschichte der Juden in Hessen, 1997), p. 233.

6. Stellv. d. Führers to Gauleitungen, 10 November 1938, Anordnung 174/38, Bundesarchiv Berlin, NS 6/231.

7. "Looting Mobs Defy Goebbels," *Daily Express,* 11 November 1938.

8. Nr. 3209, 10 November 1938, in *NS-Presseanweisungen der Vorkriegszeit,* vol. 6, pp. 1060–1061.

9. Ibid.

10. Günter Beukert, "Als Bildjournalist in der 'Reichskristallnacht,'" in Diethart Kerbs et al., eds., *Die Gleichschaltung der Bilder: Zur Geschichte der Pressefotographie 1930–36* (Berlin: Frölich and Kaufmann, 1983), pp. 191–193.

11. "Empörte Volksseele schafft sich Luft," *Völkischer Beobachter,* Berlin edition, 11 November 1938.

12. "Rede Hitlers vor der deutschen Presse (10 November 1938)," ed. Wilhelm Treue, *Vierteljahrshefte für Zeitgeschichte* 6 (1958), no. 2, pp. 175–191.

13. Ibid, p. 182. The German text is as follows: "Es war nunmehr notwendig, das deutsche Volk psychologisch allmählich umzustellen und ihm langsam klarzumachen, dass es Dinge gibt, die, wenn sie nicht mit friedlichen Mitteln durchgesetzt werden können, mit Mitteln der Gewalt durchgesetzt werden müssen."

14. *Goebbels-Tagebücher,* part I, vol. 6, 11 November 1938.

15. This insight is emphasized in Gerald D. Feldman, "The Reichskristall-

nacht and the Insurance Industry: The Politics of Damage Control," in Gerald
D. Feldman and Wolfgang Seibel, eds., *Networks of Nazi Persecution: Bureau-
cracy, Business and the Organization of the Holocaust* (New York: Berghahn,
2005), p. 296.

16. Goering's concerns regarding the consequences of the pogrom for German foreign policy were noted at the time by Hitler's military adjutant, Major
Gerhard Engel. Hildegard von Kotze, ed., *Heeresadjutant bei Hitler, 1938–1943:
Aufzeichnungen des Majors Engel* (Stuttgart: Deutsche Verlags-Anstalt, 1974),
entry for 12 November 1938.

17. At the International Military Tribunal, Goering claimed that he had
spoken with Hitler in person on the morning of November 10 and conveyed
his protests: *Der Prozess gegen die Hauptkriegsverbrecher vor dem Internationalen
Militärgerichtshof* (Nuremberg: [s.n.], 1947–1949) (hereafter IMT), vol. 9,
p. 312. In his biography of Hitler, Ian Kershaw accepts Goering's assertion but
also points out an important inconsistency in Goering's Nuremberg testimony,
namely, that Goering was not in Berlin on November 10, the day on which he
supposedly spoke with Hitler. Ian Kershaw, *Hitler: 1936–1945: Nemesis* (New
York: Norton, 2001), p. 143. Given the existence of other, incontrovertible evidence of Goering's objections to the pogrom, and given the attention that Hitler and Goebbels devoted to insurance claims over lunch in the Osteria in Munich, it is plausible that Goering communicated his concerns to Hitler or
Goebbels in some way on November 10, even if Goering's account at Nuremberg contained inaccuracies.

18. "Stenographische Niederschrift von einem Teil der Besprechung über
die Judenfrage unter Vorsitz von Feldmarschall Goering im RLM am 12. November 1938, 11:00 Uhr," IMT, document 1816-PS, vol. 28, pp. 499–540.

19. Alan E. Steinweis, *Art, Ideology, and Economics in Nazi Germany: The
Reich Chambers of Music, Theater, and the Visual Arts* (Chapel Hill: University
of North Carolina Press, 1993), p. 115.

20. *Goebbels-Tagebücher,* part I, vol. 6, 13 November 1938.

21. The presentation of these events here follows Feldman, "The Reichskristallnacht and the Insurance Industry," which is drawn from the larger work
by the same author, *Die Allianz und die deutsche Versicherungswirtschaft 1933–
1945* (Munich: Beck, 2001), pp. 233–284.

22. "Verordnung über eine Sühneleistung der Juden deutscher Staatsange-
hörigkeit," 12 November 1938, *Reichsgesetzblatt,* 1938, Teil 1, 2, Halbjahr,
p. 1579.

23. Wolfgang Benz and Barbara Distel, eds., *Der Ort des Terrors: Geschichte der nationalsozialistischen Konzentrationslager. Band 2: Frühe Lager, Dachau, Emslandlager* (Munich: Beck, 2005), p. 252.

24. Wolfgang Benz and Barbara Distel, eds., *Der Ort des Terrors: Geschichte der nationalsozialistischen Konzentrationslager. Band 3: Sachsenhausen, Buchenwald* (Munich: Beck, 2006), p. 314.

25. Ibid., p. 32.

26. Fernschreiben Nr. 14690, 16 November 1938, Bundesarchiv Berlin, R 58/276.

27. Wolfgang Benz and Barbara Distel, eds., *Der Ort des Terrors: Geschichte der nationalsozialistischen Konzentrationslager. Band 1: Die Organisation des Terrors* (Munich: Beck, 2005), p. 161.

28. This explains why, for example, some of the Jewish prisoners from Frankfurt were sent to Dachau even though most of the prisoners from that city were sent to Buchenwald. See Monica Kingreen, "Von Frankfurt in das KZ Dachau: Die Namen der im November 1938 deportierten Männer," in Monica Kingreen, ed., *"Nach der Kristallnacht": Jüdisches Leben und antijüdische Politik in Frankfurt am Main 1938–1945* (Frankfurt: Campus, 1999), pp. 55–89. The Gestapo central office in Berlin tracked the size and destination of the transports. See Blitz Berlin NUE 243 813, from Müller to Staatspolizeistellen, 10 November 1938, Bundesarchiv Berlin, R 58/276.

29. Harry Stein, ed., *Konzentrationslager Buchenwald, 1937–1945: Begleitband zur ständigen historischen Ausstellung* (Göttingen: Wallstein, 1999), p. 114; additional statistics on transports can be found in Harry Stein, "Das Sonderlager im Konzentrationslager Buchenwald nach den Pogromen 1938," in Kingreen, ed., *"Nach der Kristallnacht,"* pp. 19–54.

30. The expansion of the camps' capacity prior to the pogrom has sometimes been cited, incorrectly, as evidence that the pogrom had been planned well in advance. See, e.g., K. J. Ball-Kaduri, "Die Vorplanung der Kristallnacht," *Zeitschrift für die Geschichte der Juden* 3 (1966), pp. 211–216; and Vincent C. Frank, "Neuer Blick auf die Reichskristallnacht: Ungereimtheiten in der Vorgeschichte und bei den Folgen," *Neue Zürcher Zeitung*, 4 November 1998. In actuality, Heinrich Himmler had ordered the expansion of the camps as part of a broader campaign he wished to wage against "asocials," "work-averse" Germans, recidivist criminals, and other categories of suspects. Benz and Distel, eds., *Der Ort des Terrors*, vol. 1, pp. 156–157.

31. Stein, "Sonderlager," pp. 27–30.

32. On camp procedures see Karin Orth, *Das System der nationalsozialistischen Konzentrationslager: Eine politische Organisationsgeschichte* (Hamburg: Hamburger Edition, 1999); and Wolfgang Sofsky, *Die Ordnung des Terrors: Das Konzentrationslager* (Frankfurt: Fischer, 1993).

33. Private Reports on Jews in Germany, Wiener Library, London (hereafter Wiener Library Reports), no. 227.

34. Wiener Library Reports nos. 8, 227.

35. Stein, "Sonderlager," pp. 32–42. For reports on conditions in Buchenwald in November 1938 see also Wiener Library Reports nos. 52, 82, 162, 202, 203, and 216.

36. Stein, ed., *Konzentrationslager Buchenwald, 1937–1945,* p. 78.

37. On Dachau, see Wiener Library Reports nos. 69, 175, 184, 213, and 219. On Sachsenhausen, see Wiener Library Reports nos. 8, 77, 99, 194, 225, 227, 323, and 528.

38. Wiener Library Reports no. 194.

39. According to Benz and Distel, *Ort des Terrors,* vol. 1, p. 162, the deaths numbered 185 in Dachau and 233 in Buchenwald. They do not provide a figure for Sachsenhausen. In Stanislav Zámečník, *Das war Dachau* (Luxembourg: Stiftung Comité International de Dachau, 2002), p. 106, the figure for Jewish deaths in Dachau between 11 November 1938 and 28 February 1939 is 243.

40. Fernschreiben Nr. 14690, 16 November 1938, Bundesarchiv Berlin, R 58/276.

41. Fernschreiben Nr. 14927, 24 November 1938, Bundesarchiv Berlin, R 58/276.

42. Stein, "Sonderlager," p. 26.

43. Fernschreiben Nr. 14956, 25 November 1938, Bundesarchiv Berlin, R 58/276.

44. Fernschreiben Nr. 15032, 28 November 1938, Bundesarchiv Berlin, R 58/276.

45. Marion A. Kaplan, *Between Dignity and Despair: Jewish Life in Nazi Germany* (New York: Oxford University Press, 1998), pp. 125–129.

46. See, e.g., *Das Tagebuch der Hertha Nathorff: Berlin–New York, Aufzeichnungen 1933 bis 1945,* ed. Wolfgang Benz (Munich: Oldenbourg, 1987), pp. 119–137.

47. Fernschreiben Nr. 15431, 2 December 1938, Bundesarchiv Berlin, R 58/276.

48. Fernschreiben Nr. 638, 21 January 1939, Bundesarchiv Berlin, R 58/276.

49. Benz and Distel, eds., *Ort des Terrors,* vol. 1, p. 162.

50. Geheimes Staatspolizeiamt to Staatspolizeileitstellen, 31 January 1939, Bundesarchiv Berlin, R 58/276. The document is dated the end of January 1939, but it refers to a practice that had been in place for some time.

51. *Tagebuch der Hertha Nathorff,* p. 140.

52. Ben Barkow, *Alfred Wiener and the Making of the Holocaust Library* (London: Vallentine Mitchell, 1997), pp. 72–73.

53. See the two Fernschreiben from Heydrich to Staatspolizeistellen on 10 November 1938, 3051-PS, IMT, vol. 31, pp. 518–519.

54. Comments by Heydrich in "Stenographische Niederschrift von einem Teil der Besprechung über die Judenfrage unter Vorsitz von Feldmarschall Goering im RLM am 12. November 1938, 11:00 Uhr," IMT, document 1816-PS, vol. 28, pp. 514–515.

55. See, for example, letter from Jüttner, 29 November 1938, IMT, 1721-PS, vol. 27, pp. 485–486, in which Jüttner distributes an order from Rudolf Hess reiterating the instruction that looted items be turned over to local Gestapo offices.

56. Rundschreiben 195/38, Hess to Reichsleiter, Gauleiter, etc., 7 December 1938, Bundesarchiv Berlin NS 6/231.

57. Lothar Gruchmann, *Justiz im Dritten Reich 1933–1940: Anpassung und Unterwerfung in der Ära Gürtner,* 3rd ed. (Munich: Oldenbourg, 2001), pp. 488–489.

58. Fernschreiben, Heydrich to Staatspolizeistellen, 10 December 1938, Bundesarchiv Berlin, R 58/276.

59. Stellv. D. Führers, Anordnung 200/38, 14 December 1938, Bundesarchiv Berlin, NS 6/231.

60. Gruchmann, *Justiz im Dritten Reich,* pp. 494–495.

61. "Im Namen des Führers," judgment on Heinrich Frey, February 1939, Bundesarchiv Berlin, NS 36/13.

62. "Im Namen des Führers," judgment on Johann Hintersteiner and Friedrich Schmidinger, February 1939, Bundesarchiv Berlin, NS 36/13.

63. The decisions of the NSDAP Oberstes Parteigericht in sixteen cases are contained in Bundesarchiv Berlin, NS 36/13. A summary prepared by the court is contained in NSDAP-OPG, "Bericht über die Vorgänge . . . ," 13 February 1939, IMT, 3063-PS, vol. 32, pp. 21–29. For a summary of several cases see Gruchmann, *Justiz im Dritten Reich,* pp. 492–493; and especially Donald McKale, "A Case of Nazi 'Justice'—The Punishment of Party Members In-

volved in the Kristallnacht, 1938," *Jewish Social Studies* 35, nos. 3–4 (July–October 1973), pp. 228–238.

64. Gruchmann, *Justiz im Dritten Reich,* p. 492.

6. "A Tempest in a Teapot"

Sections of Chapter 6 appeared earlier in Alan E. Steinweis, "The Trials of Herschel Grynszpan: Anti-Jewish Policy and German Propaganda, 1938–1942," *German Studies Review* 31 (2008): 471–488, and are used here with the permission of the journal.

1. Fritz Hausjell and Theo Venus, "'. . . wie's ihm ums Herz ist.' Eine Radioreportage zum Judenpogrom 'Reichskristallnacht.' Ausgestrahlt vom Sender Wien am 10. November 1938," in *Medien und Zeit* 3, no. 3 (1988), pp. 31–33. Excerpts in Gerhard Botz, *Nationalsozialismus in Wien: Machtübernahme, Herrschaftssicherung, Radikalisierung 1938/39* (Vienna: Mandelbaum, 2008), pp. 509–512.

2. Stapostelle Bielefeld II B 2, "Rundverfügung," 14 November 1938, in Otto Dov Kulka and Eberhard Jäckel, eds., *Die Juden in den geheimen NS-Stimmungsberichten, 1933–1945* (Düsseldorf: Droste, 2004) (hereafter *Stimmungsberichte*), document 2558. Citations to the Stimmungsberichte here include document serial numbers for the complete collection on the CD-ROM accompanying the abridged printed volume.

3. Oberbürgermeister Bielefeld, "Aktion gegen Juden am 9./10.1938," 22 November 1938, *Stimmungsberichte,* document 2662.

4. The following documents are all in *Stimmungsberichte:* Landrat Büren, "Bericht für den 9.10.11.1938," 18 November 1938, document 2628; Bürgermeister Dringenberg-Gehrden, "Bericht für den 9./10.11.1938," 18 November 1938, document 2634; Oberbürgermeister Herford, "Bericht für den 9./10.1939," 18 November 1938, document 2666.

5. Landrat Halle/Westf, "Aktion gegen Juden, 18.11.1938," *Stimmungsberichte,* document 2657.

6. E.g., following in *Stimmungsberichte:* Gendarmerie Bega, "Bericht für den 10.11.1938," 18 November 1938, document 2617; Bürgermeister Amt Peckelsheim, "Bericht für den 10.11.1938," 17 November 1938, document 2722.

7. Landrat Höxter, "Aktion gegen die Juden," 18 November 1938, *Stimmungsberichte,* document 2671.

8. Bürgermeister Amt Borgentreich, "Bericht für den 10.11.1938," 17 November 1938, *Stimmungsberichte,* document 2624.

9. Stadt Minden, "Bericht für den 10.11.1938," 18 November 1938, *Stimmungsberichte,* document 2705.

10. Bürgmeister Atteln, "Aktion gegen Juden am 10.11.1938," 17 November 1938, *Stimmungsberichte,* document 2600.

11. Bürgermeister Amt Neuhaus, "Aktion gegen die Juden am 10.11.1938," 17 November 1938, *Stimmungsberichte,* document 2712.

12. Bürgermeister Detmold, "Bericht für den 9.10.1938," 18 November 1938, *Stimmungsberichte,* document 2632.

13. Bürgermeister Bad Oeynhausen, "Bericht," 17 November 1938, *Stimmungsberichte,* document 2611.

14. Bürgermeister Bückeburg, "Bericht für den 10.11.1938," 17 November 1938, *Stimmungsberichte,* document 2626.

15. Landrat Höxter, "Bericht für 10.11.1938," 18 November 1938, *Stimmungsberichte,* document 2671.

16. Ian Kershaw, *Popular Opinion and Political Dissent in the Third Reich: Bavaria, 1933–1945* (Oxford: Oxford University Press, 1983).

17. Landrat Bielefeld, "Bericht für den 10.11.1938," 18 November 1938, *Stimmungsberichte,* document 2620.

18. Private Reports on Jews in Germany, Wiener Library, London, no. 23.

19. Peter Longerich, *"Davon haben wir nichts gewusst!" Die Deutschen und die Judenverfolgung 1933–1945* (Munich: Siedler, 2006); David Bankier, *The Germans and the Final Solution: Public Opinion under Nazism* (Oxford: Blackwell, 1992).

20. Longerich, *"Davon haben wir nichts gewusst!"* pp. 132–134.

21. On the origins and application of the law, see Bernward Dörner, *"Heimtücke": Das Gesetz als Waffe. Kontrolle, Abschreckung und Verfolgung in Deutschland 1933–1945* (Paderborn: Schöningh, 1998).

22. Ian Kershaw has calculated that of the 5,650 cases of so-called Heimtücke brought before a Sondergericht in Munich during the years of Nazi rule, sixty-seven, or just over 1 percent, related to defendants who had criticized the regime's anti-Jewish policies. Of these sixty-seven cases, thirty-one were brought between November 1938 and March 1939. Ian Kershaw, "Antisemitismus und Volksmeinung. Reaktionen auf die Judenverfolgung," in *Bayern in der NS-Zeit,* vol. 2: Herrschaft und Gesellschaft im Konflikt, Teil A, ed. Martin Broszat and Elke Fröhlich (Munich: Oldenbourg, 1979), pp. 336–337.

23. United States Holocaust Museum Archive, ZC 4802, 9619.

24. United States Holocaust Museum Archive, ZC 14759. The prosecution was ultimately dropped in late 1939, after the beginning of the war.

25. United States Holocaust Museum Archive, ZC 13373, 7745.

26. Ekkehard Ellinger, *Deutsche Orientalistik zur Zeit des Nationalsozialismus 1933–1945* (Edingen: Deux Mondes, 2006), pp. 66–67.

27. An analysis by the SD of the morale reports submitted from around Germany after the pogrom concluded: "die angewandten Methoden beim Vorgehen gegen die Juden wurden insbesondere aus den Reihen der Wehrmachtsangehörigen verurteilt." SD-Hauptamt II 112, "Bericht für November 1938," 7 December 1938, *Stimmungsberichte,* document 2550.

28. *Spiegelbild einer Verschwörung: Die Opposition gegen Hitler und der Staatsstreich vom 20. Juli 1944 in der SD-Berichterstattung. Geheime Dokumente aus dem ehemaligen Reichssicherheitshauptamt,* 2 vols. (Stuttgart: Seewald, 1984), vol 1, pp. 449–451, 471–474. It should be noted that the statements documented here were given during interrogation and probably as a result of torture.

29. Wolfgang Venohr, *Stauffenberg: Symbol des Widerstands. Eine politische Biographie* (Munich: Herbig, 2000), p. 95.

30. Ulrich von Hassell, *Die Hassell-Tagebücher 1938–1944,* ed. Friedrich Freiherr Hiller von Gaertringen (Berlin: Siedler, 1988), p. 62.

31. Helmuth James Graf von Moltke to Lionel Curtis, 20 November 1938, in Ger van Roon, ed., *Helmuth James Graf von Moltke: Völkerrecht im Dienste der Menschen* (Berlin: Siedler, 1986), pp. 98–99.

32. Helmut Krausnick, ed., *Helmuth Groscurth: Tagebücher eines Abwehroffiziers 1938–1940* (Stuttgart: DVA, 1970), p. 157.

33. Saul Friedländer, *Nazi Germany and the Jews, 1939–1945: The Years of Extermination* (New York: HarperCollins, 2007), pp. 216–219.

34. Hildegard von Kotze, ed., *Heeresadjutant bei Hitler: Aufzeichnungen des Major Engels,* entry for 11 November 1938.

35. See, e.g., the following in *Stimmungsberichte:* Bezirksamt Ebermannstadt, "Bericht für November 1938," 2 December 1938, document 2635; Regierungspräsident Oberbayern, "Bericht für Dezember 1938," 9 January 1939, document 2786; Regierungspräsident Schwaben und Neuburg, "Bericht für Dezember 1938," 7 January 1939, document 2789. Longerich, *"Davon haben wir nichts gewusst!"* p. 145, suggests that the absence of criticism in the reports from early 1939 could mean that the German officials who drafted them were no longer interested in a candid assessment of public opinion with regard to

the Jewish question. My own conclusion is different: namely, that the absence of criticism in the reports reflects an actual diminution of criticism resulting from what Germans perceived as a turning-away from the barbarism of the pogrom.

36. A great deal has been written about the international response to the Kristallnacht. For useful summaries of the subject and the relevant scholarship see the special issue of the *Zeitschrift für Geschichtswissenschaft* 46 (1998), and especially the article by Hermann Graml, "Effekte der 'Reichskristallnacht' auf die britische und amerikanische Deutschlandpolitik," pp. 991–997.

37. Günther Gillessen, *Auf verlorenem Posten. Die Frankfurter Zeitung im Dritten Reich* (Berlin: Siedler, 1986), pp. 376–378.

38. Anordnung, Goebbels to Gauleiter, 10 November 1938, reproduced in Wolf-Arno Kropat, *"Reichskristallnacht": Der Judenpogrom vom 7. bis 10. November 1938—Urheber, Täter, Hintergründe* (Wiesbaden: Kommission für die Geschichte der Juden in Hessen, 1997), p. 233.

39. Nr. 3244, "Glossenkonferenz," 12 November 1938, *NS-Presseanweisungen der Vorkriegszeit: Edition und Dokumentation* (Munich: Saur, 1999), vol. 6, p. 1070.

40. Nr. 3287, 17 November 1938, *NS-Presseanweisungen der Vorkriegszeit,* vol. 6, p. 1085.

41. Nr. 3266, 15 November 1938, and Nr. 3287, 17 November 1938, *NS-Presseanweisungen der Vorkriegszeit,* vol. 6, pp. 1076 and 1084, respectively.

42. Nr. 3310, 19 November 1938, *NS-Presseanweisungen der Vorkriegszeit,* vol. 6, pp. 1095–1096.

43. *Die Juden in Deutschland* (Munich: Eher, 1936); Alfred Rosenberg, *Unmoral im Talmud* (Bayreuth: Deutscher Volksverlag, 1935); Nr. 3311, 19 November 1938, *NS-Presseanweisungen der Vorkriegszeit,* vol. 6, p. 1096.

44. Nr. 3287, 17 November 1938, and Nr. 3337, 22 November 1938, *NS-Presseanweisungen der Vorkriegszeit,* vol. 6, pp. 1085–1089 and 1105, respectively. On Frank and his institute see Alan E. Steinweis, *Studying the Jew: Scholarly Antisemitism in Nazi Germany* (Cambridge, Mass.: Harvard University Press, 2006).

45. *Die Tagebücher von Joseph Goebbels,* ed. Elke Fröhlich, 30 vols. (Munich: Saur, 1993–2007) (hereafter *Goebbels-Tagebücher*), part I, vol. 6, entry for 10 November 1938.

46. Nr. 3229, Pressekonferenz für Auslandspresse, 11 November 1938, *NS-Presseanweisungen der Vorkriegszeit,* vol. 6, p. 1065.

47. *Goebbels-Tagebücher,* part I, vol. 6, entry for 17 November 1938.

48. Nr. 3247, 14 November 1938; DNB-Rundruf Nr. 77, 15 November 1938; Nr. 3265, 15 November 1938; and Nr. 3276, "Streng vertrauliche Mitteilung an die Schriftleitungen," 15 November 1938, all in *NS-Presseanweisungen der Vorkriegszeit,* vol. 6, pp. 1071, 1074, 1076, and 1079, respectively.

49. Nr. 3287, 17 November 1938, *NS-Presseanweisungen der Vorkriegszeit,* vol. 6, pp. 1084–1085.

50. Ibid.; Nr. 3290, 18 November 1938, *NS-Presseanweisungen der Vorkriegszeit,* vol. 6, p. 1090.

51. Nr. 3276, "Streng vertrauliche Mitteilung an die Schriftleitungen," 15 November 1938, and Nr. 3287, 17 November 1938, *NS-Presseanweisungen der Vorkriegszeit,* vol. 6, pp. 1079 and 1084, respectively.

52. Radio programming schedules for Reichsrundfunkgesellschaft in Bundesarchiv Berlin, R 78/1309–1310.

53. *Goebbels-Tagebücher,* part I, vol. 6, 27 November 1938.

54. Dirksen to Foreign Ministry, 17 November 1938, *Documents on German Foreign Policy 1918–1945* (hereafter DGFP), series D, vol. 4 (Washington, D.C.: United States Government Printing Office, 1951), document 269.

55. Dieckhoff to Foreign Ministry, 14 November 1938, DGFP, document 501.

56. *Goebbels-Tagebücher,* part I, vol. 6, 20 November 1938.

57. Michael Marrus, "The Strange Story of Herschel Grynszpan," *American Scholar* 57, no. 1 (Winter 1988), p. 73; Helmut Heiber, "Der Fall Grünspan," *Vierteljahrshefte für Zeitgeschichte* 5 (1957), pp. 142–145.

58. Institut für Zeitgeschichte, Munich (hereafter IfZ), Zs 618, Zeugenschrift Friedrich Grimm.

59. Memo by Diewerge, 11 November 1938, Bundesarchiv Berlin, R55/2079; Zeugenschrift Friedrich Grimm, Zs 618, IfZ. On Grimm's relationship to France see Roland Ray, *Annäherung an Frankreich im Dienste Hitlers? Otto Abetz und die deutsche Frankreichpolitik 1930–1942* (Munich: Oldenbourg, 2000).

60. Zs 593, Zeugenschrift Diewerge, IfZ.

61. Their association, it is worth noting, endured beyond the collapse of Nazism, as both men continued to move in the same extreme right-wing political circles in North Rhine–Westphalia in the 1950s. While Diewerge was a key member of the Naumann Circle, Grimm served more in the role of an apologist and legal consultant. Norbert Frei, *Vergangenheitspolitik: Die Anfänge der Bundesrepublik und die NS-Vergangenheit* (Munich: Beck, 1996), pp. 165–

166, 380–383; Ulrich Herbert, *Best: Biographische Studien über Radikalismus, Weltanschauung und Vernunft 1903–1989,* 3rd ed. (Bonn: Dietz, 1996), pp. 449–453.

62. Diewerge to Kastner, 24 November 1938, Bundesarchiv Berlin, R55/21007. The story, which had absolutely no basis in fact, had originated in Johannesburg and then made its way to Diewerge in Berlin via the Foreign Office. See AA to Promi, 6 December 1938, Bundesarchiv Berlin, R55/21007.

63. Grimm to Diewerge, 12 January 1939, Bundesarchiv Berlin, R55/20979.

64. *Politische Justiz: Die Krankheit unserer Zeit* (Bonn: Scheur, 1953), pp. 118–119. See also ZS 618, Zeugenschrift Friedrich Grimm, IfZ.

65. This is evident in the book that Diewerge published about Grynszpan in 1939, *Anschlag gegen den Frieden* (Munich: Eher, 1939), as well as in a manuscript prepared in 1939 and published in 1942 by Friedrich Grimm, *Der Grünspan Prozess* (Nuremberg: Willmy, 1942).

66. Memo by Diewerge, 19 December 1938, Bundesarchiv Berlin, R55/20979.

67. Beate Kosmala, "Pressereaktionen in Polen auf den Novemberpogrom 1938 in Deutschland und die Lage der polnischen Juden," *Zeitschrift für Geschichtswissenschaft* 46 (1998), pp. 1034–1045.

68. Memo by Grimm, 2 May 1939, Bundesarchiv Berlin, R55/20982.

69. Report from Deutsche Botschaft, Paris, 28 March 1939, Politisches Archiv des Auswärtigen Amtes, Berlin, R 46854.

70. See especially Memo by Grimm, 18 March 1939, and Memo by Grimm, 28 April 1939, both in Bundesarchiv Berlin, R55/20983.

71. Memo by Diewerge, 24 January 1939, Bundesarchiv Berlin, R55/20979.

72. Diewerge to Goebbels, 6 June 1939, Bundesarchiv Berlin, R55/20985.

73. Diewerge to Goebbels, 20 April 1939, Bundesarchiv Berlin, R55/20979; Diewerge, *Anschlag gegen den Frieden.*

74. Deutsche Botschaft, Paris, to AA, 24.7.39, Politisches Archiv des Auswärtigen Amtes, Berlin, R 46856.

75. "Betrifft: Grünspann-Prozess," August 1939, Politisches Archiv des Auswärtigen Amtes, Berlin, R 46856.

76. The circumstances of Grynszpan's capture by the Germans were quite complicated. The clearest presentation is Marrus, "Strange Story," pp. 74–75.

77. Documents in Politisches Archiv des Auswärtigen Amtes, Berlin, R 46856.

78. Grimm, "Denkschrift über die in Paris im Juni–Juli 1940 von der

deutschen geheimen Feldpolizei in der Grünspan-Sache beschlagnahmten Akten," no date, Politisches Archiv des Auswärtigen Amtes, Berlin, R 27518.

79. Anklageschrift, 16 October 1942, Bundesarchiv Berlin, R60II/79.

80. Diewerge to Goebbels, 29 October 1941; Diewerge to Staatssekretär, 13 November 1941; and Aktenvermerk "Betrifft Grünspan-Prozess," 5 December 1941, all in Bundesarchiv Berlin, R55/20985.

81. *Goebbels-Tagebücher,* part II, vol. 4, entries for 2 and 3 April 1942. Freisler was nevertheless soon rewarded for his loyal service to the Nazi movement when Hitler appointed him to the presidency of the Volksgerichtshof, where he would later notoriously preside over the show trials of many members of the anti-Nazi resistance.

82. Diewerge to Goebbels, 29 October 1941, Bundesarchiv Berlin, R55/20985.

83. Alfred Gottwaldt and Diana Schulle, *Die "Judendeportationen" aus dem Deutschen Reich 1941–1945* (Wiesbaden: Marix, 2005), p. 68.

84. "Führerinformation," March 1942, Bundesarchiv Berlin, R55/20985. Schlegelberger himself had been well aware of the details of the "Final Solution" at the time the Grynszpan trial was being prepared. See *Trials of the War Criminals before the Nuernberg Military Tribunals,* vol. 3: *The Justice Case* (Washington: United States Government Printing Office, 1951), especially pp. 646–650.

85. *Goebbels-Tagebücher,* part II, vol. 3, entry for 27 March 1942; Jeffrey Herf, *The Jewish Enemy: Nazi Propaganda during World War II and the Holocaust* (Cambridge, Mass.: Harvard University Press, 2006), pp. 222–223. Note 133 on p. 343 indicates that some of the most extreme antisemitic propaganda posters were distributed in March 1942.

86. For example, Bormann to Goebbels, 1 April 1942, Bundesarchiv Berlin, R55/20985, and *Goebbels-Tagebücher,* part II, vol. 4, entry for 2 April 1942. Goebbels's deputy also met with Hitler to discuss the trial: Zs 618, Zeugenschrift Friedrich Grimm, IfZ.

87. Henry Picker, *Hitlers Tischgespräche im Führerhauptquartier, 1941–1942* (Stuttgart: Seewald, 1963), entry for 26 March 1942, p. 210.

88. "Ablauf der Hauptverhandlungen gegen Grünspan" and "Voraussichtlicher Ablauf der Hauptverhandlung gegen Grünspan," April 1938, both in Bundesarchiv Berlin, R55/20985.

89. "Besprechung über den Grünspan-Prozess," 7 April 1942, Bundesarchiv

Berlin, R55/20985. In 1943, Kittel was to publish an article on precisely this subject in a journal sponsored by the Propaganda Ministry. See Gerhard Kittel, "Die Behandlung des Nichtjuden nach dem Talmud," *Archiv für Judenfragen* (1943), pp. 7–17. It is reasonable to assume that this article was related to Kittel's preparations to testify in the Grynszpan trial. On Kittel's activities as an academic expert on Jews see Steinweis, *Studying the Jew,* pp. 66–76.

90. Herf, *Jewish Enemy,* pp. 113–114.

91. On Schönemann see Philipp Gassert, *Amerika im Dritten Reich: Ideologie, Propaganda und Volksmeinung 1933–1945* (Stuttgart: Franz Steiner, 1997), especially pp. 117–127; quotation p. 42.

92. Friedrich Schönemann, *Die aggressive Wirtschaftspolitik der Vereinigten Staaten in Südamerika und die Stellung Deutschlands* (Stuttgart: Ferdinand Enke, 1939), pp. 51–52; Friedrich Schönemann, *Amerika und der Nationalsozialismus* (Berlin: Junker und Dünnhaupt, 1934), pp. 11–12. In 1943, i.e., subsequent to the events described here, Schönemann published *Die Vereinigten Staaten von Amerika* (Berlin: Junker und Dünnhaupt, 1943), which also called attention to the dangers posed by Jewish power in America.

93. Telegramm, Schleier to AA, 30 January 1942, Politisches Archiv des Auswärtigen Amtes, Berlin, R 27515.

94. Schnellbrief, Günther to AA, 21 March 1942, Politisches Archiv des Auswärtigen Amtes, Berlin, R 27515.

95. Michael R. Marrus and Robert O. Paxton, *Vichy France and the Jews* (New York: Basic Books, 1981; reprint: Stanford: Stanford University Press, 1995), pp. 58–63; Gerhard L. Weinberg, *The Foreign Policy of Hitler's Germany: Starting World War Two, 1937–1939* (Chicago: University of Chicago Press, 1980), p. 529.

96. "Fragen an Bonnet," April 1942, and a two-page fragment of an undated report (folios 261–262), both in Bundesarchiv Berlin, R55/20985; Günther to Krümmer, 30 April 1942, Politisches Archiv des Auswärtigen Amtes, Berlin, R 27515; *Goebbels-Tagebücher,* part II, vol. 3, entry for 13 February 1942. After the war, Bonnet denied that he would have followed through on the plan to testify. See Marrus, "Strange Story," p. 76.

97. "Ablauf der Hauptverhandlungen gegen Grünspan" and "Voraussichtlicher Ablauf der Hauptverhandlung gegen Grünspan," April 1938, both in Bundesarchiv Berlin, R55/20985.

98. The first mention of the allegation was in a Gestapo report drafted in

the autumn of 1941. The report itself has not survived, but its existence is referred to in "Führerinformation," 17 April 1942, Bundesarchiv Berlin, R55/20985.

99. Hans-Jürgen Döscher, "Das Attentat auf den deutschen Diplomaten Ernst vom Rath am 7. November 1938: Neuere Forschungen zu den Hintergründen," *Geschichte in Wissenschaft und Unterricht* 54 (2003), pp. 241–244; Hans-Jürgen Döscher, *"Reichskristallnacht": Die Novemberpogrome 1938* (Munich: Propyläen, 2000), pp. 167–171.

100. Zs 593, Zeugenschrift Diewerge, and Zs 618, Zeugenschrift Friedrich Grimm, IfZ.

101. *Goebbels-Tagebücher,* part II, vol. 3, entry for 24 January 1942.

102. Memo by Freisler, 23 January 1942, Bundesarchiv Berlin, R55/20985.

103. Diewerge to Goebbels, 2 April 1942, Bundesarchiv Berlin, R55/20985.

104. Döscher claims that the Justice Ministry added the sodomy charge in an effort to torpedo the trial. Döscher, *"Reichskristallnacht,"* p. 165. Goebbels, however, did not interpret the action in this way. Instead, he concluded that the lawyers in the Justice Ministry were "foolish" (*töricht*), politically naive, and "psychologically not very adept." *Goebbels-Tagebücher,* part II, vol. 4, entries for 5 and 14 April 1942.

105. *Goebbels-Tagebücher,* part II, vol. 4, entry for 17 April 1942.

106. Memo by Krümmer, 16 April 1942, Politisches Archiv des Auswärtigen Amtes, Berlin, A-AA R 27515.

107. Führerinformation, 17 April 1942, Bundesarchiv Berlin, R55/20985.

108. Zs 593, Zeugenschrift Diewerge, and Zs 618, Zeugenschrift Grimm, IfZ.

109. Serge Klarsfeld, *Vichy-Auschwitz. Die "Endlösung der Judenfrage" in Frankreich* (Darmstadt: Wissenschaftliche Buchgesellschaft, 2007), pp. 53–77, 408–409.

110. Marrus and Paxton, *Vichy France,* pp. 227–234.

111. *Goebbels-Tagebücher,* part II, vol. 4, 12 and 14 May 1942.

112. "Führerinformation" 1942 Nr. 60, 3 July 1942, reproduced in Döscher, *"Reichskristallnacht,"* p. 184.

113. Döscher, *"Reichskristallnacht,"* p. 172.

114. The theory of Grynszpan's survival was promoted in Heiber, "Fall Grünspan." For a persuasive refutation see Ron Roizen, "Herschel Grynszpan: The Fate of a Forgotten Assassin," *Holocaust and Genocide Studies* 1/2 (1986), pp. 217–228.

115. Döscher, *"Reichskristallnacht,"* p. 173.

116. Max Domarus, *Hitler: Reden und Proklamationen 1932–1945* (Neustadt: Schmidt, 1963), vol. II, p. 2237; Herf, *Jewish Enemy,* pp. 261–262.

7. "Defendants and Witnesses Openly Hold Back with the Truth"

1. Reinhard Henkys, *Die nationalsozialistischen Gewaltverbrechen: Geschichte und Gericht* (Stuttgart: Kreuz, 1964), pp. 191–197; Annette Weinke, *Die Verfolgung von NS-Tätern im geteilten Deutschland: Vergangenheitsbewältigungen 1949–1969* (Paderborn: Schöningh, 2002), pp. 40–43.

2. Institut für Zeitgeschichte, Munich (hereafter IfZ), Urteil, SG Bremen, 11 February 1948, Gb 11.06.

3. Lists of cases classified by Staatsanwaltschaft, compiled in 1947 (appended to Wolf to Weigert, 15 July 1947), OMGUS collection, IfZ.

4. Andreas Eichmüller, "Die Strafverfolgung von NS-Verbrechen seit 1945: Eine Zwischenbilanz," *Vierteljahrshefte für Zeitgeschichte* 56, no. 4 (2008), pp. 621–640; and Edith Raim, "The Punishment of Crimes against Jews in West Germany, 1945–1950," paper presented at "Lessons and Legacies" conference, Northwestern University, November 2008. These sources represent the results of a major survey of postwar trials for Nazi crimes undertaken by the Institut für Zeitgeschichte in Munich.

5. This conclusion is based on the presence of only a handful of such cases in a collection of East German trial materials formerly deposited in the Bundesarchiv Berlin, Aussenstelle Dahlwitz-Hoppegarten, copies of which can be found in the United States Holocaust Memorial Museum Archive, RG-14. An official East German summary of prosecutions for Nazi crimes published in 1965 includes only two such cases in a list of several hundred notable trials conducted after the creation of East Germany. See *Die Haltung der beiden deutschen Staaten zu den Nazi und Kriegsverbrechen: Eine Dokumentation* (Berlin: Ministerium der Justiz der DDR, 1965), pp. 55–56. Once completed, the survey of East German trial records currently under way at the Institut für Zeitgeschichte, Munich, will allow for a more precise estimate. Existing scholarship on the adjudication of Nazi war crimes in the Soviet Zone and East Germany offers no specific insight into the way Kristallnacht-related cases were handled. See, for example, Weinke, *Die Verfolgung von NS-Tätern;* and Christian Meyer-Seitz, *Die Verfolgung von NS-Tätern in der Sowjetischen Besatzungszone* (Berlin: Spitz, 1998).

6. Thomas Albrich and Michael Guggenberger, "'Nur selten steht einer dieser Novemberverbrecher vor Gericht': Die strafrechtliche Verfolgung der Täter der so genannten 'Reichskristallnacht' in Österreich," in Thomas Albrich et al., eds., *Holocaust und Kriegsverbrechen vor Gericht: Der Fall Österreich* (Innsbruck: Studien Verlag, 2006), pp. 26–56.

7. A good example is the town of Memmingen, where sixty-nine investigations were opened in 1946 and 1947, only one of which ultimately went to trial. Information from IfZ database courtesy of Dr. Andreas Eichmüller.

8. Urteil, LG Giessen, 12 April 1950, IfZ, Gg 01.33.

9. Michael Stolleis, *The Law under the Swastika: Studies on Legal History in Nazi Germany,* trans. Thomas Dunlap (Chicago: University of Chicago Press, 1998), pp. 175–178.

10. See, e.g., Oberstaatsanwalt Bamberg to Generalstaatsanwalt Bamberg, 24 February 1947, OMGUS collection, IfZ.

11. Urteil, LG Marburg, March 1952, IfZ, Gm 03.07.

12. Urteil, LG Aschaffenburg, 19 November 1948, IfZ, Ga 05.01.

13. OMGUS Legal Division to Judge J. W. Madden, 1 March 1946, as well as numerous documents from 1946 and 1947 with subject "Criminal Prosecution before German Courts of Former Party Members for Acts against Humanity Committed against German Nationals," OMGUS collection, IfZ.

14. Oberstaatsanwalt Aschaffenburg to Generalstaatsanwalt Bamberg, 25 February 1947, OMGUS collection, IfZ.

15. Urteil, LG Aschaffenburg, 19 November 1948, IfZ, Ga 05.01; Urteil, LG Hanau, 14 February 1949, IfZ, Gh 04.03.

16. Urteil, LG Giessen, January 1949, IfZ, Gg 01.08; Urteil, LG Marburg, 1951, IfZ, Gm 03.04; Urteil, LG Giessen, 12 September 1949, IfZ, Gg 01.30; Urteil, LG Giessen, 8 April 1948, IfZ, Gg 01.41; Urteil, LG Coburg, 8 September 1949, IfZ, Gc 02.01/2.

17. Urteil, LG Marburg, 17 August 1951, IfZ Gm 03.11; Urteil, LG Giessen, 7 March 1951, IfZ, Gg 01.43; Urteil, LG Darmstadt, 16 July 1948, IfZ, Gd 01.25.

18. Urteil, SG Bremen, 11 February 1948, IfZ, Gb 11.06.

19. Urteil, LG Hanau, 14 February 1949, IfZ, Gh 04.03. Also see Urteil, LG Darmstadt, 16 July 1948, IfZ Gd 01.25; and Urteil, LG Darmstadt, 14 December 1945, IfZ, Gd 01.28.

20. Urteil, LG Giessen, 22 December 1948 (and revised judgment of 31 May 1949), IfZ, Gg 01.31.

21. Urteil, LG Giessen, 3 November 1948, IfZ, Gg 01.37.

22. *Die Verfolgung nationalsozialistischer Straftaten im Gebiet der Bundesrepublik Deutschland seit 1945,* ed. Bundesjustizministerium (Bonn: n.p., 1964), pp. 78, 81, 83, 84, 87, 88, 90, and 93.

23. Urteil, SG Bremen, 11 February 1948, IfZ, Gb 11.06.

24. Wolf to Weigert, 15 July 1947, OMGUS collection, IfZ.

25. See *Allgemeine Wochenzeitung der Juden in Deutschland,* 30 December 1949, 20 January 1950, 10 March 1950, 19 January 1951.

26. Albrich and Guggenberger, "'Nur selten steht einer dieser Novemberverbrecher vor Gericht,'" pp. 32, 43, 46, and 48.

27. Norbert Frei, *Adenauer's Germany and the Nazi Past: The Politics of Amnesty and Integration,* trans. Joel Golb (New York: Columbia University Press, 2002), pp. 5–25.

28. Ibid., p. 8.

29. Urteil, LG Giessen, 18 November 1949 (and revised judgments of 18 November 1949 and 24 March 1950), IfZ, Gg 01.21.

30. Urteil, LG Giessen, 14 April 1949, IfZ, Gg 01.24; Urteil, LG Giessen, 13 November 1947, IfZ, Gg 01.27; Urteil, LG Giessen, 12 April 1950, IfZ, Gg 01.33.

31. See, for example, the pamphlet authored by Hermann Graml, *Der 9. November 1938* (Bonn: Bundeszentrale für Heimatdienst, 1953), of which subsequent editions were published in 1954 and 1957.

32. The following discussion is drawn largely from Y. Michal Bodemann, "Reconstructions of History: From Jewish Memory to Nationalized Commemoration of Kristallnacht in Germany," in Y. Michal Bodemann, ed., *Jews, Germans, Memory: Reconstructions of Jewish Life in Germany* (Ann Arbor: University of Michigan Press, 1996), pp. 179–223; Harald Schmid, *Erinnern an den "Tag der Schuld": Der Novemberpogrom von 1938 in der deutschen Geschichtspolitik* (Hamburg: Ergebnisse, 2001).

33. Schmid, *Erinnern an den "Tag der Schuld,"* p. 78, note 41.

34. Jeffrey Herf, "Philipp Jenninger and the Dangers of Speaking Clearly," *Partisan Review* 56 (1989), pp. 225–236. For an alternative interpretation that is critical of Jenninger see Elisabeth Domansky, "'Kristallnacht,' the Holocaust and German Unity: The Meaning of November 9 as an Anniversary in Germany," *History and Memory* 4, no. 1 (1992), pp. 60–94.

35. An audio recording and the full text of the speech are available at www.mediaculture-online.de (accessed 25 May 2009).

36. The following is drawn largely from Harald Schmid, *Antifaschismus und Judenverfolgung: Die "Reichskristallnacht" als politischer Gedenktag in der DDR* (Göttingen: V and R Unipress, 2004); see also Thomas C. Fox, *Stated Memory: East Germany and the Holocaust* (Rochester, N.Y.: Camden House, 1999).

37. Schmid, *Antifaschismus und Judenverfolgung*, p. 91.

38. This point is emphasized in Fox, *Stated Memory.*

39. Bodemann, "Reconstructions of History," pp. 196, 219.

40. Some examples appear in the "Note on Sources."

41. E.g., Wolfgang Benz, "Applaus, Beteiligung, Missbilligung: Zum Verhalten des Publikums in der 'Reichskristallnacht,'" *Zeitschrift für Geschichtswissenschaft* 46 (1998), pp. 961–971; and most recently Michael Wildt, *Volksgemeinschaft als Selbstermächtigung: Gewalt gegen Juden in der deutschen Provinz 1919 bis 1939* (Hamburg: Hamburger Edition, 2007).

Note on Sources

1. The project is described on the website of the Institut für Zeitgeschichte, Munich, at http://www.ifz-muenchen.de/verfolgung_von_ns-verbrechen.html (accessed 25 May 2009).

2. Citations to the reports in this book refer to the original documents as made available electronically through the Wiener Library. The reports have now been published as *Novemberpogrom 1938: Die Augenzeugenberichte der Wiener Library London,* ed. Ben Barkow, Raphael Gross, and Michael Lenarz (Frankfurt: Suhrkamp, 2008).

3. Heinz Boberach, ed., *Meldungen aus dem Reich 1938–1945: Die geheimen Lageberichte des Sicherheitsdienstes der SS,* 18 vols. (Herrsching: Pawlak, 1984); *Deutschland-Berichte der Sozialdemokratischen Partei Deutschlands (Sopade),* microfilm edition (Dortmund: Institut für Zeitungsforschung, 1967).

4. Otto Dov Kulka and Eberhard Jäckel, eds., *Die Juden in den geheimen NS-Stimmungsberichten, 1933–1945* (Düsseldorf: Droste, 2004).

5. Examples of the vast literature of local studies are Gerold Bönnen, "Der Novemberpogrom 1938 in Worms und seinem Umland im Spiegel staatsanwaltschaftlicher Ermittlungsakten der Nachkriegszeit," *Der Wormsgau* 19 (2000), pp. 155–182; Anselm Faust, ed., *Die "Kristallnacht" im Rheinland: Dokumente zum Judenpogrom im November 1938* (Düsseldorf: Schwann, 1987); Andreas Heusler and Tobias Weger, *"Kristallnacht": Gewalt gegen die Münchner*

Juden im November 1938 (Munich: Buchendorfer, 1998); Herbert Reyer, ed., *Das Ende der Juden in Ostfriesland: Ausstellung der Ostfriesischen Landschaft aus Anlass des 50. Jahrestags der Kristallnacht* (Aurich: Verlag Ostfriesischer Landschaft, 1988); Barbara Suchy, ed., *Düsseldorf, Donnerstag, den 10. November 1938: Texte, Berichte, Dokumente* (Düsseldorf: Mahn- und Gedenkstätte Düsseldorf, 1989); Josef Wißkirchen, ed., *Reichspogromnacht an Rhein und Erft 9./10. November 1938. Eine Dokumentation* (Pulheim: Verein für Geschichte und Heimatkunde e.V. Pulheim, 1988).

Acknowledgments

I began this book while I was still based at the University of Nebraska–Lincoln. I am grateful for travel support from the UNL Harris Center for Judaic Studies and a Faculty Development Leave that enabled me to spend a significant amount of time in Germany. Peter Gengler, my research assistant, compiled an excellent index to the Wiener Library reports. Completion of the book came after my move to the University of Vermont (UVM), and for their encouragement and advice I would like to thank my colleagues in the Department of History and the UVM Miller Center for Holocaust Studies, especially Frank Nicosia and Jonathan Huener, and my assistant, Philip Pezeshki.

Much of this book was researched and written at the Institut für Zeitgeschichte in Munich. I have benefited immensely from the hospitality, professionalism, and knowledge of the staff at the Institute. I would like to thank especially Edith Raim, Andreas Eichmüller, Giles

Bennett, Thomas Schlemmer, Hans Woller, and Dieter Pohl. I am also grateful to the staff of the archive of the Center for Advanced Holocaust Studies at the U.S. Holocaust Museum, especially Henry Mayer; to the staff of the Bundesarchiv in Berlin; and to the staff of the Politisches Archiv des Auswärtigen Amtes, also in Berlin.

Richard S. Levy of the University of Illinois–Chicago read the entire manuscript and made numerous valuable suggestions for improvement. I am deeply grateful for his intellectual guidance over the years. I am also indebted to the following colleagues on both sides of the Atlantic who took an interest in this project and who helped in many different ways: Doris Bergen, Michael Berkowitz, Michael Brenner, Christopher Browning, Bruce Campbell, Robert Ericksen, Norbert Frei, Henry Friedlander, Philipp Gassert, Geoffrey Giles, Peter Hayes, Angela Hermann, Peter Longerich, Eberhard Jaeckel, Christiane Kuller, Jürgen Matthäus, David Messenger, Andreas Nechama, Oliver Pollak, Ron Smelser, Sybille Steinbacher, Ray Stokes, Dietmar Süß, Winfried Süß, and Gerhard Weinberg.

Joyce Seltzer, my editor at Harvard University Press, encouraged me at every stage of this project. Her rigorous criticism of my drafts improved this book immeasurably, as did Christine Thorsteinsson's meticulous copyediting. The book also benefited greatly from the reports of two anonymous readers commissioned by Harvard University Press.

My largest debt, as always, is to my wife and colleague, Susanna Schrafstetter, who provided indispensable intellectual advice and psychological support. Her father, Fritz, was too young to have experienced the Kristallnacht personally, but he most certainly would have done the right thing had he had the chance. This book is dedicated to him.

Index